GOD SO LOVED
THE WORLD

Elizabeth Goudge

GOD SO LOVED
THE WORLD

Coward-McCann, Inc., New York

For My Godchildren

Mark, John, Caroline, and Andra Elizabeth

Contents

GOD SO LOVED
THE WORLD

Chapter 1

THE WORD WAS MADE FLESH

God so loved the world, that He gave His only
begotten Son, that whosoever believeth in Him
should not perish, but have everlasting life.
                                   —St. John III:16

1.

THIS is the story of that almost unbelievable humbling,
the life that God lived when he came down from
heaven and lived upon earth as a man. In a particular human
body, born of a mother belonging to a certain race of people,
nearly two thousand years ago in the country of Palestine, God
lived and died for us men and for our salvation. The fact of this
humility is so glorious that it is beyond human understanding,
but the limitations of race and time and place put a sort of picture
frame about the glory, so that we can look at it without being
blinded. And we must look at it, because the picture in the frame
is the most important thing in this world, or in any other.

Man had forgotten what God looked like. In the beginning
God made man and loved him, and man put God at the center

3

of his life, looked at him, humbly worshiped him, loved and served him, and was happy. Man loved God of his own choice because God had given him free will. Unless God had given man the gift of choice he would have been incapable of love, because it is the nature of love that it cannot be compelled but must be freely given. And then came that worst tragedy of human history. Man turned away from God and put himself in the center. He chose to love and serve himself instead of God, and for a man to think himself more worthy of attention than God is pride, the most detestable of all the sins and the root of all the others. To serve God is to serve holiness and life eternal and to attain to them; to serve self is to serve sin and death and to die eternally.

To save man from this death the great love of God chose to do two things, to show himself to man all over again in his eternal beauty and to lift up the great weight of sin that kept man a prisoner and carry it away, that man might be free to rise up and turn from self to God and serve and love him as he used to do in the beginning.

And the way of God's choice was the way of this humbling. He came down to earth and lived as a man among men, that they might see and hear and touch eternal beauty, and he took upon himself the dreadful suffering and death that are the result of sin, though he himself was sinless, and in this way lifted the load and carried it away.

This great showing-forth and deliverance God accomplished for us in the person of his son, who is one with him, the Word of God, the brightness of the everlasting light and the image of his goodness. The mystery of the Holy Trinity, the Father and the Son made one by the Holy Spirit of Love, Three Persons and yet One God, is beyond our understanding, but what we must understand is that the adorable beauty which we see in Jesus of Nazareth is the beauty of God himself and that the suffering and death endured for us by him are the suffering and death of God.

But still he has left to us the power of choice. We need not look at him and love him unless we want to. We need not turn from ourselves to him unless we choose. But if we have once looked at him, even though we have seen him only dimly, we find we can't do anything else but try our very hardest to put him in the center of our lives.

This humbling began very far back in history, in God's choice of the people who should be especially his people. He did not choose to belong to one of the powerful nations of the world, or even to one of the cleverest or most civilized; he chose the people of Israel, a shepherd people whose story, like his own, has much joy in it but great hardship and sorrow too. But the people of Israel had one great treasure, and that was a truer idea of God than other nations possessed. Ever since that turning from God which we call the Fall man has been like a lost creature trying to find the way home, and the religions of the world are his blundering attempts to find again the God whom once he saw and loved so well. And in this search the people of Israel came closest to the reality. They worshiped one God and they knew that he was the Creator of the world, holy and just, not capricious and cruel like the many gods of other nations. And so it was to this poor and struggling nation who knew the most about him that God came.

For centuries before he was born they knew that he would come to them. Their prophets told them about him, calling him by many wonderful names, the Messiah, the Deliverer, the Holy One of Israel, the Son of Man. But most of them imagined he would come as a conqueror who would deliver his people from their earthly enemies and establish an earthly kingdom. Very few realized that the enemy he was coming to fight was man's selfishness, that he would conquer by suffering, and that his king-

5

dom would be the spiritual kingdom of those who love God.

Palestine, where the nomad people of Israel found a home at last, is a small country, and beautiful, but dry and mountainous and not very productive. And it is so wedged in between countries larger and wealthier than itself that throughout its history it has had little peace. Foreign armies have been perpetually marching across it, fighting battles on its soil, oppressing its people, or taking them into slavery. Its history has been rather like the history of Poland in our own day, wedged in between Russia and the nations of western Europe and nearly crushed to death between them. And it is this small and oppressed bit of country that the Creator of the whole immense universe called especially his own when he lived on earth.

The people of Israel enjoyed in their history a few short periods of freedom and prosperity, but God did not choose one of them in which to come among his people. Instead he chose a moment when they were having a difficult time. Rome had conquered nearly all Europe, as well as Palestine, and we can visualize the people of Israel enduring much the sort of life that the French people endured after Hitler conquered France. Many of the men in high places had made friends with the enemy for the sake of the comfort and security that this friendship brought them, but the rest of the nation was heavily taxed. They were not badly treated if they did what they were told, and the Romans were efficient rulers, but the people of Israel have always been a proud and independent people and the loss of their freedom was bitter to them. In Palestine at that time, as in France during the last war, there was a vigorous underground movement. In France, the Maquis, in Palestine, the Zealots. If the Romans caught the Zealots engaged in active rebellion they executed them, and their way of torturing and killing rebels was the dreadful way of crucifixion. It was no unusual thing in Palestine at that time to see crosses set up beside the road and men

6

dying on them in agony. The outward life of the country, the tending of the vineyards and olive groves, the plowing of the fields, the sowing and gathering of the crops, the lives of the farmers and shepherds and artisans and their families in the small villages perched upon the hilltops went on normally enough, but underneath it was much hidden anxiety and grief and pain, and into the middle of it all came God. And there was nothing of their life that he did not share with his people, and does not today share with us, because we are his people if we love him, and he is as close to us as he was to them, when they heard his voice and saw his face and put out their hand and touched him.

2.

And now we come closer to him and think of his mother.

She lived in Nazareth, in Galilee, in the north of Palestine. We can imagine ourselves travelers approaching Nazareth on the evening of a day in early spring. All around is a scene of great beauty, for the February rains are just over and the country is now fresh and green. Behind us as we toil up the steep rocky path is the beautiful plain of Esdraelon; to the east are the mountains of Moab, while the snow-capped peak of Mount Hermon shines out against the sky. There were many trees in Palestine in those days. The lower slopes of the hills are wooded with cedars and oaks and ilexes, and all about us as we climb up to the village are terraces of vines and olives. Though it is such a steep climb up to Nazareth the village itself lies sheltered in a hollow surrounded by steep hills. The white houses are small, the poorer houses roofed with branches, the larger ones with small stone domes. Some of the bigger houses

7

have gardens about them planted with fruit trees, figs and citrons, almonds and pomegranates. The almond trees are just coming into bloom, and here and there is a froth of pink blossom over a garden wall. The atmosphere is crystal clear and the sky a deep blue flecked with golden clouds. The color on the hills is very wonderful, purple and rose and tawny orange, and the shadows sharp and dark.

We are in Nazareth now, walking up a narrow cobbled lane between the houses. The men have not yet come home from their work in the fields and the people whom we pass are the women and children. They are poor people, and the women wear long dresses of blue and brown cloth that they have woven themselves on their looms, with white veils on their heads to protect them from the sun. But they have woven bright garments for their children, and the little things run along beside them looking very gay, the boys with small round caps on their heads, or turbans bound round with a fillet in imitation of their fathers, the little girls with veils like their mothers. Most of the women are going to the spring to fetch water, so that their husbands and sons can wash themselves before they sit down to the evening meal. Some of them carry their waterpots on their shoulders; others balance them on their heads. The spring at Nazareth, today called Mary's Fountain, gushes out from the hillside, clear and very cold.

The women linger here, exchanging village gossip with each other, sometimes lowering their voices to talk a little of the sorrows and dangers of the times. But as much as they can they like to forget these and talk of the small, happy affairs of the village that make up the brightness of their lives. They are pleased that Joseph-bar-Jacob, the village carpenter, is going to marry Mary, the daughter of Anne. They like Joseph and they are talking about him as they stand by the spring, taking their turn to fill their waterpots. "He is a just man," they say of him.

8

And they mean a good deal by that great word "just." They mean that Joseph is trustworthy, that when he has given his word he does not go back on it, and when he has undertaken a job of work he does it as well as he can right through to the end. And they mean also that he is a good man, whose life is clear as the mountain air and whose words and deeds are kind. Mary is lucky, they say, that he has chosen her for his wife, and Anne is lucky that she can give her daughter into such safe keeping. And then they pause in their talk because Mary herself is coming up the lane with her waterpot.

What does she look like? No one seems to have written down a description of her, but we are told that she belonged to a tribe that in appearance was very like the modern Bedouin Arab. That means that she is olive-skinned and slender, with soft dark eyes. Girls married very early in Palestine in those days, and she is about fourteen or fifteen years old. She wears a blue homespun dress with a white veil on her dark hair, and on top of her head is a pad with the waterpot balanced on it. She has trained herself not to touch the pot with her hands as she walks, and this has taught her to hold her back straight and her head high and to walk with the grace and dignity of a queen.

Out of all the women who have ever lived upon this earth, or who will ever live, this village girl is the one whom God chose to be the Mother of his Son, and so we know that she was as perfect as a woman can be, lovely in mind and in spirit as well as in body, and like all lovely people very much beloved. She must have been strong and sturdy too, like all country girls trained to hard work, and we know from all that happened afterward that she was extraordinarily brave. So the other women were glad to see her at the spring, and she was glad to see them. They talked to her about Joseph, and her cheeks flushed pink with happiness and her eyes were bright with laughter as she lifted her waterpot from her head and held it beneath

9

the gushing water. She stayed and talked to them all for a little while before she turned to go home, one hand now holding the full pot steady on her head, walking very slowly and carefully so as not to spill the water, looking about her as she walked at the great beauty of the world and thanking God for it in her heart. The greatest moments of our lives often come upon us unawares, and perhaps she did not know, as she walked home with her waterpot, that before the night had fallen upon this lovely land something would have happened to her that would have changed her from a girl into a woman, and opened for her a door into heaven that would never again be shut.

The great artists of the world, painting their pictures of the Annunciation, have all imagined that it happened while Mary was saying her prayers. Her home, like others in Palestine, was built round a small inner courtyard, with the chief windows and doors opening into it. The windows in the outer walls were mere slits, so that the noise and glare of the outer world was shut out. The room where Mary prayed was cool and quiet with no sound in it except the whisper of leaves from the fig tree growing in the courtyard. The Eastern people do not kneel to pray, they stand, and Mary stood with bent head and arms crossed upon her breast, and praised God and thanked him, and asked him to have mercy upon his handmaid. Perhaps she used her own words, or perhaps the words of the psalms of David that she would have known by heart. "Praise the Lord, O my soul," and "Have mercy upon me, O God, after thy great goodness."

It is not difficult to imagine the thoughts that were uppermost in her mind as she prayed. Day by day she heard the talk at the spring. She knew all about the suffering of her country and being so loving a girl she must have carried the sorrow of it always with her. And like all her people she was watching day by day for the Holy One of Israel who would come to deliver his people. As a little girl she had sometimes looked out from one of the narrow outward facing windows of her home to see if she could catch a sight of him riding up from the valley below with his sword at his side, or run to the courtyard door at the sound of a strange footfall in the street, to see if it were he at last. Perhaps now, like King David, she cried in her heart with the voice of all her people, "I am poor and needy, make haste unto me, O God. Thou art my help and Deliverer; O Lord, make no long tarrying." But against this dark background of the sorrow and longing of her people the thought of her own joy sprang up like a flower—Joseph, and the children they would have, and their home where they would all live together. She prayed that it might be a happy home. And then through the door that opened on the courtyard the light of the setting sun streamed so gloriously that she looked up, and in that moment the door was no longer just the door into the courtyard but a door opening from earth into heaven.

Mary has left a record of what happened to her then. She thought that an angel came to her, stepping from heaven into her little room. Her people had always loved and reverenced those servants and messengers of God, the angels. King David had thought of the clouds and the winds as angels and had dared to imagine them carrying God himself across the sky upon their wings. "He rode upon a cherub and did fly; yea, he did fly upon the wings of the wind." Isaiah had seen the terrible six-winged seraphim who stand about the throne of God, great and awful presences who yet veil their faces with their mighty wings before the even more awful presence of God. Jacob had seen a ladder set up between earth and heaven and the angels passing and repassing upon it. Abraham and other holy men had spoken with angels as a man speaks with a man, and received from them the commands and the comfort and the strength of

God. To four of these loving and lovely spirits, who sometimes at God's command humble themselves to stoop beneath the low lintel of the door of earth and come to us, the people of Israel had given names—Raphael, Gabriel, Cassiel, and Michael. Mary believed it was Gabriel who came to her that day. She has left no description of what he looked like; perhaps, like the angel whom St. John saw on the Island of Patmos, "a rainbow was upon his head and his face was as it were the sun," and the light blinded her. That is really all that people who have looked into heaven are able to tell us about it—that it is "light." But she knew what he said to her.

"Hail, thou that art highly favoured, the Lord is with thee. Blessed art thou among women."

In this story of an almost unbelievable humbling this angelic humility takes its place, this coming in of Gabriel to Mary, this greeting of a young girl by a great angel with words of gentle courtesy. Some of the old painters have shown Gabriel kneeling before Mary, like a courtier before his queen, as he spoke his Salutation.

Mary was "troubled," wondering "what manner of salutation this should be." She must have been afraid, too, because Gabriel's next words brought her the comfort of God to the frightened.

"Fear not, Mary, for thou hast found favour with God."

Then she knew quite certainly for always that God loved her, and that whatever happened to her through the rest of her life she would never have to be afraid again. This certainly steadied her spirit, made it calm and peaceful like a still pool, so that she was able to accept the amazing revelation of God that followed, as the quiet water is able to receive the reflection of the sky and stars above it. She was to be the mother of the Holy One of Israel, for whom she had watched so long, the mother of the Son of God. Her watching and waiting was nearly ended now.

12

In a few months' time she would hold the Son of God in her arms, and he would be her Son too. She, Mary of Nazareth, a fourteen-year-old girl whom the great world had never even heard of, she and no other was to be his mother. The angel told her this, and almost unbelievable though the revelation must have seemed to her yet her quiet and loving spirit was able to believe it.

Yet though she was no longer frightened she was appalled by the greatness and the mystery of this thing that she was asked to do. This child, her child, was to be the Son of the Lord God of Israel himself, not of Joseph. She was asked to be the Mother of God. How could she be? How could she do it? Who was she that this honor should come to her? She was not strong enough to bear it. "How shall this be?" she cried out to Gabriel. And we can picture her no longer standing but crouched down on the ground with her face buried in her hands. This is how humble men and women always feel when God calls them to do some great thing for him. How can I do it? How can I possibly do it?

The answer is always the same answer, the one that Gabriel gave to Mary. "The Holy Ghost shall come upon thee and the power of the Highest shall overshadow thee." Not in their own strength, Mary, do the servants of God do the work to which he calls them, but in his. What a man or woman cannot do by themselves they can do when God is with them, for with God nothing is impossible.

And so the second great certainty came to Mary, and she lifted her head and opened her arms and said, "Behold the handmaid of the Lord; be it unto me according to thy word."

She knew a third thing now, that she loved God, who loved her and whose power would never fail her. She had nothing to give him but herself and so she gave herself. She loved him so much that she wanted only one thing now, to do his will whatever it should cost her.

13

3.

It was to cost her a very great deal. She was to have great joy in her life, but great suffering too, and both of them so piercing that only a woman as strong and stouthearted as Mary would have been able to endure them without breaking.

Her worries began almost at once, for Joseph was deeply troubled when he found that she was to have a child who would not be his but the direct gift of God to her. He, too, had been watching and waiting for the Holy One of Israel, and he knew the prophecy of Isaiah that foretold that a virgin of Israel would be the mother of the Messiah. But he had not expected this virgin to be Mary. It must have seemed as though this girl whom he loved had suddenly been taken away from him. He felt shut out. She was no longer the Mary whom he knew but someone mysterious and strange whom he could not understand. He did not know what to think about it all, and in his unhappiness and bewilderment he felt that he could not now marry her.

And then one night, after he had lain awake tormented by his doubts, he fell deeply asleep and dreamed that the door opened into heaven for him too, and an angel came to him out of the light with this same glorious message that had come to Mary. "Fear not." He, too, like Mary when the light shone upon her, received into his soul, to the utmost extent to which he was able to bear it, the knowledge that the Almighty and Eternal Lord God loved him, loved Joseph, the obscure carpenter of Nazareth, a poor and humble man, and had called him to be the foster father of his Son. When he woke up there was no more doubt or bewilderment left in him. He wanted only to do one thing, and that was to obey the God who loved him and whom he loved. From that moment onward he did not question anything but just did quietly and at once what he was told.

About this time, perhaps while Joseph was so troubled and because she felt he would be happier if she went away, Mary paid a visit to her cousin Elisabeth who lived up in the hills in the country of Judea, southward from Galilee. Perhaps she traveled part of the way with friends who took care of her, and then parted from them at the foot of the hill upon whose summit was perched the small white town where Elisabeth lived.

It was later in the year now. The valleys were green with the waving corn and all over the slopes of the hills above them was spread the glory of the spring flowers—scarlet and purple anemones, blue speedwell, blood-red pimpernel, yellow daisies, cyclamen, and violets. Marigolds were a flame of gold under the sun, and the midday heat drew out the good smell of the aromatic things that Isaiah loved. He wrote that the Lord said, "I will plant in the wilderness the cedar, ... and the myrtle, and the oil tree; I will set in the desert the fir tree, and the pine, and the box tree together."

Mary in her blue dress, under the blue sky, must have climbed upward among the flowers most joyously. Even though she was worried about Joseph she put the worry away from her, for this was a day made for joy. Pulling a sprig of Isaiah's loved myrtle, she remembered him and the glorious and glowing words in which he described the Son of God. "And his name shall be called Wonderful, Counsellor, ... The Everlasting Father, The Prince of Peace." And this Wonderful One would be her child. God was giving to his people, through her, their Saviour. "Comfort ye, comfort ye, my people, saith your God." Not much longer now. Soon God would stoop from heaven to lay his Son in her arms, and her arms would give him to the world. She marveled at the humility of God. He could have given his Son to the world without her help. He could have sent him down from heaven in a blaze of glory. Yet he did not choose this lonely and lofty way, he chose to bend low and whisper to her, "You and I." Yet this, she knew, is always God's way, for God is love.

Mary must have spent the whole of the rest of her life thanking God for the way in which he had honored her, and one of her songs of thanksgiving, the Magnificat, has been sung all down the centuries for love of her. Perhaps she began to make it up as she climbed the hillside, to fit a tune to her words and to sing it to the accompaniment of the wind in the pine trees. "My soul doth magnify the Lord, and my spirit hath rejoiced in God my Saviour. For he hath regarded the low estate of his handmaiden; for, behold, from henceforth all generations shall call me blessed. For he that is mighty hath done to me great things; and holy is his name."

4.

Meanwhile in a small house in the town at the top of the hill Elisabeth was sitting at her window waiting for Mary, and she too was praising God because to her and to her husband, as well as to Mary and Joseph, there had come the great "Fear not," and to her too God had whispered, "You and I."

Elisabeth was married to a priest called Zacharias, and they had grown old together serving God. They had one grief: they had no child. They had prayed long and earnestly to God to give them one, but the years had passed and still there was no child. So then after the foolish fashion of men and women they had imagined that God had not heard them. They had learned a good deal in a long life but not yet that God never fails to answer prayer. But he answers it in the way and at the moment that is best for everybody, and man, who cannot see the wonderful pat-

tern that God is weaving with the lives of us all, gets discouraged
if the way is not to his liking and the moment delayed.

Elisabeth's baby had to be delayed because God had chosen
her child to do a particular piece of work for him at a special
time. It had been foretold that a great prophet should be born
upon the earth who should prepare the way of the Christ. In
those days, when a king decided to visit the cities of his kingdom,
a messenger would be sent running before him through the
wilderness to tell the people he was coming, so that they could
prepare their city and make ready to receive the king. Isaiah had
described this forerunner. "The voice of him that crieth in the
wilderness, Prepare ye the way of the Lord, make straight in
the desert a highway for our God." And to Elisabeth and
Zacharias God gave the great honor of being the mother and
father of the forerunner.

It was revealed first of all to Zacharias. He was in Jerusalem,
the holy city of Israel. He had finished his work as a priest in the
Temple, and he was in the last week of his service there. The
Temple at Jerusalem was very beautiful. King Solomon had
built the first Temple but it had been destroyed by enemy inva-
sion, and then rebuilt, and now it was being rebuilt once more
by Herod, the Jewish king who in obedience to the Roman
Emperor ruled this conquered country for him. It was built of
marble and white limestone, inlaid with beautiful mosaics, with
great open courts grouped about the inner Temple, the Holy
Place, and the Holy of Holies. Day by day the people gathered
in the court outside the Holy Place to pray, but they did not go
into the Holy Place, into which only the priests might go. They
entered it in turn, perhaps only once in their lives, and burned
incense there just as the dawn was breaking. Into the Holy of
Holies only the High Priest might go, and he only once a year.

The day came when it was the turn of Zacharias to enter the

17

Holy Place for the last time. Old and white-haired, dignified in his priestly garments of purple and white, he made his way through the Temple courts with two assistant priests on either side of him, and as he went he struck a gong to tell the people that the hour had come for the burning of the incense. The coming of man to God and God to man, their meeting and union, is a thing so full of mystery that man has always had to use symbols to help him to understand a little of the wonder of it. The smoke rising up from the burning incense was a picture of the prayers of the people rising up from their penitent hearts, and Zacharias burning the incense in the Holy Place was giving them to God.

When the assistant priests had made everything ready, they withdrew, leaving Zacharias alone to burn the incense. Standing before the altar in the Holy Place he could see the door leading to the Holy of Holies. To many Israelites this small windowless room was the most sacred place in the world because it was the symbol of the presence of God dwelling with his people. Alone in the quietness Zacharias bowed his head and worshiped, as Mary had done in the quiet room at Nazareth.

And as the smoke of the incense ascended, and he lifted up the prayers of his people to God, once more the door opened and the glory of heaven shone through. Zacharias saw an angel formed all of light standing at the right side of the altar and like Mary he was terrified. And then to him too there came the great "Fear not," and he was comforted, and as the turmoil of his terror quieted it seemed that he heard a voice telling him that his prayer had been heard. He was to have a child and he must call him John. "Thou shalt have joy and gladness and many shall rejoice at his birth." The voice itself was glorious as light, each word falling like a flake of fire to lighten the darkness of his fear and drive it away. "He shall go before him to make ready a people prepared for the Lord." The forerunner. He was being told that he was to be the father of the forerunner. But he could not believe it. He was old, and Elisabeth was old, and they had given up hope of this child so long ago. It was too wonderful to be believed. He wanted more proof than this light that blinded him and this voice speaking right inside his soul that might both of them be nothing but delusion. He could not believe without some sort of solid proof. Again came the voice in his soul, flooding it with light.

"I am Gabriel that stand in the presence of God, and am sent to speak unto thee, and to show thee these glad tidings."

But still he cried out for his proof, and the voice came again. "Behold, thou shalt be dumb, and not able to speak until the day that these things shall be performed, because thou believedst not my words, which shall be fulfilled in their season."

The light faded and the door was closed. Slowly he came back to himself. It seemed to him that he had been on a long journey and had been an immense time away. He remembered who he was, and where he was. Outside the Holy Place the people were waiting for him. He had offered their prayers to God and now he must go back to them and bless them. Staggering a little, because he was a very old man and he had just experienced great fear, great gladness, and great doubt, he came out to them and saw the astonishment on their faces. . . . So he *had* been a very long time away. . . . He raised his hand and tried to pronounce the blessing that was always given at this time, "The Lord be merciful unto us and bless us, and lift up the light of his countenance upon us, and give us peace," but he could not because no words would come. He had his proof. He was dumb. But it seemed to the people that blessing came to them from the light upon his face. Because of the light they knew that he had seen a vision.

He went home and as he could not speak he must have written out an account of what had happened for Elisabeth to read. But perhaps she knew already. Perhaps God had already said to her, "You and I. I will put your son in your arms and you shall give him to my people to prepare the way."

5.

There was a light step in the courtyard and a voice called "Elisabeth! Elisabeth!" Looking through the window Elisabeth saw Mary standing beneath the old fig tree which grew beside the well. She looked happy and eager yet shy and humble at the same time, for she was young and Elisabeth was old and Elisabeth had known her all her life, had loved her like her own child, and now she must find it hard to believe that this child Mary had been chosen out of all the women of Israel to be the Mother of the Holy One. But Elisabeth did not find it hard to believe because she was humble too, and like all the humble she had a great reverence for other people, even those whom she knew in and out through and through and had held in her arms when they were small. With her old face flooded with awe and joy she came to Mary, and holding the girl's hands in hers, she bent her head as though she did honor to her Queen.

"Blessed art thou among women," she said, "and blessed is the fruit of thy womb. And whence is this to me, that the Mother of my Lord should come to me? For, lo, as soon as the voice of thy salutation sounded in mine ears, the babe leaped in my womb for joy. And blessed is she that believed, for there shall be a performance of those things which were told her from the Lord."

Then Mary put her arms round Elisabeth's neck and kissed

20

her and clung to her, not at all like the Queen whom Elisabeth had greeted but like the child whom she had always loved as her own. Then they went together out of the blazing sun of the courtyard into the cool dim house. Mary stayed with Elisabeth for three months, and we can imagine them sitting together and making clothes for their babies, and talking of the wonderful thing that had happened to them both. When she was alone Mary sang as she sewed, for now she had completed her song of praise and she thanked God not only that he had so honored the poor and humble people of the world, in choosing a peasant girl to be the Mother of his Son, but for his faithfulness, too. Men had wondered sometimes, as the long and bitter years went by, if he had forgotten his promise to send his Son to help them. But he had not forgotten. There is no forgetfulness in God. "In him is no variableness neither shadow of turning."

6.

"The day spring from on high hath visited us," said Joseph, and Mary answered softly, "To give light to them that sit in darkness and in the shadow of death, to guide our feet into the way of peace."

Over their heads the night sky blazed with stars and the frosty road rang sharply beneath the donkey's feet. The donkey stumbled now and then, for it was tired and Joseph limped as he walked because his feet had got sore with so much tramping over stony hill paths. It might have been thought that Mary had the best of it, warmly wrapped up in a thick cloak and sitting on the donkey's back, but she was really the most tired of the three. Her eyes looked enormous in her white face and her voice as she answered Joseph was hoarse with weariness, yet when Joseph looked at her anxiously she smiled, and then he smiled too. Throughout the long and weary journey from Nazareth to Bethlehem they had both been extraordinarily happy, for they had given themselves utterly to do the will of God, and now its movement was like a great wind that carried them along.

Mary and Joseph had wondered sometimes, during the first weeks after they were married, about the prophecy which had said that the Holy One of Israel would be born at Bethlehem. "And thou, Bethlehem, in the land of Judea, art not the least among the princes of Judea, for out of thee shall come a Governor that shall rule my people Israel." And yet here they were at Nazareth, and the time for the baby's birth was coming near. And then one day a Roman soldier had come riding into the village, and when he had gathered all the people together he had read them a proclamation. The government was going to hold a census, an official numbering of the population for the purposes of taxation, and each man must go with his wife to the city from which his family had originally come, to record their names and give an account of their circumstances. This meant that Joseph and Mary must go to Bethlehem, because he was descended from King David and Bethlehem was David's city. Their neighbors must have been horrified, for such a long journey in winter would be very bad for a young girl expecting her first baby. But Mary and Joseph were not horrified for they saw in this journey the movement of the will of God and they were not afraid.

Yet they must have needed all their courage. We are not told anything about their journey, and so it is only supposition that they kept up their hearts by repeating the hymn of praise that Zacharias had composed when his son John was born and his speech was restored to him again. Yet surely they did, because

22

it was so lovely a prophecy of the coming of their child.... The day spring from on high. Light in darkness. The way of peace. ... They had only to reach their journey's end and it would all come true.

"Look, Mary!" said Joseph.

Mary straightened herself and looked eagerly in the direction in which Joseph was pointing. Bethlehem, like most of the old cities of this country, is built upon the summit of a rocky hill, and clear-cut against the sky they could see tall cypresses and squat houses black and white under the moon. The sight of it put new life into them, and it did not seem long before they were passing beneath the archway in the city wall and entering the narrow streets.

Bethlehem tonight was full of bustle and noise. Roman soldiers guarded the gateway, and the cobbled streets were crowded with the many travelers who had come like Joseph and Mary to register their names.

Joseph asked his way to the inn, but when they reached it his heart sank. The inns at that time were just a yard surrounded by a high wall and a colonnade, with rooms for the travelers under the arches. But the yard of this inn was full of camels and donkeys being unloaded, and jostling, tired, bad-tempered travelers, with the harassed innkeeper moving about among them, and one glance told him that the rooms all round were full too. "To guide our feet into the way of peace." He wanted peace for Mary, but it did not look as though he would find it in this inn.

We do not know who it was who suggested that they should go to the stable. Perhaps the innkeeper fetched his wife and she, seeing how ill Mary was, took her quickly to their own stable as the only quiet place she could think of. The old houses of Bethlehem are built over caves in the limestone rock. You can

23

corners of the earth it seemed that the light was the music and the music was the light.

"Glory to God in the highest, and on earth peace, goodwill towards men."

Peace had come down to dwell with men forever. No matter what the suffering, the fighting, the storms, the distress, nothing now could ever take from the lovers of God the gift of his peace. Men could never again doubt the goodwill of God toward them, for God had given his own Son to be born, to live, to die, for their salvation. God's goodwill was incarnate now as a little child lying in a manger.

The moment of vision passed and the door was shut in heaven. The night was quiet again, lit only by the moon and the stars and the flames of the fire. But the shepherds did not doubt the truth of what they had heard and seen. They did not even waste time talking about it. "Let us go now," they said to each other, and we are told, "They came with haste" to the place where their Saviour lay. We do not know how they found the way. Perhaps by the time they got to Bethlehem dawn was not far away and they saw the morning star shining like a lamp over the roof of the little house that was built over the cave. They went in and found him wrapped in his swaddling bands, lying in the warm hay in the manger hewn out of the wall, with Mary and Joseph loving and watching him there, and the gentle beasts looking on in amazement. In the fitful lantern light they could see him like a flower in the hay, and they knelt down and worshiped and adored. They saw him with their own eyes and their joy must have been almost too great to be borne.

Light looked down and beheld Darkness,
"Thither will I go," said Light.
Peace looked down and beheld War,
"Thither will I go," said Peace.

THE WORD WAS MADE FLESH

Love looked down and beheld Hatred,
"Thither will I go," said Love.
So came Light and shone;
So came Peace, and gave rest;
So came Love, and brought Life,
And the Word was made Flesh, and dwelt among us.

—Laurence Housman

Chapter 2

THE DESIRE OF ALL NATIONS

A light to lighten the Gentiles, and the glory of
thy people Israel.

—St. Luke II:32

1.

IT IS only a journey of five miles from Bethlehem to Jerusalem, and when their baby was still not many days old
Mary and Joseph took him there that they might present him
to God in the Temple. All the fathers and mothers of Israel
brought their babies to God in this way, very much as we bring
our babies to be baptized in church.

The scene is the same beautiful Temple where Gabriel came
to Zacharias. We picture a priest standing at the top of a flight of
marble steps, and the mothers standing at the foot of them with
their babies in their arms, Mary among them, patiently waiting
her turn to lay her baby in the priest's arms that the priest might
bless him and offer him to God. Joseph was beside her carrying
a wicker cage with a pair of turtle doves or two young pigeons in

28

it, for when a baby was presented to God the father always offered a sacrifice.

To us it seems dreadful that worshipers coming to God's Temple should have brought live animals and birds with them, and that these should have been killed and burned upon the altar of sacrifice in one of the great open-air courts. But all through the centuries of their history the people of Israel had offered sacrifice in this way. Just as the smoke from the incense was a picture of prayer rising up to God so these sacrifices made a picture to them of their penitent souls offered to God in sorrow for their sins. When they saw the flames leap up they felt that God had accepted their penitence and that they were made one with him again. If they had no birds or beasts of their own they had to buy them, and it cost them something to offer this gift of their penitence to God. Well-to-do people could afford to sacrifice goats and sheep, but the very poor could only afford the turtle doves or pigeons that Joseph brought.

Mary's turn came, and she and Joseph went up the steps together, and she laid her baby in the priest's arms, and then she and Joseph bent their heads while the priest blessed their son and lifting him up offered him to God. Sometimes this is called the first sorrow of Mary, because this moment at the beginning of Our Lord's life when she saw him lifted up and given to God is a picture of the moment at the end of his life when she saw him lifted up upon the cross and given to God again. At both these moments, at the beginning and the end, he was taken from Mary. All she could do was to stand by and watch.

To the priest who blessed him, and to the other fathers and mothers, Our Lord was just one baby among all the rest, not very important because his parents had only brought two birds in a wicker cage as a sacrifice, but there were two people in the Temple that day who did know that their God and Saviour had come among them. Simeon and Anna were old and holy people

29

who were always waiting for the coming of the Christ, and to Simeon it had been revealed that he should not die until he had seen his Saviour. He knew that day that this was the moment for which he had been waiting all his life, and he came to the Temple and was watching and waiting when the fathers and mothers came with their babies. He knew at once which of all those babies was his Lord and King and with a cry of joy he held out his arms, and Mary, after one glance at his transfigured face, put her baby into them. And Simeon cried out aloud and blessed God and said, "Lord, now lettest thou thy servant depart in peace, according to thy word, for mine eyes have seen thy salvation, which thou hast prepared before the face of all people; a light to lighten the Gentiles, and the glory of thy people Israel."

Then Simeon gave her baby to his mother again, and blessed her and Joseph, and looking at Mary he said to her, "This child is set for the fall and rising again of many in Israel." He saw in that moment how the presence of the Christ among them would test men. The holiness of God would shine out from him and in that light they would see themselves for what they were. They would not like what they saw, and the proud among them would hate him for showing it to them and fall into the deadly sin of turning away from him, while the humble, hating themselves, would rise up out of themselves to him. And then looking at Mary in her youth and happiness it seems that he saw her as she would be when the time of the second offering came, and her youth had gone and her happiness had turned to anguish, for he said to her, "A sword shall pierce through thy soul."

And then old Anna came. She spent all her time in the Temple praising God and praying to him. She knew, too, that this baby was her Lord, and bent her head and worshiped him, and praised God that she had lived to see him with her own eyes.

And Joseph and Mary took their baby back to Bethlehem, to

the house where they were staying while Mary grew strong, and they marveled at all these strange things that were happening.

2.

When Our Lord grew to manhood he said one day to the poor men gathered about him, "How hardly shall a rich man enter into the kingdom of heaven," and perhaps he remembered as he spoke the story Mary had told him of the rich men who came to Bethlehem to worship him, and how bitterly hard the way had been for them.

This story is so strange and mysterious that we can go on thinking about it forever and still find something fresh to think about. In the book of Isaiah there is a verse which seems to foretell their coming. "And the Gentiles shall come to thy light, and kings to the brightness of thy rising." And so because of this verse, and because of the splendor of the gifts that they brought, lovers of Our Lord throughout the years have thought of these men as kings, and they have thought of them also as representing the three races of mankind, the men of Asia, Africa, and Europe, and they have given them names, Caspar, Melchior, and Balthazar.

But all that St. Matthew actually tells us about them is that they were three wise men and that they came from the east. But those three words "from the east" tell us something about their journey. They must have crossed the desert of Arabia and the mountains of Moab, and it must have been a long and bitter journey during which they endured hunger and thirst, fever, heat, and cold, and ceaseless danger from wild beasts and desert tribesmen. If they had not been men of great courage and

determination they could not have endured and persevered. We
long to know how it was that they set out upon their journey.
When they reached Jerusalem they explained their presence by
the one quiet sentence, "We have seen his star in the east and
are come to worship him," and that is all we know. Yet from it
we can learn a little. All through the ages wise men have loved
to study the stars. The Greeks believed at one time that great
heroes became stars when they died. Other wise men have
thought of the stars as guardian angels, believing that people
born in certain months are under the protection of particular
stars. Shakespeare wrote in one of his sonnets,

> Till whatsoever star that guides my moving point on me
>   graciously with fair aspect,
> To put apparel on my tattered loving and show me worthy
>   of thy sweet respect.

The three kings must have been men of science, astronomers
who studied the stars, and seeing a new light in the sky have
believed it to be the protector of a great hero coming upon the
earth. As this star was very glorious so this hero almost must be
very glorious; he could be no less than a very great king. And
so guided by the star they set out upon their long journey. And
that is all we can know.

Yet in our own minds we can't help giving a name to that
star of "fair aspect," and calling it Gabriel, who stands in the
presence of God and brings men to that presence. Those poor
and simple men, the shepherds, were in their humility so near to
God that they could actually perceive the angel and accept his
message as the truth without a shadow of doubt in their minds.
And their journey to their Saviour was a very short one. But the
journey is not so easy for clever men. For them Gabriel is not
the child's angel of intuition, near and swift and warm, but the

angel of reason, cold and distant like a star in the sky. Long and difficult thought brings them to their Saviour, and the way can be hard and may take years.

But the kings came at last to the land of Israel and made their way, as was natural, to the chief city of the country, to Jerusalem. They rode through the city on their camels, travel-stained and tired, but majestic and awe-inspiring men whose strange appearance made an instant and startling impression upon the crowds thronging the narrow streets. And the question which they kept crying aloud as they rode was equally startling. "Where is he that is born king of the Jews?" They did not ask, where is he who will be king, but who *is* king. They were asking for no child born to a reigning monarch, who would be king one day, but for one who was king *now*, king at this very moment.

The expectation of the Christ was always like a living fire burning in the heart of every man and woman of Israel. They never knew when he might suddenly appear among them, and they so longed for him to come and deliver them from Rome that this expectation could easily flame up into revolt at any rumor of his coming. And this question of the kings seems to have started just such a rumor. One man whispered to another, "They say he is born." The news flashed right through the city and reached the palace, and when Herod heard it "he was troubled, and all Jerusalem with him."

He was troubled because he did not want revolt. The birth of some child whom the people would believe to be the Christ would disturb the order he had struggled for years to maintain. He was called Herod the Great because he had succeeded in making his people live in obedience to Rome, and that had been a great achievement. He had crushed any attempt at rebellion with dreadful cruelty, but with success. He had been a very clever king, and now that he was an old and dying man he did not want failure at the last. He asked where it was prophesied

33

that the Christ should be born, and when he was told it was at Bethlehem he sent for the three kings and questioned them about the star. Then he sped them upon their way to Bethlehem with words that sounded most kindly and courteous.

"Go and seek diligently for the young child; and when ye have found him bring me word again, that I may come and worship him also."

But behind the courtesy his words have a sarcastic ring. It is not likely that he believed in the Christ; but he wanted to find out if a baby had been born whom the people really believed to be the Christ, so that he could get rid of the child at once.

That evening the kings traveled the five miles to Bethlehem and to their joy the star went before them and brought them to the house where the baby was, shining low over the roof so that they could make no mistake. Perhaps the house to which Mary and Joseph had moved was the innkeeper's little house above the stable, perhaps another, but in any case it would have been a humble place, not accustomed to receiving visits from royalty. As the star was shining over the roof it must have been already dark when the kings arrived. They had left their servants with the camels in the street below and climbed the stone steps with the starlight and lantern light glinting upon their swords and bright raiment, and the rich gifts they carried so carefully. They were not taken aback at finding their king in this poor little house; they did not care where they found him if only they could come to him at last; they "rejoiced with exceeding great joy" as they knocked at the humble door and stood waiting with reverently bowed heads.

Joseph heard the jingle of the camels' bells and the sound of strange voices in the lane, and opened to them at once. The happy shepherds had praised God for the heavenly thing that had happened to them, and told everyone about it, so that by this time Joseph must have been quite accustomed to all sorts of men and women and children coming to see the baby; yet he must have been astonished to see those strange and magnificent foreigners standing there like figures out of a dream, looking at him so humbly and eagerly. As it was already dark Mary would have put her baby to bed some hours ago, but she had realized by now that though he was hers he belonged to everyone else, too, and she must share him gladly and graciously. So as Joseph bowed at the door, she smiled at the three kings, and lifting her sleeping son from his cradle sat with him on her lap to show him to them. All his life Our Lord was always at the mercy of everyone who wanted him, and scarcely had a minute's peace, yet he never lost patience. So he was patient now and did not cry when the voices and bright lights woke him up.

The three kings "fell down and worshiped him," adoring him in the Eastern fashion with their foreheads touching the ground. And then they dared to lift themselves up and look at him, and knew a joy greater than anything they had ever dreamed of. To see him with their own eyes, to worship him, was worth all that they had suffered, worth the long journey, the weariness, hunger, and thirst, the danger and the pain. It was so much worth it that in this moment of joy all they had suffered was forgotten as though it had never been. They poured themselves out in adoration before him and all that they had and were they laid at his feet.

For the gifts of gold and frankincense and myrrh symbolize the utmost that a man can give to God. The gold is our wealth— our money, our talents, our health, and our strength. The frankincense is our prayer—our souls adoring God, our minds thinking about him, our hearts loving him, our wills resolved to serve him only. And the spice called myrrh, that is used in the East to embalm the bodies of the dead, is our pain—our griefs and disappointments, the aches and the illnesses of our bodies, and our death. In those three kings kneeling there we can see ourselves.

They knelt there for us all. Yet though they gave, for themselves and for us, the utmost that a man can give, how little it is in comparison with God's great gift to them and to us, the gift of his Son who is himself.

For God gives, too, to the utmost, and the greatness of God's gift as well as the tiny content of our own is symbolized by the gold and frankincense and myrrh. For Our Lord is our King, our Priest, and our Sacrifice, who rules over us, prays for us, and died for us. It was the greatest King who has ever reigned, the only utterly holy Priest, the only perfect Sacrifice, whom the kings saw in that child, and when they remembered this they bowed themselves in worship all over again.

They left their splendid gifts there and they looked their last on the child, yet not sadly, knowing they would see his face again when he and they had each died for the other; and they kissed a fold of Mary's shabby dress, bowed to Joseph, and went away. But they did not go back to Herod for in their sleep that night God told them in a dream to go back to their country another way, and not through Jerusalem. Their journey would have seemed easy this time, for they traveled light. They had given all that they had to God.

And Joseph and Mary were alone again with their baby, and Mary "kept all these things and pondered them in her heart."

3.

As we follow the story of Our Lord's life we shall see that there is nothing at all that men can suffer that he did not suffer too. One of the greatest miseries which men endure is that of banishment from their own country. Thousands of men and women and children were driven from their homes in the last war, and many have never been able to return to them, and the people of Israel have endured the wretchedness of exile over and over again all through their history. And the sorrow of exile was the first of the sorrows that came to Our Lord.

King Herod was a man who let nothing whatever hinder him from doing what he had decided to do. He had made up his mind that this child whom he feared his people might hail as the Messiah should be got rid of, and the fact that the kings did not return to Jerusalem, to tell him which of all the babies in Bethlehem was the one they had worshiped, did not turn him from his purpose. He gave the order that all the children in Bethlehem under two years old should be murdered. Such cruelty seems to us unbelievable, but Herod was a man so intensely cruel that he had murdered his own wife and children when he had suspected them of treachery. And he was an old man, and dying, and perhaps hardened and embittered by his pain. He gave the order and it was carried out. Yet it was only over the bodies of those children that Herod had power, and paradise waited for their happy spirits. They were the first of the martyrs to die for Our Lord, and the only ones who actually died before he did. The company of his martyrs is past counting now, but when he himself passed from the martyrdom of his cross to Paradise it was just that little band of children who met him joyously at the gate.

King Herod was no doubt satisfied with what he had done, but the one baby whom he had wanted to kill was the only one who escaped. Joseph had another of his dreams, in which an angel of God warned him of what was to happen, and told him to take Mary and her baby to Egypt and to stay there until it was safe to come back again. He obeyed at once, as he always did, though he must have felt something very like despair, wondering if he would ever again get back to his own village,

37

and the work that he loved, and the quiet life with Mary in their own home that he longed for. And this journey down into Egypt with a young wife and a small baby would be full of danger and difficulty. And when they got there how would he support them, in a foreign country, among people who did not even speak his language? And then he remembered the great "Fear not," and the assurance of God's love that had come to him then. The despair passed and he gave himself once more to do the will of God.

Joseph and Mary and their baby must have followed the old caravan road to Egypt that Joseph traveled when he too went into exile. We know nothing of that journey except that it must have been full of danger and difficulty. Once again Mary had to ride upon a donkey, aching with weariness, her arms numb with the weight of the child, and Joseph would have tramped beside her, tired and footsore. At first they must have been terrified lest Herod's men should overtake them, and kill their baby after all, and when that dread was left behind there would have been the fear of the unknown in front of them. For Joseph and Mary were mortal man and woman and even the greatest of God's saints, who have experienced his love and given him their trust, occasionally have panic-stricken thoughts that don't quite keep pace with their faith. And when they had left their own land behind and entered Egypt there would have been the heat of the desert by day and the cold at night, the sudden dust storms choking them, and the fear of losing the way. There must have been days when they hadn't enough to eat, and the water in their water bottles ran short. Joseph and Mary would not have minded so much for themselves as for their child. In Bethlehem they had rejoiced in the health and beauty of their baby but now they had to see him weary and fretting. Small babies can be wonderfully patient when they are ill and miserable, but their very patience breaks the hearts of those who love them.

Somewhere in Egypt they found a place to live, perhaps in some small mud-walled house in a village by the Nile. Some Egyptian man and his wife, poor people like themselves, were kind to them, and Joseph was put in the way of earning a living, and Mary given clothes for her child. It is strange to think that dark-skinned Egyptian women would have held Jesus in their arms and rocked him and sung songs to him. Perhaps they sang him the song of the Pharaoh Ikhnaton, the song of the God who is One, and never knew that they held him in their arms. Yet Mary and Joseph must have felt very homesick, and when Mary sang to her child perhaps she sang the children of Israel's song of exile, "By the waters of Babylon we sat down and wept, when we remembered thee, O Sion." When we adore Our Lord for all that he suffered for our salvation we sometimes forget all that his father and mother suffered too.

Yet the time passed, and was not as long as it seemed, and once more in his sleep the great angel stood by Joseph and told him that Herod was dead and that they might go home.

4.

The life of Our Lord is like a great symphony. It has three movements, with a silence between each when we are left wondering what is happening. The first movement is the music of his babyhood and boyhood, the second of his ministry and suffering and death, and the third of his resurrection. The first movement has one small break in it, not the deep silence that divides the other movements but a pause, dividing the babyhood from the boyhood, and the pause is one of twelve years.

Yet if we feel shut out from these years we have no right to

39

complain, for they do not belong to us but to Mary and Joseph. After all the dangers and difficulties, the strange comings and goings, at last they had their little boy to themselves in their own home. Joseph worked at his carpenter's bench again and Mary kept house, and their child was the joy of their lives. He was a happy child, and no little boy could have had a lovelier home than Nazareth. The hills about the village were a perfect playground for all the children who laughed and played there with him. From the northern hills they could see the deep blue Mediterranean, and the ships with their colored sails entering the harbor of Ptolemais. Down below them in the valleys ran two important roads, and they could see the Roman legions tramping by and hear the bells of passing caravans. In the spring they would run and tumble on hillsides carpeted with flowers, and pick great bunches of them to take home to their mothers, and watch the colors changing on the eternal hills. And we are not kept quite shut out from the peace and beauty of these days, for in this pause, as in the deeper silences, there is just one lovely sentence in the Bible that tells us something of what was happening. This is the flash of light that shines out now.

"And the child grew, and waxed strong in spirit, filled with wisdom; and the grace of God was upon him."

The sturdy little body grew stronger and more beautiful every day. The strong spirit that was to uphold so many through his earthly life, and that upholds us all today and now, showed itself in the courage of this little boy, in his gift of leadership and power of comfort. The greatness of his mind was already apparent in his humor, good sense, and love of learning. And the grace of God, the life of God, shone out in that glowing vitality which is a lovelier thing than beauty and indestructible while life shall last.

He was twelve when Joseph and Mary decided that he was old enough to go with them to Jerusalem for the Passover feast.

This feast was celebrated once a year, in the spring, and it was the greatest of the Jewish festivals because it commemorated the greatest event in their history—their deliverance from slavery in Egypt and the beginning of their journey to find the home that God had promised them. All the people of Israel who could leave their homes went on pilgrimage to Jerusalem for the feast and offered their sacrifices in the Temple. From all the small towns and villages perched upon the hilltops all over the country came companies of men and women and children, some of them riding upon donkeys, others walking, and all wearing their gayest clothes. The anxieties that pressed upon them they put away from them now, for it was a time for happiness. They laughed and talked as they journeyed and looked about them at the springtime beauty of their land; the high and distant hills splashed with heavenly color, the nearer ones striped silver and green with the vines and olives, the waving green corn in the valleys, and the fields full of flowers. At night they camped out near some village or inn, setting up their tents under the olive trees, lighting campfires, and sitting about them before they went to sleep, listening to the little tunes that the shepherd boys played on their pipes, and singing the songs of Israel. In the midday heat they stopped to rest by some wayside well and watched the little lizards darting out over the stones, and heard the crickets chirping. They got footsore and tired sometimes, but on the whole it was a happy journey, and every day Jerusalem came a little nearer.

To Our Lord it must have been a time of wonder and delight. He had been a much-traveled baby, but he could not remember that, and so this to him was the first journey of his life. When he became a man he loved his country and his people very deeply, and this journey would have revealed to him the beauty of the one and the life of the other. With eager delight he looked at the villages and fields and hills, at the men and women going about their business and the patient beasts at their toil, and stored all these things in his memory and like his mother pondered them in his heart. His strong young body would have exulted in the walking that tired his father and mother. While their elders were sitting resting in the shade the boys would have run races and climbed trees and played games, and Jesus would have run the fastest and tackled trees that baffled the others, and had brilliant ideas for new and wonderful games. But if he did things always a bit better than they did the other boys would not have disliked him for it because he never boasted about his exploits. He did not seem to think about them at all. For the boy who ran and laughed and played with the other boys was God, and in such humbling there could be no place for pride.

Perhaps as the little company from Nazareth made its way south it was joined by a company from another hill town, and among these were Zacharias and Elisabeth and their boy. Then Jesus was happier than ever for he had John with him for the rest of the journey. For these two cousins loved and admired each other and had each of them a very great reverence one for the other.

His first sight of the holy city must have held Our Lord silent and still with awe. It was a city larger than anything he had ever dreamed of, built high upon its hill of Mount Sion, with palaces and houses, towers and domes all enclosed within the old, powerful, tawny-colored walls that rose up so fiercely from the bare rock. A fine city yet rather a terrible one, with something stark and cruel in the look of it.

The noise and traffic in the narrow streets must have confused the country-bred boy, but people and what they were, and how they felt and what they did, always interested him so much that he would not have shrunk away from it. Wide-eyed, bombarding

42

Joseph or John with eager questions, he would have watched them all go by, pilgrims, priests, and merchants, rich men and poor men, splendidly dressed Roman officials and beggars in their rags, tramping legionaries, camels and donkeys, dogs and children. Perhaps one or two of them, some worried Roman official borne by on his litter or one of the tired slaves who carried it, noticed the boy, and the memory of the fresh beauty of his face made a hard day not so difficult as it might have been.

But for Our Lord the crowning glory of it all was the Temple. This was the house of God and the heart of Israel. Here was the Holy of Holies where God's presence dwelled, and before it in the Holy Place the smoke of incense rose up from the altar. Here he had been brought as a baby and given to the God whom he loved and worshiped with all the strength of his heart and mind and soul, and who through all his short life had always seemed nearer to him even than Joseph and Mary and John, closer even than his own breath and blood. This was the house of his God and Father and in coming to it he had come home.

He went to the Temple services with Joseph and Mary and stood with them to pray, but sometimes he went off by himself to pray alone, and they let him go, glad that he should learn to find his way about the holy place that meant so much to every Israelite. If they allowed him more freedom than parents usually give to children of twelve, that was natural, for if he was fearless he was trustworthy and sensible too, and never seemed to come to any harm.

And so it was that on the last day of the feast he discovered the quiet court where the Rabbis, the teachers of the Jewish religion, were instructing the young boys who came to them as pupils. Jesus had been instructed too, at home in Nazareth, but not by such wise and learned men as were teaching here. In Nazareth they had not been able to tell him the half of all that

43

he longed to know. His brilliant eager mind thirsted for knowledge. He wanted to know all about the history of his people and his religion, and to understand the law. Above all he wanted to read all the Scriptures, and have them explained to him, so that through them he might reach out to a deeper knowledge of his God and Father, and of his Father's purpose for him. He took his place quietly among the other boys and sat down to listen, his chin propped on his hands, his eyes fixed on the old Rabbi who sat with a roll of the Scriptures on his knees, talking to them of the Hope of Israel. As he listened Our Lord's heart beat hard, as it always did when men talked of the Christ. In five minutes he had forgotten all about the little party of travelers who today were to start the homeward journey to Nazareth. It was, he knew, his Father's will that he should be here, listening and learning, and he had known long before he had been old enough to put what he knew into words, that to do the will of his Father was the reason why he had come into the world.

Mary and Joseph had been traveling for a whole day before they found that Jesus was missing. Possibly it had been arranged that he should travel the first bit of the journey with Zacharias and Elisabeth and his beloved John, and his parents thought he was safely with them; and they, when Jesus did not join them, would have thought he was with his parents. In great anxiety Mary and Joseph looked for him among all their friends, and when they could not find him they went back to Jerusalem, where they spent three days searching for him. Mary must have been in misery all those three days. This was the first time that she had been parted from her son, and in her sorrow there was a foreshadowing of the anguish she would feel when he died. Then, as now, it was on the third day that he was given back to her again.

She and Joseph found him at last in the quiet court of the

Temple, and now he was not only listening to the Rabbis but asking them questions. The questions of an intelligent boy of twelve are frequently too much for a poor grownup, and as this boy was wise beyond his years and athirst for knowledge the Rabbis must have been quite tired out. To rest themselves they asked him questions, too, and were astonished at his understanding and answers.

Mary interrupted with a cry of anguished reproach. "Son, why hast thou thus dealt with us? Your father and I have sought thee sorrowing."

He went at once to comfort them but could not understand Mary's reproach. "How is it that ye sought me?" he asked her. "Wist ye not that I must be about my Father's business?" Why had she been worried? Did she not understand that he had to do his Father's will, and that when he was away from her that was what he was doing? He was quite safe doing his Father's will.

But Mary and Joseph had had a bad fright and just at this moment they were incapable of understanding anything except that he must come home with them at once, and they would not take their eyes off him again until they had got him safely back to Nazareth.

"And he went down with them, and came to Nazareth, and was subject unto them."

There is sadness in that sentence, the sadness of the boy who had to say good-by to Jerusalem the holy city, to the beautiful Temple that was his Father's house, and the learned men who could have taught him so much if he had stayed with them. It must have been bitterly hard to say good-by, but quietly and obediently he turned his back on it all and went home to little Nazareth.

This self-denial of the boy Jesus makes us think of some of

45

the other denials of Our Lord's life. Good and fine men always have many gifts, though they do not excel equally in all that they do because being imperfect their growth is uneven, like that of a tree that puts out some branches that are perfectly grown and some that are twisted or stunted. But Our Lord was a perfect man, he had all the gifts that a man can have in perfection, and perfectly balanced. We do not always realize how talented he was because for our sakes he denied himself the use of so many of them. He could have been the finest scholar who has ever lived, the greatest ruler, politician, artist, musician, or poet. We can see his great gifts shining through all his words and deeds, yet for our sake he denied himself their full use. Hard work for God and man took up all his time; there was none left in which to enjoy himself reading books and writing poems. Because he never happened to say that he found this self-denial hard we need not think that he found it easy. A very talented man always finds it very hard indeed if he cannot use to the full the powers that are his; he feels restless and thwarted and at times even a bit desperate.

But once he had wrenched himself away from the beautiful Temple and the wise teachers and the quiet court the boy Jesus would not have stayed sad for long. Whatever it was that his heavenly Father wanted him to learn from those Rabbis he had already learned it by the time his earthly father came to fetch him. And if he had to leave the Rabbis he had his loving and most perfect mother.

"His mother kept all these sayings in her heart."

If she had not understood in the Temple about his having to do his Father's will that was only because she had been so stunned by the fright he had given her. As soon as she got over it she would have understood. Her great love and understanding were his all through his life.

5.

We come to a silence, a break of eighteen years between the music of the first part of the symphony and of the second. Upon his return home Nazareth took the boy Jesus and hid him away, and we do not see him again until he is thirty years old. We call this silence the hidden years. We feel we would give anything to know about them, yet why should we? They don't belong to us. His self-giving is like a stream that widens out and out. The years of his childhood belonged to Mary and Joseph, and in these years of his boyhood and young manhood he gave himself to his family and friends and the bit of earth where he lived. It is what comes after that belongs to us. In that self-giving the stream became a mighty flood that embraces all the world.

Yet in this pause, too, there is one shining sentence that tells us something. "And Jesus increased in wisdom and stature and in favour with God and man."

The intelligent, eager little boy growing up into a very wise man, one of those men to whom people go when they are in any sort of trouble, and he straightens out their muddles and comforts their sorrows with his understanding, and bolsters up their weakness and idiocy with his courage and good sense.

The perfect child's body that Mary had held in her arms growing into a perfect man's body, tall and strong, made for hard work and hard endurance, a body characterized by those physical graces that are the outward signs of spiritual gifts. Brave and sensible men who know what they have to do, and do it come what may, walk with a quick firm step and keep their backs straight. Truthful men look you straight in the eyes with a glance which is not easy to meet if you yourself don't happen to be as truthful as they are. Clearheaded men talk easily and naturally and are a delight to listen to, and when they have a

47

keen sense of humor, and the imagination and power of observation of the artist and poet, they are such good company that other people make it very difficult for them ever to be alone. Men with a deep, strong, unselfish love for their fellow men have a smile that, when they see you, flashes out like light over their faces and makes your own cold heart glow with warmth and comfort. Men who for years have been growing in holiness and the love of God have in their faces a beauty that cannot be described, but as we grow older we learn to recognize it, and it makes us feel that if to love God in the beauty of holiness can make a man look like that then it is the one thing supremely worth doing; and the life that gives us the chance of trying to do it is, whatever its suffering, most precious to us.

The Evangelists have left no record of Our Lord's physical appearance, but perhaps they did not think that necessary. They have shown us what he was, and if we think of that long enough and hard enough we find that we have such a clear picture of him in our minds that if we meet him one day at a turn in the road we shall know him.

He was "in favour with God and man." He could not possibly have been anything else.

Our Lord's relatives are often mentioned in the gospels, and so we can think of him in these hidden years as taking his place in the family. As his eldest son Joseph would have taught him his own trade of carpentering and Our Lord would have learned to make tables and stools, looms for the weaving, plows, and yokes for the oxen. We picture him hard at work in the carpenter's shop that opened on the village street, singing as he worked because he liked work and was doing it supremely well. As Joseph got older and less strong he would have left the hardest work to his son and Our Lord's body would have gained strength and learned endurance through the handling of the heavy saws and planks of wood. Carpentering was not the only trade he knew

48

about. His parables show us that he understood all the work that countrymen do. He knew about the work in the vineyards, about plowing and sowing and reaping and the keeping of sheep. When he had finished helping his own father he would go and help other men who perhaps were old or ailing and had no strong young son to lend them a hand.

As we think of the work that he must have done picture after picture of him flashes across our minds. We see him doing the work of some old shepherd who was sick and leading the sheep home over the hills, talking to them in the sheep-and-goat language that Eastern shepherds know. Sheep do not usually follow a shepherd who is not their own, but they would have followed the God who made them. We see him working in the harvest fields, tirelessly swinging the heavy scythe, gathering the grapes or the olives, pruning the fig trees and quinces. He would have enjoyed the tending of the land, of living creatures and growing things, for it was service to this lovely bit of earth that was his home, and service to the God and Father who had made all things good.

He knew how to make bread, too, and perhaps when Mary was ill or tired he made it for the family. He must have been a wonderful elder brother to all younger children, able to turn his carpenter's skill to the making of toys and his artist's imagination to the fashioning of stories and games. He would have comforted the little ones in all their troubles and when the naughty ones got into a scrape he would have known exactly what to do. And he would have taught them by word and example to reverence the religion of Israel, to be constant and faithful in the keeping of the Sabbath and the saying of their prayers, to love God and keep his commandments.

It seems that sometime during these years Joseph died, and Jesus would have strengthened him in his dying, comforted Mary, and then taken the burden of the family upon his shoulders. He must have had much to do for his village and family, for he was thirty years old before he was able to leave Nazareth.

This life of hard work, strenuous and faithful for all to see, had its roots in a life that no one saw, the life of prayer that he lived alone with God. Many saints have had a great deal to say about their experiences in prayer, and have even written books about it, but about his life with his Father Our Lord was silent, for it was something too holy to be spoken of, and went so deep that no words could have described it. And we, when we think of it, must think of it upon our knees, knowing only this about it, that it was the source of the power and strength and love that wrought out our salvation.

Teach us, good Lord, to serve thee as thou deservest:
To give and not to count the cost;
To fight and not to heed the wounds;
To toil and not to seek for rest;
To labour and not to ask for any reward
Save that of knowing that we do thy will.   Amen.
                                        —St. Ignatius Loyola

Chapter 3

FOLLOW ME

Repent ye: for the kingdom of heaven is at hand.
—St. Matthew III:2

1.

WE HAVE come now to the central movement of the great symphony. In nearly all symphonies the first movement is one of grace and charm, sometimes light and gay, but in the second we move on to the Andante, mounting to a climax of strength and power, sometimes full of sadness. The third movement is nearly always one of triumphant joy.

Our Lord is thirty years old now, an age when a man's powers have reached their full development, when he is physically and mentally at his strongest. The work that he had to do for his own family and village is finished and his work for us all lies before him. And John the Forerunner comes out of the wilderness to prepare the way.

He had been living for a long time in the wild mountains of

Judea, praying alone to God, wearing only a rough coat of camel's hair, keeping himself alive on locusts and wild honey, and sleeping in caves in the rocks. He must have been cold and hungry and bitterly lonely, but he did not mind what he endured if through prayer and discipline he could become the sort of man whom God could use to prepare the way for the coming of the Christ. John knew that he had to be like a trumpet sounding at dawn, like an ax with a keen cutting edge. He had to cry aloud to men to wake up, for their Lord was coming. With hard, almost brutal words he had to show them exactly what detestable sinners they were, break their pride, which was like a barred door keeping God out, that they might repent and let him in through the smashed-up door that is humility. He could not do this unless he had woken up himself, unless he was himself sorry and humbled. And this alertness, this penitence, he learned in the wilderness, and through the pain of that time God purged him and strengthened him and fitted him for all he had to do.

John began his preaching in the valley of the River Jordan, preaching with such power that presently crowds of people were streaming out from the towns and villages of Judea to listen to him. All sorts of people came, men and women, rich and poor, soldiers, merchants, rabbis, and priests from the Temple, and they crowded about him where he stood thundering at them from a rock, and listened in astonishment to the startling things that he had to say. He told them who he was in the words of the prophet Isaiah. "The voice of one crying in the wilderness, Prepare ye the way of the Lord, make his paths straight." And then he painted for them a picture of this Lord that frightened them. The Christ was coming to purge Israel. He was coming as a woodman with an ax in his hands to cut down the rotten trees. He was coming as a farmer to the threshing floor to separate the wheat from the chaff, to burn the chaff and destroy it. He was coming with the Holy Ghost and with fire, coming in the awful holiness of God to burn away their sin.

John, like Our Lord after him, could use words as a surgeon uses a knife, painful, sharp words that cut away deception from men's minds as a poisonous growth in a body is cut away. "Generation of vipers," John thundered at learned and highly esteemed men who until now had had no doubts about their own worth and distinction, "who hath warned you to flee from the wrath to come?" Vipers. Venomous little snakes that men encounter in their path with wrath and kill right off without thinking twice about it.

Everyone who heard John was startled, shocked, and scared. "What must we do?" they asked.

"Repent ye!" he cried. "Repent! Repent! Repent!"

And many of them repented. They came to John and humbled themselves to tell him all the viperish things that they had done and thought and said, and when he found that they were truly sorry and ashamed he took them down to the River Jordan and baptized them, immersing them that they might understand that the love of God had washed away their sins. He was gentle with them then, and told them what they must do that they might please the God who had forgiven them. Those who were well off must share with those who were not so rich. The businessmen must not charge prices higher than was right and honest. The soldiers must do their work without violence, speak the truth, and be content with their wages. What God wanted of each of them was that he should be honest, generous, and kind, do his work as well as he could, and come what might, be cheerful about it and not grumble.

Like all teachers and prophets John had disciples, young men whom he instructed, who loved him and helped him in his work as sons help their father. These men and many others realized his greatness, and they found it difficult to believe that he was a mere man. Some of them thought that he was the prophet Elijah reborn upon this earth, and others felt sure that he was not the Forerunner of the Christ, as he said he was, but the Christ himself. Like all the saints John was a deeply humble man, and when he knew what they were saying he was in great distress. "I am not the Christ," he cried out. "I am the voice of one crying in the wilderness. There cometh one mightier than I after me, the latchet of whose shoes I am not worthy to stoop down and unloose."

John baptized in the River Jordan in Judea. The river flows swiftly and the water is fresh and clear. The climate in the sheltered Jordan Valley is almost tropical. Flowering trees grow upon the riverbanks, among them the tamarisk with its feathery pink flowers and willows with their silvery leaves. The birds love these trees, and morning and evening their song mingles with the music of the flowing water.

One day John was baptizing in the Jordan. He stood knee-deep in the river and one by one his penitents came to him and he dipped up the water and poured it over them, and spoke to them just the few words that would help and comfort them. It was a day of light, one of those brilliant days that sometimes end in thunder. The streaming silvery sunshine danced on the water, on the leaves that rippled as the wind passed over them, and lit with beauty the wet faces of the penitent men, who knowing themselves forgiven of God turned to smile at John as they said good-by. As time went on he became very tired, and the light dazzled him. There was a pause in the stream of penitents, and he shut his eyes for a moment. Then he heard a light, quick, firm footfall. It had a dear familiarity about it and his heart leaped. It always had leaped when he heard that step. His mother had told him that when he was a baby in her womb his whole small body had leaped for joy at the approach of the Mother of Jesus, carrying her son, too, a baby in her womb.

"John!"

He swung round and opened his eyes. Yes, it was he, coming down the path through the trees, taking off his coat as he came. His eyes met John's, and his smile flashed out like light over his face. Making himself one with the company of the penitents he had come to John to be baptized too. Before John could stop him he had stepped down into the water and was humbly waiting, this cousin and friend of John's whose shoe's latchet he was not worthy to stoop down and unfasten.

John in his humility was in even deeper distress than he had been when they asked him if he was the Christ. "I have need to be baptized of thee," he said, "and comest thou to me?"

Jesus answered gently, "Suffer it to be so now: for thus it becometh us to fulfill all righteousness."

Then John understood. They had both of them always obeyed those laws of their earthly country that were right and just. Jesus had always shared the obedience of his people, even though he was the God to whom all obedience is due. The first law of the heavenly kingdom that he had come to establish was that a man should humble himself and be sorry for his sins before he could enter into it.

So Jesus bent his head, and John baptized him. Then he stood erect again, the silver water shot through with sunshine streaming off him, and went up "straightway" out of the water. John watched with humble love, and it seemed to him that all the light of the bright day gathered itself about that quickly moving figure. It was as though the very heavens opened and the light shone down. John, gazing till his eyes ached with loving, thought he saw wings in the light, that bent themselves protectively over Jesus, as though the light was some actual living presence. From the shining light there came to him then a sense of such purity, such peace, that he thought of a dove. He shut his eyes and a voice pealed like thunder in his ears. "This is my beloved Son, in whom I am well pleased."

2.

Before he began his work John had gone up alone into the mountains to fight temptation, to fast and pray and listen to the voice of God, and now Our Lord did the same thing. He had no sins to be purged away by discipline and pain but before he began his work for the salvation of the world he had to meet and fight temptation. Those whom penitence has admitted to the kingdom of God are not set free from temptation. As the servants of God grow in humility and devotion to Our Lord so temptation assails them more and more violently. The devil gets desperate when he sees a soul drawing day by day nearer to God. He goes all out in the fight and uses every weapon that he can. The holier the man the worse the temptation, and Our Lord being entirely holy endured such an agony of temptation as no man had endured before. Yet that he did endure, and conquered, has put hope into the heart of every sinner ever since. There is not a single temptation that can come to us that did not come to him, and he knows everything there is to know about it. When we are fighting the devil we feel very far away from Our Lord, but we are really very close indeed, because he has been there before us and is fighting with us.

The times of greatest suffering in Our Lord's life came at the beginning and the end of his three years' ministry. At the end he suffered at the center of a crowd of brutal men, with noise and confusion all about him, but at the beginning he suffered by himself at the center of silence. It is hard to endure being looked at while you suffer, and it is also hard to suffer quite alone. Both these kinds of endurance Our Lord knows about.

Leaving behind him the happiness of his day of baptism, the Jordan Valley with its light and flowing water, its birds and flowers, with his staff in his hand he tramped away across the stony waste that sloped from the valley, and climbed up into the mountains that the three kings crossed when they came to worship him. These mountains are beautiful in the distance with their wonderful colors of blue and amethyst, but near at hand they are savage and cruel, with a striped and tigerish look. Only a brave and adventurous man would have chosen such a place for his battleground, and chosen for the armor of his fighting spirit the loneliness of the cold nights and the hot days, a bed of stones and the pains of a starving body.

Our Lord seems to have told no one about the worst part of this fight; like his prayer it must have been something that went far beyond the experience of ordinary men, and if words had existed that could describe it they would not have understood. But he did tell his disciples about the three last temptations that came to him, for they were temptations that come to us all throughout our lives, and to help us he told us how he himself met and mastered them.

As the forty days' fight drew to a close Our Lord was "an hungered." That is to say, he was exhausted and in pain, and had such a craving for food that he felt he could not keep sane if he did not get it. Men who nearly starved to death as prisoners of war, men who were adrift on rafts from torpedoed ships, know what he felt like; and he knows what they felt like. And the devil put this thought into his mind. "Look at that stone lying there. If I am the Son of God I can turn that stone into bread." He knew he was the Son of God, and he also knew that his sinlessness had brought him into such perfect union with his

Father that the power of God could flow through him to change the substance of material things in whatever way God willed. But it must be in the way God willed, not the way he willed, and he knew it was not the will of his Father that he should use this power to help himself. He had come into the world to live and suffer as a man, and he must not do for himself anything that could not be done by a man's natural skill and courage, nor shirk any of the human suffering that would be the natural consequence of many of the things that it would be his duty to do or say.

Every day we are up against this temptation to do what we want instead of what God wants, and most of the time the devil conquers us. We use the gifts God has given us to help ourselves in the way that we choose, instead of giving them back to God to be used by him for his children in the way that he wills. God wants us to face and tackle some difficulty or responsibility or pain, and we shirk it like a horse refusing a gate. And then tired out with the exhausting business of trying to please ourselves, and seldom succeeding, and trying to find another way round than the way of the five-barred gate, and getting lost, we look for fresh strength in the wrong place, in the amusements and luxuries of the world that buoy you up for the moment and then leave you feeling weaker and sillier than you did before. But we find our salvation in the answer that Our Lord gave the tempter. "Man shall not live by bread alone, but by every word of God."

The only possible way to live is to give ourselves to God to do his will, which is his word. And the word of God is not only the command of God but the strength of God, for they are inseparable; he never tells us to do anything without giving us the strength to do it. And his strength is the only source of our strength; it never lets you down and it lasts forever.

58

The stone remained a stone and was not made bread, and Our Lord remained weak and in pain. Whenever we are tired or ill we suddenly begin to have doubts about the things we knew with absolute conviction only a short while before. The truths upon which we have based our lives seem all at once to give way beneath us. It is a dreadful feeling and it came flooding over Our Lord now. Was he really the Son of God? He felt that he must prove it to himself in some way, or he could not go on. Men who are exhausted often have queer visions and now Our Lord thought that he was standing upon a pinnacle of the Temple in Jerusalem. Below him were the Temple courts, with the smoke going up from the altar of sacrifice, and the courts were thronged with people. He heard a voice saying to him, "If thou be the Son of God, cast thyself down from hence: For it is written, He shall give his angels charge over thee, to keep thee; and in their hands they shall bear thee up, lest at any time thou dash thy foot against a stone."

Though it was the voice of the tempter it seemed the voice of common sense. Why should he not put his sonship to the test in some such way as this? Why should he not ask God to give him a sign, show him in some unmistakable way that he was truly the Christ? He would attempt some humanly impossible feat and cry out to God for the help of his angels in accomplishing it. If the help was forthcoming then he would know without any shadow of doubt that he was the Son of God. And so would all the people who would witness the wonder. They would be spared the agony of doubt, the indecision they would have to suffer, if he came among them without any great sign from heaven to show them who he was. This temptation must have been harder to fight than the other for it struck at him not only through his own doubt but through his love of his people. Yet he fought and conquered, answering the evil voice that had dared to speak to

59

him in the words of the Scriptures that he loved with words from the same Scriptures.

"It is said, Thou shalt not tempt the Lord thy God."

To tempt is to test, and to put God to the test is not only an insult to his majesty but destroys the whole glory of faith. As love that is compelled is no love, so faith that is compelled is no faith. Faith in God is loving God so much that you believe he exists even though your bodily eyes cannot see him, and do what he tells you to do though you have no way of proving that the voice you hear in your soul is his voice, and journey toward the place he tells you to go to without knowing if it is really there. It is like a charge in the dark of blindfolded men, and it takes great courage. Faith grows out of love and is inseparable from courage. Our Lord chose now, for himself and for his people, the way of courage. He would not ask God for a sign, and when later they asked him to give them one he would not give it to them. And he will not give it to us either. Day after day, over and over again, right up till the end of our lives, we have to fight this temptation of doubt and cowardice and walk the way of faith as he did.

But the devil had not finished with him yet. It seemed to Our Lord that he was no longer standing upon a pinnacle of the Temple, looking down on the crowded courts below, but upon the summit of a high mountain looking down upon the kingdoms of the world, and he saw them bathed in glory, infinitely beautiful and desirable. And the tempter's voice said, "All these things will I give thee, if thou wilt fall down and worship me."

The voice speaking to Our Lord was the voice of the power of evil. We who are such tiny specks in the great universe, and are always within us so deeply and tremblingly conscious of our weakness and nothingness, cannot help worshiping power. And we can worship which power we choose, the power of God

60

triumphant now and forever in the world of the spirit, or the power of evil triumphant in this world only for as long, and in so far as men yield themselves to it. Men who worship the power of God in humility and love are given the power of God that they may grow in humility and love, and their very growth is their reward, for it does not end in this world but carries them right on to God himself in eternity. Men who worship the power of evil in pride and selfishness are given the power of evil that they may grow in pride and selfishness, and this growth can lay hold of great rewards in this world, it can grasp all the material possessions and satisfactions that there are, and find great delight in them for the brief moment before they dissolve in the dust of death.

It seems to us almost unbelievable that Our Lord could have been tempted to worship the power of evil, yet he would not have been true man if it had not been so, for no man escapes this temptation. It is so subtle that they do not always see it for what it is. They think they want power over their fellow men, that they may rule them for their good, or they think they want wealth that they may use it to help other people, and are unaware of the pride and selfishness that are really at the root of their longing. Yet if they attain to earthly power, even though they are good men to begin with, more often than not they are evil men when they come to the end of it all.

Our Lord knew that with the great talents that were his he could have been a greater conqueror than Alexander and ruled a wider empire than Caesar. Gripped in the awful power of this temptation, his eyes enchanted by the glory of the kingdoms of this world, he must have seen more and more clearly, as the temptation mounted, the beauty of the earthly kingdom which he could have founded. He would have ruled in wisdom, justice, and generosity, and compelled men to wisdom, justice, and generosity. His rule would have imposed upon them a heaven upon earth that would have lasted until the day of his death, and hardly a moment longer.

And what good would that have been to the men and women whom he loved? A forced and worthless happiness over almost as soon as tasted; and his Father had sent him into the world to win for them an eternal joy. He saw this temptation for the evil thing it was, fought and conquered it, and like a compass needle turning back to the north his allegiance returned to his Father.

"Thou shalt worship the Lord thy God, and him only shalt thou serve."

In the tormented man tearing himself away from the vision of the glory of the earthly kingdom that might have been his, we see again the little boy turning away from the earthly Jerusalem and going so patiently back to Nazareth.

There was no more the evil power could do. The great pitched battle was over and the devil left Our Lord "for a season." Only for a season. He would be back again, and the fight go on right up till the end, but just for the moment he was conquered and the powers of evil sank away down from the mountain and left it to the peace of God.

In his second temptation Our Lord had refused to compel the angels to help him but they came freely now and "ministered unto him." Perhaps the dawn was breaking when the door of heaven opened, and they came out of the east with wings of flame. Our Lord felt no less spent and weary because they had come, for physical ease was a thing he had refused, but he knew they were there. "He shall give his angels charge over thee, to keep thee; and in their hands they shall bear thee up, lest at any time thou dash thy foot against a stone." Without them it would not have been possible for a starving man to have climbed down the mountain and tramped over the stony waste back to the valley. But they were there and Our Lord got home safely.

62

3.

After the fight in the wilderness, and before the next great fight begins, there comes a pause of peace and happiness as Our Lord gathers about him the first of the band of eager young men who became his disciples.

From the wilderness he had returned "in the power of the Spirit" into Galilee, and this power was with him now in these first days of his preaching and teaching. His message was the same as John's, "Repent: for the kingdom of heaven is at hand." They must have worked together for a short while, tramping through the Jordan Valley, aflame with the love of God and the love of the souls of men—rivalry made a thing impossible by the greatness of their love.

Our Lord's first disciples were a gift from John, and in nothing more than in the selflessness of this gift do we see the greatness of John. Now that the Christ had come he knew that his own work was over. "He must increase, but I must decrease," he said. There was no bitterness in that, only the quiet and humble acceptance of a fact. And he was immensely happy to draw back into the shadow in the presence of the shining of his Lord. He said he was like the friend of the bridegroom, "which standeth and heareth him, rejoicing greatly because of the bridegroom's voice: this my joy therefore is fulfilled." But he guessed that his death was not far away, and like all men who face their end he wanted to leave his wealth to the person he loved best in the world. But he had no earthly wealth. He possessed nothing but the love and loyalty of the best of his spiritual children. That he gave to Our Lord.

One day, surrounded by a group of his disciples, John saw Jesus coming toward them and he said, "Behold the Lamb of God, which taketh away the sin of the world."

63

It was a startling thing to say. John had been able to assure men that God would have mercy upon the penitent, but he had not been able to do more than that. Now he told his disciples that this man coming toward them, perfect like one of the unblemished lambs that were offered upon the altar of sacrifice at Jerusalem, would pick up the burden of the sin of the world, take it on his shoulders and carry it right away. For this man was the Christ.

The next day John was standing with only two of his disciples, two young fishermen, and they saw Jesus passing by. One of these two was the young John who became Our Lord's greatest earthly friend after the death of the elder John; and the other was Andrew who at the end of his life died a martyr's death for Christ. John the Baptist must have known of what greatness these two as yet untried young men were capable. Probably of all his disciples they were the ones he loved best; especially the young John with his great gift of loving friendship. He repeated the same words again: "Behold the Lamb of God," and this time the words were not only a statement but a command. We can picture John the Baptist, after he had spoken, turning quietly away and leaving his two disciples. For a moment, perhaps, they hesitated, then they too turned and followed the figure of the younger man moving quickly and lightly along the path through the trees. How could they do anything else? They had heard his voice and seen his face and to follow him seemed the only thing worth doing in the world.

If Our Lord was going anywhere "straightway" they must have had to hurry to catch up with him. He heard their running footsteps and turned round, and his smile was like light flashing over his face.

"What seek ye?" he asked them.

They did not answer that question. Perhaps they found it

difficult to explain that it was just himself they wanted. Instead they said, "Master, where dwellest thou?"

He said, "Come and see."

In those words there is not only the welcome of a good host to his friends but a most charming gaiety, a hint of fun. Once he had left Nazareth Our Lord never had a home. The place where he lived now was probably a rough tent, or a shelter of green branches built upon the riverbank; it was not exactly a king's palace, but with a king for a host it must have felt like one.

It was toward evening. Our Lord waited upon his guests, lighting a little fire of sticks and laying before them such food as he had, perhaps a loaf of bread and a handful of dates. He liked preparing meals for his friends. After his resurrection he would get breakfast for those same men upon the shore of the Sea of Galilee, only a few miles from the riverbank where he was getting supper for them now. While they ate and talked together the moon rose and laid a path of light upon the river, and shone through the branches of the trees upon the face of the Son of God. It was then perhaps that Andrew got up and slipped away. He had a brother, Simon. He must fetch Simon that he also might look upon the face of the Christ and hear his words. John had a brother, too, James, whom he loved, but he did not go to fetch him then for he could not leave Our Lord. And so for the first time these two friends were alone together. Years later John wrote, "And the Word was made flesh and dwelt among us, (and we beheld his glory, the glory as of the only begotten of the Father,) full of grace and truth." Sitting there on the ground at Our Lord's feet the young John looked up into his face and saw the glory, and the grace was like new life poured into him and the truth searched him through. There was born in him then that great love of Our Lord that transformed his whole life and through him has changed other lives also. For John, even more than the other Evangelists, has through the heavenly

65

splendor of the words that he wrote about Our Lord brought countless men and women to love him too.

Then Andrew came back with Simon, and Jesus turned from John to welcome another man who would live and die for him. Simon was an older married man, a fisherman too, stocky and strong, outspoken and downright, a complete contrast to the young and sensitive John. He stood before Our Lord, touching his forehead and breast in salutation as Eastern men do, and gruffly murmured a greeting, and Our Lord looked at him and loved his sturdiness. "Thou art Simon, the son of Jona," he said, "thou shalt be called Peter, a rock."

This must have surprised Simon. In spite of his sturdy body he had never thought of himself as having anything rocklike in his character. He was an impulsive man, apt to rush into impetuous speech and action, and then finding himself not able to carry through what he had started or to make good his protestations. But Our Lord understood him. He was like a child who seeing a beautiful thing runs after it and falls headlong. But he saw the true and beautiful thing when another child would not have seen it, and out of the grief and humbling of many tumbles would grow a steadiness and strength that would not fail.

Simon Peter and his brother Andrew had a friend called Philip, who like them came from Bethsaida, a little town built on the shore of the Sea of Galilee. Jesus met him next day and said to him, "Follow me," and Philip looked in his face and knew that he would always follow him. Men who have found Our Lord can never rest until those whom they love have found him too, and so now Philip hurried off to fetch his friend Nathanael, as Andrew had already fetched Simon, and John had fetched his brother James.

"We have found the Christ," said Philip to Nathanael, "and he is Jesus of Nazareth, the son of Joseph."

But Nathanael seems to have been in a bitter mood, enduring some grief that was making him miserable, and as the miserable often do he gave a very nasty answer. "Can any good thing come out of Nazareth?" he said.

Philip did not waste time arguing with an embittered man, he just said, "Come and see."

And Nathanael came, and Jesus, looking into his eyes, knew him to be a man straight and true, without falsehood. "An Israelite indeed," he said, "in whom is no guile."

Jesus with the keen sight of great holiness "knew what was in men," and though he knew their sins, too, it was always the good in them upon which he immediately laid his hand. The sin he would purge away but the good he would take and love and make perfect. He had seen the hidden strength in Peter and now, ignoring the bitterness, he saw Nathanael's truth.

Nathanael was startled. He had never seen Jesus of Nazareth before and yet he was looking at him and speaking to him as though they were old friends. "Whence knowest thou me?" he asked.

Jesus answered, "Before that Philip called thee, when thou wast under the fig tree, I saw thee."

Only Our Lord and Nathanael knew just what happened under that fig tree. We can only guess. Had Nathanael been praying there? Asking God for strength to bear his grief? Weeping over it? Whatever it was, Jesus knew about it, and looked at Nathanael with such love and understanding that his bitterness vanished. "Master," he cried out, "thou art the Son of God; thou art the King of Israel." And from that moment he belonged body and soul to his Lord.

These were the first six, two pairs of brothers and two friends, James and John, Andrew and Simon Peter, Philip and Nathanael. They were the first stones of the living Church that Our Lord has built, every stone the spirit of a saint.

67

4.

Upon this time of happiness there falls a shadow which for Our Lord must have been a bitter grief. John the Baptist was arrested and imprisoned.

After the death of Herod the Great his kingdom had been divided into three parts by the Romans. Later on, Judea became a Roman province, and two of Herod's sons, Herod Antipas and Philip, became the rulers of Galilee and the desert region to the northeast of it. Herod Antipas, Tetrarch of Galilee, had fallen in love with Herodias, Philip's wife, taken her from her husband and made her his own wife, which was contrary to Jewish law as well as being an act of treachery to his brother, and John had courageously told him exactly what he thought of him.

He was imprisoned in the terrible fortress of Machaerus. The Jordan flows from the Sea of Galilee down to the desolate valley of the Dead Sea. It is sunk so deeply in the earth that nothing will grow there. The cliffs above it look twisted and tortured and the rocks near the water are covered with salt and slime. High up in the bleak mountains overlooking this dreary place was the fortress. The concentration camps where today the men who will not submit to tyranny and wickedness are sent to die are a modern version of Machaerus. When Our Lord heard of John's arrest he must have known that he would not see his friend again in this world, and men and women in Europe who have seen those they love taken away to concentration camps can understand the anguish that he felt.

But no one saw his grief. Serene and steady he went quietly on with the work that had to be done, and the next thing was to call his disciples more closely to him. Though Andrew and the young John had been John the Baptist's gift to him one cannot believe that he would have allowed them to leave John the

68

Baptist entirely while he was still a free man. But now John the Baptist had been taken away from them all and the time had come for Our Lord to make these young men his own.

The story of how he did it is one of the loveliest in the Gospels, and the scene of it is the Sea of Galilee—that was the scene of so very much of Our Lord's work for his people and for us all. As later on in this story we shall watch him praying, preaching, and healing in this land of Galilee, it is good to have a clear picture in our minds of the background against which his figure moves.

The name Galilee has a country sound about it but in reality the district about the large inland lake was a busy place, humming with activity and alive with the comings and goings of the men of many nations. Our Lord had not come into the world to lead the life of a hermit; he had come to save the souls of men, and wherever sinning, sorrowing, suffering men and women were to be found there was Our Lord in the midst of them. The western shore of the lake was ringed round with towns and villages, the biggest of them being Tiberias, Magdala, and Capernaum. On the hills behind Tiberias Herod Antipas had built his beautiful summer palace, and from the harbor of Tiberias his barges set out for pleasure trips upon the lake. Among the mountains on the eastern shore were Greek cities. The old caravan roads from Tyre and Sidon, and the Roman highways leading from Antioch to Jerusalem, and from Damascus to the Egyptian frontier—all met at the Sea of Galilee. When Our Lord walked along the roads of Galilee he would have met Roman legions on the march, Phoenician merchants, jugglers, and gladiators going to the amphitheater at Tiberias or to the Greek cities among the eastern mountains. It was a busy industrial district, with die works, pottery works, and ship-building yards. There was a flourishing fishing industry and the fish caught in the lake were pickled and sent to Jerusalem.

In those days the hills of the western shores were wooded, and among the trees were gardens bright with lilac, nasturtiums, carnations, and geraniums. From these gardens came the sound of running water, and there were always plenty of birds about— sparrows, swifts, pigeons, cranes, and kingfishers. The bare hills on the other side of the lake, seven miles away, were mauve and pink beyond the blue water, and to the north snow-covered Mount Hermon rose up against the sky. The lake was often crowded with shipping, but sailors had to keep their weather eye open, for storms on the Sea of Galilee can blow up very suddenly. The west winds sweep down from the mountains, and water that was smooth one moment is tempestuous the next. Life in the midst of so much activity, and surrounded by such beauty, made the Galileans a very individual people. The more rigid Jews of Jerusalem laughed at them for this individuality and made fun of their country dialect, but they had an independence of mind and an idealism that the men of Judea lacked; and Our Lord in his wisdom chose the men of Galilee for his first disciples.

There were innumerable little coves, as well as the cities and villages about the Sea of Galilee, from which one could look up and see hillsides terraced with vines and olives or patched with fields of corn. An open-air preacher could ask for no more perfect place in which to talk to a crowd of people than one of these coves. Hundreds of men and women could sit on the shore in the sunshine, and the natural amphitheater of the hillside behind them made it easy for them to hear the preacher's voice. Our Lord was preaching one day in one of these coves. Some fishing boats were drawn up on the shore, and near them fishermen sat on the rocks mending their nets. They were Peter, Andrew, James, and John, and as they did their work their eager minds drank up his words as the thirsty earth drinks up the rain. Today we thank God for the receptive minds of the men of Galilee, for they remembered Our Lord's teaching so vividly, and wrote it down so freshly, that when today we read what he said it is as though we were not reading at all but sitting and listening with the crowd in the cove. There was such a big crowd that Our Lord was nearly pushed into the lake. But he was never at a loss for a quick and humorous solution of all the problems that beset him. If he was being pushed into the lake then he'd go on the lake, and he called out to Peter and asked him to lend him his boat as a pulpit. The impulsive Peter flung his net aside, leaped to his feet, and ran laughing to help Our Lord into the boat and push it out from the shore. And here, with the boat rocking a little on the ripples, Our Lord sat and taught.

He wore a long flowing talith, or coat, of blue or white, over a loose robe woven all in one piece, without seam, and a white turban bound round the head by a cord and falling to the shoulders to protect him from the hot sun. Almost we can see the grace and dignity of his still figure, the strength and beauty of his sunburned face as he talked to the absorbed crowd on the shore, and hear his clear and most lovely voice that was music to the ears of those who listened and strength and comfort to their souls. Those nearest to him heard as well, as accompaniment to his words, the sound of the little ripples slapping softly against the side of the boat. It is one of the loveliest sounds in the world, and no lover of Our Lord can hear it today without aching to hear, too, the sound of the Master's voice.

Latin, Greek, and Aramaic were all spoken in the towns and villages about the Sea of Galilee, thronged as they were by Romans, Greeks, and Jews, and it is likely that Our Lord with his scholar's gift could speak some Latin and Greek as well as his native tongue, but these were his own people to whom he was preaching now and he spoke Aramaic.

What did he talk about, after he had settled himself in the boat? He looked up at the curve of the hill behind the cove and saw a young man going backward and forward in a field up there, his basket of seed held upon his left hip, his right arm moving in that immemorial gesture of generosity that is the sowing of the seed. Our Lord would have remembered one of the psalms. "They that sow in tears shall reap in joy. He that goeth forth and weepeth, bearing precious seed, shall doubtless come again with rejoicing, bringing his sheaves with him." In the young man up there he saw a picture of himself, who had come forth from heaven bearing the precious seed of the Word of God that he would sow in the hearts of men with so much pain, he being himself the Word, his person and his teaching and his actions all one in their revelation of the Father. The seed spun out into the sunlight from the hand of the sower, and some of it fell upon the hard wayside from which the birds would snatch it away, as the devil snatches away the Word from our hearts when we have heard or seen a little but have not bothered to try to understand. And some fell upon stony ground, where it would spring up quickly but without striking deep root, and wither away as quickly in the hot sunshine, as the Word does in our hearts when trouble comes and we have neither courage nor perseverance. And other seed fell among thorns that would choke it, as the Word can be choked in our hearts by our absorption in the worries and deceitful riches of this world. And some fell upon the good ground from which the green corn would spring and the golden sheaves be reaped with gladness, as God reaps his joyous harvest of love from hearts that are honest and good. And Our Lord smiled, and lifted up his voice and said, "A sower went forth to sow...."

When the parable was finished he turned instantly to the man who had lent him his boat. Peter had helped him and now he was going to help Peter. Our Lord was the most grateful man who ever lived. No one could do him even the smallest service without being startled almost out of their wits by the splendor of his gratitude. For real gratitude is a most unusual thing. Most of us are either ungracious grudging brutes when people do things for us, because it insults our pride to be helped, or else we take it as a matter of course, so high an opinion have we of our deserts. Only the truly humble can be truly grateful.

"Launch out into the deep," Our Lord said to Peter, "and let down your nets for a draught."

Peter did not think it would be any good; they had spent the night fishing and had not caught anything. But he did what he was told and rowed out into the lake, Our Lord and Peter and Andrew in the first boat, John and James following in the second. Philip and Nathanael were most likely among the crowd and they came running and jumped into the boats too. The busy lakeside receded from them, and floating between the blue water and blue sky, they were very quiet. Peter cast the net, skillfully and accurately, so that it spread out smoothly over the water before the lead weights drew it down. Perhaps he looked a little grim, for he had been doing this all night quite uselessly. Then he gave a shout; for the bell-shaped net had enclosed a shoal of fish—so many of them that the boat keeled over and the net began to break. More shouts brought James and John to the rescue and for a short while the men worked in a tense silence, filling the two boats with the gleaming, leaping, silver fish. When they had finished the boats were so heavily laden that they were weighed down in the water, and with all their strength they rowed for the shore to land the catch before the boats sank beneath the weight of it.

There was not a spare oar for Peter, and released from the nets, he swung round and dropped at Our Lord's feet like a shot bird. The others, straining at the oars, were startled by the cry that came from him. "Depart from me; for I am a sinful man, O Lord." The splendor of divine gratitude, the sense that he

73

had of great power unleashed, had brought him suddenly to the edge of an abyss, that great bottomless abyss that is the difference between the holiness of God and the sin of man. He was terrified. There is no more frightening moment than that in which a man first sees the fact of himself as he is against the fact of what God is. The difference is something which he feels he cannot bear. Actually, for a moment or two, he wants God to leave him so that he may not have to bear it. But that God does not do. Instead he flings across the abyss the sure bridge of his love.

"Fear not!"

Speechless, trembling, Peter looked up into the eyes of God and knew himself beloved. He stumbled to his feet and Our Lord reached out a hand to help him up. "Fear not; from henceforth thou shalt catch men."

Andrew, James, and John, attending to the rhythmical swing of their oars, did not speak. It was not necessary. Peter had spoken for them all, and Our Lord's answer had gripped them all to him as it had gripped Peter. They had caught the fish and he had caught them, and he and they together would catch so many souls for God that they would be past counting. They came to the shore and beached the boats and worked hard unloading the fish. But they were not the same men who had left the shore. Before, they had been prepared to be his disciples in their free time, but now they were ready to forsake all they had, their homes, their work, their comfort, and their security, to follow the Lamb of God wherever he might lead them.

5.

There is another story of the calling of a disciple. He too comes from the Sea of Galilee but he is a very different type of man to the others. He is not a fisherman but a taxgatherer, and his name is Matthew.

Everybody, except Our Lord, disliked the taxgatherers. They hated them only a little less than they hated Herod Antipas. All merchandise brought into Herod's province, whether it was silks and spices brought by road or fish brought in from the lake, was taxed, and Herod's income from his customhouses was a large one. If the taxes bore heavily on the merchants they must have been a crushing burden upon the poor fishermen. Our Lord's fishermen-disciples can have had no love for Matthew, who sat in his little customhouse at the quayside at Capernaum and defrauded them of hard-earned money for the benefit of the hated tyrant in his palace up on the hill.

But Our Lord, seeing Matthew sitting behind his table with its piles of money, saw something in him that he liked immensely, as he had instantly liked Nathanael's truth. In spite of the good income that he earned, and the comfortable life that it gave him, was Matthew hating his work, hating the contempt that other men felt for him, above all hating the evil man who was his master? We picture him a well-fed, plump little townsman, perhaps a bit vulgar and ostentatious in dress and manner, but with the eyes of a lost dog looking for the kind of master whom a nice dog can run after to the world's end. His dog's eyes must have followed Our Lord as he went back and forth between the town and the lakeside, and compared what he saw with the other man up on the hill.

Our Lord came to him "at the receipt of custom." Perhaps the fishermen-disciples owed Matthew money and he came himself to pay it, for he was meticulous about things like paying taxes. In the shadow of the customhouse, with the bright lake and the hot sunshine behind him, the tall Son of God stood before the little taxgatherer and courteously laid the coins on the table, and Matthew looked up at him with his dog's eyes and knew him for the master he longed for. Our Lord turned to go, and the awful desolation that seizes on a dog when he sees his master going away without him overwhelmed poor Matthew. Our Lord smiled. "Then follow me," he said. And leaving the custom-house, and the neat little piles of money on the table, Matthew got up and followed him.

It must have been a shock to the other disciples when Our Lord brought one of the hated taxgatherers to them to be their brother, though perhaps by this time they had realized that life with Our Lord was likely to be a series of shocks. And perhaps, too, by this time they had learned something of his own love and tolerance.

Before Matthew finally gave up his wealth and his comfortable home to become a poor man for love of Our Lord he gave a feast for his new master. Our Lord had honored him by choosing him for his disciple, and this was his way of honoring Our Lord. He invited his own friends too, and as taxgatherers were disliked so much his friends were not the most respectable members of society. But Our Lord went among them all, humble and friendly, courteous and most kind, and made of the party something so delightful that no one who was there ever forgot it. But the respectable men of the city, the Scribes and a very strict set of religious men who called themselves Pharisees, "those who separate themselves," were horrified that Our Lord should have gone to such a party and taken his disciples with him.

"They that are whole need not a physician," he answered them, "but they that are sick. I came not to call the righteous but sinners to repentance."

76

Naturally a doctor goes among those who need him and not among those who don't. The common sense of this answer silenced them, but they found another matter for reproach. John's disciples, those who had not joined Our Lord, lived very austere lives, fasting and praying, and so did the disciples of the Pharisees, but Our Lord's disciples ate and drank like other men and appeared to be thoroughly enjoying themselves. Our Lord had the practical answer to this complaint too. "Can the children of the bridechamber mourn, as long as the bridegroom is with them?" The disciples gathered about their master were like the friends of the bridegroom gathered about him on his wedding day. Our Lord was in love with the souls of men as a bridegroom is in love with his bride, and they felt their souls drenched in his love as day by day their bodies were drenched in the sunshine of the blue days. Just to be with him made them so gloriously happy that they could do nothing but rejoice.

And then he described their joy as being like new wine, something so bright and sparkling that it could not be poured into old bottles or they would burst. Just now the old traditional penances and fastings could not hold their joy, any more than an old worn-out coat can hold a patch of strong new cloth. The Pharisees had been imprisoned in their rigid traditions so long that they had come to think that only the old things are good. They only liked old wine. New things, they thought, must be bad just because they were new. And so for the fresh original ideas that sparkled through Our Lord's teaching, for the heavenly freshness of Our Lord himself, they could feel nothing but dislike. They closed their hearts against his love and so they could not experience his joy.

But the disciples could, and to think a little of what their joy was like helps us to feel it too. In Palestine the sun does not rise slowly and gradually, as it does in America; it leaps suddenly into the sky, and the world that a moment before was cold and dark is suddenly warm and brilliant and palpitating with light. This is the sort of change that had come over Peter when, in his misery and penitence, he had fallen at Our Lord's feet and Our Lord had said to him, "Fear not," and pulled him to his feet again to be his servant forever. And over Matthew when he stepped out of the dark little customhouse into the sunshine with Our Lord beside him. And over Nathanael when Our Lord's understanding wrung from him the cry, "Thou art the Son of God; thou art the King of Israel." To each of the disciples the change had come a little differently, but it had been the same sun that had changed their darkness into light.

It is a human instinct to long for a perfect companionship with some one person. All men and women have this longing, and many become embittered because in their journey through life they do not find this companion. But the disciples did find him. Each man found himself, for the first time in his life, loved and understood with a perfect love and an absolute understanding. This understanding included the wickedness in him as well as the good, and this at first would have caused him misery and shame, as it did to Peter, but gradually the misery would have been lost in a sense of relief and rest. The relief that comes to men when they let go of their pride is a wonderful thing, and so is the restfulness of being with someone who knows the worst. You don't have to pretend any more. And when, knowing the worst, you find that they still love you, the wonder of it is so great that it seems to make the whole world new. We need not envy the first disciples because they had, and have, this joy. We are Our Lord's disciples too, even though we come at the tail end of the great procession, a lot of little black pigs tagging along behind the stately white sheep. The sun can rise for us, too, in just the same way.

There is a sentence in the book of Revelation which describes the life of the saints in heaven. "They follow the Lamb whithersoever he goeth." When St. John wrote those words was he remembering the happiness of those first days in Galilee? They were in heaven already, simply being with him, for that is heaven, and our heaven starts on earth.

> Jesu I now begin
> To love thee day and night.
> My soul from earth to wean
> I shall do all my might.
> 'Twas all my love to win
> Jesu became my knight.
> —Bodleian Ms.
> XVth Century

Chapter 4

THE WATER OF LIFE

As the hart panteth after the water brooks, so
panteth my soul after thee, O God.
—Psalm XLII:1

1.

IT WAS nearly time for the spring Passover feast, when all
good Israelites who could make the journey went on pilgrimage to the Holy City. Jerusalem was always Our Lord's
chief battlefield, and a great fight awaited him there, but before
they left Galilee he and his disciples said good-by to those
idyllic early days by attending a joyous festival. They, and Mary
the Mother of the Lord, were invited to a wedding at Cana of
Galilee, a village not far from Nazareth.

Jesus and his disciples walked there over the flower-covered
hills, and perhaps they talked of the kingdom of heaven, and
Our Lord tried to make his children understand the great power
of this life that they were living now, this life of love that was
the life of the kingdom.

80

He said it was like a grain of mustard seed that a man takes and sows in his field, a seed so small that it is almost invisible, yet it grows into a great tree and the birds come and take shelter among its branches. And he said it was like a bit of leaven hidden in a lump of heavy dough and transforming it into the bread by which mankind is fed. The life of love could grow in the same miraculous way. From something hidden in the hearts of a few men it could grow into something that would transform the world.

And its value was as great as its power. It was like treasure hid in a field, which when a man had found he gladly sold all that he had to buy the field and possess the treasure. It was like a pearl of great price, a thing so precious and lovely that a pearl merchant would part with every other jewel just to possess this one perfect thing.

The disciples' hearts would have burned within them as their Master talked to them, for he himself was love and life and king and kingdom. He was the great tree whose branches sheltered them, the leaven that had transformed their heavy useless dough, their treasure and their pearl of such great price.

And so talking of heavenly love they came to Cana to the festival of earthly love and were received there with honor, for Our Lord's preaching had made him famous now all over Galilee, and he had earned the title of Rabbi, which means Teacher. Mary's pride in her son must have made this one of the happiest days of her life. Perhaps she had not yet seen his disciples, and Our Lord would have said, "This is *my mother*," with joy and pride; for Mary was young still, and beautiful, and he loved her more than any son has ever loved his mother. The disciples would have greeted the Mother of their Lord with reverence, and John, who would one day be as her own son to her, must have loved her on sight.

It was a happy feast, with old friends greeting each other and

81

the women wearing treasured wedding garments that had been handed down to them from their mothers and grandmothers. The bride's face was hidden behind her veil but the bridegroom's laughing countenance was shining like the sun for all to see, and his groomsmen were rejoicing round him. The disciples reminded each other of what their Master had said about the children of the bridechamber, and agreed that those young groomsmen were no happier than they were.

In the middle of the feast, with everybody laughing and talking, eating and drinking, and the music of the lutes sounding softly, Mary glanced through the door of the room where they feasted into the courtyard outside and saw a group of servants gesticulating and arguing in great distress. She got up and slipped outside to see what had gone wrong. Something indeed had gone very wrong. The wine had given out. The light wines of the East are not so strong as ours and are drunk to quench thirst, as we drink lemonade, and the guests had been so unusually thirsty that there was none left. The people of the East do not treat hospitality in the lighthearted way that we do. They regard it as something sacred. An Eastern host would rather starve than fail to offer food and drink to a stranger who came to see him, and for the wine to give out at a wedding would be such a disgrace that neither host and hostess nor servants would ever get over it. In this dilemma Mary sent for her son.

"They have no wine," she said to him briefly but tragically when he stood beside her.

The calamity was so great that everyone in the courtyard turned to Our Lord in stricken silence, yet hopefully, for they knew of old what skill he had in averting disaster.

Our Lord said to his mother, "Woman, what have I to do with thee? mine hour is not yet come."

This answer has always been a puzzle. It sounds a curt impatient answer, and Our Lord had God's own great patience and would never have spoken curtly to the mother he loved so much. The words that Our Lord spoke to his mother in Aramaic, remembered years after, were eventually written down in Greek. Did the writer's memory fail him a little here? What Mary heard, most gently spoken, was possibly this, "Mother, don't hurry me. Wait a moment."

For this was a moment when it was not possible for Our Lord to do what was wanted "straightway." It was the moment of the unfolding of his first great miracle. That wonderful catch of fish is called "the miraculous draught of fishes," but though Our Lord had known where the shoal was, the actual fish had been there in the sea at the time. Now, for the sake of his friends, he was going to do what for his own sake he had refused to do when he was starving in the wilderness. Then he would not change the substance of stone into the substance of bread. Now he was going to change water into wine.

Before the mystery of the power of his holiness our reverence shrinks away, yet we can realize that this first miracle must have been hard for him. We see later in the Gospels that none of his miracles were performed without cost, and this first one must have cost him a great deal. The bringing forth of his power perhaps wrenched his whole being. He could not do it all in a moment.

Mary had quickly understood. To cover the pause she had turned to the servants and said, "Whatsoever he saith unto you, do it." How very many times she must have said that to children when they had got into trouble, and had run off to find Jesus and ask him what they ought to do.

In Eastern homes, when guests arrived, they always washed their dusty feet before they went into the house, and water was kept in the courtyards for this purpose. Six empty pots stood now in the courtyard.

"Fill the waterpots with water," Our Lord said to the servants.

They must have thought that a useless thing to do, just as Peter had thought it quite useless to cast the net yet again, but like Peter they found it impossible to do anything but obey, and they filled the pots up to the brim.

"Draw out now, and bear unto the governor of the feast," said Our Lord.

And when they poured the water out of the pots into the flasks it was not water, but wine, and when the guest of honor tasted it he told the bridegroom that this wine that they were drinking last of all was best of all. It was cool and refreshing and life giving, like the water springs for which the hart in the psalm so greatly longed.

Our Lord and Mary went back to the house again, having saved the household from disaster and made of this feast a joyous thing up to the very end.

After the feast Our Lord and his disciples went back to the Sea of Galilee, to Capernaum, and Mary went with them for "not many days." These days must have passed all too quickly for her, and then she had to say good-by and go back to Nazareth, and Our Lord and his disciples set out for Jerusalem.

2.

These days of travel were great days for the disciples. There were no crowds now pressing upon them to hear the Rabbi preach, and they had their Master to themselves. In the cool mornings, before they began the day's march, in the evenings under the stars, they prayed together. Twice a day every devout Jew recited certain passages from the Scriptures called the "Shema," which means "Hear," and they would have recited it together. The first thing the disciples heard in the morning would have been Our Lord's voice starting the recitation, "Hear, O Israel: the Lord Our God is one Lord. And thou shalt love the Lord thy God with all thy heart, and with all thy soul, and with all thy might." And the last thing they heard him say at night would have been the words, "I am the Lord your God."

Now, as always, he had so much to teach them about that prayer to God which is for his children the very breath of life, that breathing out which is the offering of themselves in love to him and that breathing in of his grace without which they cannot live. When they said to him, "Lord, teach us to pray," he repeated to them sentence by sentence the "Our Father" which is the perfect pattern of prayer for all time. First we worship and adore our heavenly Father. Then with the prayer that his kingdom of love may come in our hearts we have the intake of the breath, which we breathe out again with the offering of ourselves to do his will. Quietly we breathe out to our Father the story of our needs and the needs of those we love, and ask him to supply them. Then we ask him to forgive us our sins and to grant that we may forgive each other; for unless we forgive each other we cannot ourselves breathe in his mercy. Then we end by begging him to defend us from all evil things that could possibly separate us from him, for apart from him we have no life.

He told them that they must never cease from prayer. "Men ought always to pray and not to faint," he said, and he told them the story of the unjust judge, and the importunate widow who came to him demanding justice. She went on and on begging and imploring him for justice until at last, just because she wearied him so, he gave it to her. If an unjust earthly judge answers ceaseless, persevering prayer, will not the just Judge of all the world do the same? He taught them that God loves to give good gifts to his children, even as earthly fathers do. He said to them, "If ye then, being evil, know how to give good gifts unto your children, how much more shall your heavenly Father give the Holy Spirit to them that ask him?" And he said, "Ask, and it shall be given you; seek, and ye shall find; knock, and it shall be opened unto you. For every one that asketh receiveth; and he that seeketh findeth; and to him that knocketh it shall be opened."

And so journeying they came in sight of the Holy City, towering up upon Mount Sion, its tawny walls challenging and fierce under the hot sun. Our Lord would have quickened his pace, so that the disciples found it hard to keep up with him. From now onward his life would be all fighting, an unceasing fight for the souls of men against every evil which men and devils could bring in array against him, and it would have been with the bearing of a soldier that he walked now toward Jerusalem. Yet the disciples, when they caught up with him and looked at his face, would have seen it alight with joy. For once more he was coming to his Father's house, not this time as a little boy who would sit at the feet of the Rabbis but as a Rabbi himself, with the right to stand and teach in the beautiful courts of the Temple. The Passover feast commemorated the redemption of the people of Israel from slavery in Egypt and the birth of the nation. He would teach his people how through penitence they might find redemption from their sins and new birth in the kingdom of heaven. Perhaps in his eagerness he repeated the 84th psalm.

"My soul longeth, yea, even fainteth, for the courts of the Lord; my heart and my flesh crieth out for the living God. Yea, the sparrow hath found an house, and the swallow a nest for herself, where she may lay her young, even thine altars, O Lord of Hosts, my King and my God. Blessed are they that dwell in thy house: they will be always praising thee."

They entered the gates of the Holy City and mingled with the crowds thronging the narrow streets. There is a tradition that Zebedee, the father of John and James, was a Galilean fish merchant who also had a business in Jerusalem and supplied rich men with their fish, including the high priest. If this is so John and James knew Jerusalem well and would have taken Our Lord to their father's house to lodge there.

As soon as the courtesy of a guest allowed, Our Lord went straight to the Temple. But here his joy in being once more in "the courts of the Lord" was turned to flaming anger. For one of them had been turned into a market. The men who sold oxen and sheep and doves for the Temple sacrifices had brought their animals and birds right inside the Temple and were selling them there. And the money changers had set up their little tables and were doing business right inside the house of God. The Temple court that should have been orderly and peaceful, a place where people could pray and be quiet and think about God, was dirty and noisy and desecrated. The frightened beasts, conscious as animals so often are that their death was close, were lowing and bleating in their distress. Men were shouting at them, arguing, bargaining. The Temple guard, a band of armed policemen whose business it was to keep order in the Temple, was there to prevent men from coming to blows, but it was not their business to control the noise. The Scribes and Pharisees were passing back and forth, but they did not care that God's house was being used in this way because those who did business in the Temple court had to pay for the privilege, and the Temple funds were enriched by the desecration. If you have ever seen a country market place on market day, with rapacious men trying to get their money's worth and cunning men trying to do them out of it, and remember the noise and nastiness, and then if you think of picking up that market place and putting it down in the nave of a cathedral, you will know what that Temple court was like.

What happened now shows us how terrible is the righteous anger of God. We are accustomed to think of anger as a wicked thing, and so it is with sinners whose anger is caused by hurt pride or intolerance or hatred, but God's anger is the fire of his holiness blazing out upon the darkness of sin and it is the purest thing there is, and the most terrifying.

Our Lord seized a rope and quickly knotted it into a scourge, and with this weapon in his strong hands he came striding down upon the crowd, driving them all before him, men and beasts alike. He seized the tables of the money changers and flung them down, scattering the money all over the paving stones.

"Take these things hence!" he cried, his voice rising clear and strong above the turmoil. "Make not my Father's house an house of merchandise!"

For a little while there must have been indescribable noise and confusion; men shouting and crying out in anger and fear, as they dodged and ducked to escape the scourge and scrambled after the rolling, spinning coins, the animals stampeding, the tables crashing down, and the tall white-robed figure flashing among them with the terrible scourge and the still more terrible voice that was like the trumpet of an avenging angel ringing in their ears. If any of them looked at his face they saw the fire of God's holiness there and dared not look again. Once panic starts in a crowd there is no stopping it. Like wind sweeping the corn it swept over those men and beasts. They turned all one way and fled.

The court was cleared. The Temple guard was there but they did not attempt to stop him. The Scribes and Pharisees were there but they seem to have been powerless. One fearless young man armed with nothing but a twisted bit of rope dominated the whole of that crowd and did with it exactly what he wanted to do with it. It was another miracle, a miracle this time of sheer courage.

By the evening of that day the whole city was blazing and humming with the story of what had happened. In the house of the high priest and in all the houses of the great there was

anxious consultation. Who was this terrible young man who had
fallen on them like a star from heaven? Obviously, a very dangerous young man, of the type to turn rebel and cause very seri-
ous disturbance. They could do nothing at present for they were
in a very weak position; the whole city knew that the young man
had protested against a great wrong, and with superb courage.
They could do nothing but watch him, and wait. But Our Lord
had humiliated these proud men, and the humiliation of the
proud very soon turns to hatred. Our Lord knew that; he had
known it when he knotted his bit of rope into a scourge. But he
never recoiled from hatred, he faced it as a white stag faces the
hounds, knowing that though the hate of wicked men can destroy
the body that is all that it can do.

The disciples were awed and a little afraid. They remembered
the words of the 69th psalm, "The zeal of thine house hath eaten
me up." There had been no human witnesses of Our Lord's
battle in the desert, and so for them this was the first revelation
of the steel within the meekness and gentleness that had so enchanted them through those first days in Galilee. There was a
sword in the beautiful scabbard, they knew now.

In the days that followed he preached to the great Passover
crowds that thronged the Temple courts and the streets of the
city, calling them to repent, telling them of the kingdom of
heaven, that spiritual country whose citizens are those who love
each other and their God. Standing upon a flight of steps in one
of the Temple courts he looked down at just such a crowd as one
may see any day in a great city, a crowd both terrible and pitiful.
He saw the pinched gray faces of the very poor who never had
enough to eat, the misshapen bodies of men who had carried too
many burdens, and the bent shoulders of the tired women. He
looked down upon faces twitching with pain or blotched by
disease, into eyes glazed with grief or fear. He looked into the
bewildered faces of those who are longing for they know not

what, into the eyes of the hopeless, the dying, the persecuted, the persecutors, the rich, the poor, the proud, the humble, and he saw them all with that keen sight of the love of God that caused him such agony that in the end it broke his heart.

"Come unto me all ye that labour and are heavy laden and I will give you rest." His soaring voice was like wings lifting them, folding them, cradling them. "Take my yoke upon you and learn of me, for I am meek and lowly of heart and ye shall find rest unto your souls. For my yoke is easy and my burden is light." No matter what their trouble, if they would only come to him and hold fast to him he would bear it with them and they would have rest. He would teach the proud and the unsatisfied how to be meek as he was meek, and the torment of their restlessness would be quieted. The farmer lays his yoke upon the oxen who are his servants and the yoke is sometimes heavy to carry, but the yoke that he would lay upon his servants would be easy to bear for it was the yoke of love. For love, the Holy Spirit of God, is winged, and as you carry love the wings unfold and carry you.

They could believe all that he told them while his voice was ringing in their ears, for he spoke as they had never yet heard a man speak. In all that he said there was the authority of a conviction deeper than any conviction they had ever known. There were many in those Passover crowds who listened to him who believed that he was indeed the Christ of God, and that they might know that his promises were backed by the power of God that is always greater than any sin or suffering, however terrible, he healed many who were sick.

But the men who hated him asked for a sign. They said, "What sign shewest thou unto us, seeing that thou doest these things?"

The temptation to give them a sign was one he had already met and conquered, and he would not give it to them. But standing in the Temple he drew his perfect body to its full height and said, "Destroy this temple and in three days I will raise it up." They thought he spoke of Herod's Temple but he spoke of his body that was the Temple of the Holy Spirit of God. He knew even then, that though they would kill his body God would restore it to glorious life once more.

3.

Among the Pharisees there was a man who did not hate him, and his name was Nicodemus. He must have been a timid man for he had not the courage to come openly to Jesus and talk to him; he came by night. Our Lord took him up to the roof of Zebedee's house, where no one would see him, and here under the stars, with the sleeping city spread out below them, they talked. John, in whose home they were, must have been with them, sitting so quietly in the shadows that Nicodemus soon had forgotten his presence, because it is he who has recorded this conversation, and recorded it in such a way that we feel every word of it bit deep into his memory. It is in the third chapter of St. John's gospel and reading it the words come to us as they must have come to John, like the music of great poetry, sounding at first so easy in its lovely rhythm and yet really too deep for understanding.

When Our Lord taught many people together, a crowd of all sorts of people of all ages, he taught them by telling them stories like the parable of the sower, for the mind of a mixed crowd is as simple as the mind of a child, and stories are easy for children to remember. Our Lord's stories are like flowers folded about a drop of precious honey. He knew that the stories, remembered, would one day unfold in the mind, and the truths within them be revealed. But when he talked to one person alone he spoke straight out to their hearts without any need of stories. Nicodemus was one of the learned men of Israel, a member of the Sanhedrin, the supreme council and court of justice of the Jewish people, and he and Our Lord talked to each other as one Rabbi to another, the one searching for the truth and the other trying to help him to find it.

"Rabbi," said Nicodemus, "we know that thou art a teacher come from God, for no man can do those miracles except God be with him."

Jesus said, "Verily, verily, I say unto thee, Except a man be born again, he cannot see the kingdom of God."

This "verily, verily, I say unto thee," "indeed and indeed I tell you," comes over and over again in the gospels. Our Lord used it when something that he was saying mattered very much, when he was pleading almost with desperation that a man should understand, remember, do something that was of tremendous importance to him. It rings out through his teaching just as the great "Fear not" rings out when the door of heaven is opened. Whenever it comes it is almost like an alarm bell ringing in our ears.

Nicodemus cried out to Our Lord as Mary had cried out to the angel, "How?" A man cannot be born again when he is old. He cannot go back into his mother's womb.

Our Lord was fighting for the soul of Nicodemus and the "verily, verily," rings out again. "Verily, verily, I say unto thee, Except a man be born of water and of the spirit he cannot enter into the kingdom of God. That which is born of the flesh is flesh; and that which is born of the Spirit is spirit."

A man cannot enter into the kingdom of heaven without a change as absolute as that of the entry into this world which we call birth or the entry into the world to come which we call death.

A man must be washed clean in the waters of repentance, he must be emptied of selfishness and filled with God's spirit of love, and that is the greatest change that can possibly happen to him. As the body of the baby is made from the physical body of his mother so the changed spirit of man is made by the indwelling of the Holy Spirit of love.

"Marvel not that I said unto thee, Ye must be born again," said Our Lord. "The wind bloweth where it listeth, and thou hearest the sound thereof, but canst not tell whence it cometh, and whither it goeth: so is every one that is born of the Spirit."

As the spirit of love, like the wind, is beyond our understanding, so our own reborn spirits are beyond our understanding. We cannot understand how God brought them into being and we do not know where he is taking them or what he is going to do with them. We can only trust God and commend our spirits into his hands.

But still Nicodemus cried out, "How can these things be?"

And Our Lord said, "Art thou a master of Israel, and knowest not these things?" You are a wise man, you have studied much, do you not know that there is mystery beyond mystery that you will never understand? And then Our Lord said sadly that men would not believe the things that he told them about the kingdom of heaven here on earth; they would not believe that it was possible to lead the life of love; they would not even try, so how could they expect to understand the mysteries of heaven? But he understood them, for he had come down from heaven, and was in heaven even now.

He looked down at the sleeping city below him and thought of the thousands of men and women whom it held, suffering and sick with sin, men and women whom he had come to save, and as his heart ached over them all he remembered that when the children of Israel had been sick and dying in the wilderness Moses had made a brazen serpent and lifted it up on a pole, and they had looked at it and lived. That had been a picture of his own death on the cross, and he began to tell Nicodemus about his death. He said, "As Moses lifted up the serpent in the wilderness, even so must the Son of Man be lifted up: That whosoever believeth in him should not perish, but have eternal life."

And then he spoke the most glorious words that have ever been spoken in the whole history of the world.

"For God so loved the world, that he gave his only begotten Son, that whosoever believeth in him should not perish, but have everlasting life."

And then Our Lord said something that reminds us of what Simeon said to Mary in the Temple, when he told her that the presence of her child among them would test men and show what they were. He said that he had come into the world as the light of the world, and that those who could not endure to see their sin would hate his light and turn away from it into their own darkness, but the humble lovers of the truth would come to him.

Was Nicodemus humble enough to come to him? Did Our Lord win the fight for his soul? We think that he did, for it was Nicodemus who helped Joseph of Arimathea take Our Lord's body from the cross and lay it in the grave.

4.

The Passover feast ended, and journeying home to Galilee Jesus and his disciples had to pass through Samaria, and they came to a village called Sychar. Samaria is a district between Judea and Galilee which the disciples regarded as enemy country. For the Samaritans were of a different race from the Jews and they hated each other. Their hatred had begun far back in their troubled history. After the death of Solomon civil war broke out and when it was over his kingdom was divided into two, the southern kingdom of Israel and the northern kingdom of Judah. Then the Assyrians invaded the country and carried most of the people of the northern tribes into captivity. A couple of centuries later the Babylonians swept down upon the south "like a wolf on the fold," sacked Jerusalem and destroyed Solomon's Temple, and the southern tribes too were taken into exile. Fifty years later some of these last exiles struggled back and heroically began to rebuild their Temple, and they found living in Samaria a race of Assyrian colonists who had intermarried with the remnant of the northern tribes. This race would gladly have made friends with the returned exiles at Jerusalem, but they would have nothing to do with them. To the Jews marriage with other nations was a sin and they hated equally the Israelites who had married the Assyrians and the Assyrians who had married them. From then on the Samaritans lived in their own bit of country as a race apart. They had their own Temple built upon the summit of Mount Gerizim close to Sychar, and here they offered their sacrifices and worshiped God as the Jews did at Jerusalem, and the rivalry between the two Temples was as bitter as the hatred between the two races.

Just outside Sychar was a well called Jacob's well, because it was close to the bit of ground that Jacob gave to his son Joseph. It was an old well then, and it is still there today, with a church built over it to keep it safe, for if it was venerated then because it was Jacob's well, it is still more venerated today because beside it Our Lord sat and rested.

He and his disciples reached the well about noon, after a long journey, and they were so hungry that the disciples decided to go to Sychar and buy food; and they must have been very hungry indeed if they were willing to buy food from the hated Samaritans. But Our Lord was so tired that he could not get any further, and instead of going with them he sat by the well to rest. And John stayed with him, because again it is John who tells us what happened. John must have been anxious about his Master and we can imagine him sitting down quietly a few paces away, so that Our Lord should not have to talk to him but yet should have him there if he wanted him.

We do not often hear of Our Lord being tired, but now he was "wearied." And if we think of all that he had done in Jerusalem, of the cleansing of the Temple, and the hatred it had brought upon him, of the great crowds pressing upon him, of the preaching and the healing and all that it meant in terms of the outpouring of love and strength and courage, we can realize a little how utterly tired out he must have been.

Beside the old well, with the flight of steps leading down to it, there was a small archway with a stone bench under it, and here Our Lord rested, thankful for the shade and the quiet. He longed for a drink, but the water was deep down in the well and there was nothing to dip it up with. He leaned back against the cool stone and hoped it would be a long time before the disciples returned.

But if Our Lord ever found himself in possession of a moment of peace he never kept it for long, and presently there was the sound of sandaled feet upon stone and looking up he saw a Samaritan woman coming down the steps to the well with her pitcher on her head. He smiled at her and asked her if she would give him a drink.

The woman was utterly astonished. For one thing it was not the custom for a Jewish man to greet a woman out of doors; even if she was his own mother or wife he would pass her in the street in silence. And then she was a Samaritan, one of the hated race to whom no Jew spoke if he could help it. But Our Lord never paid any attention to customs that had in them neither kindness nor good sense, and hatred, whether it was race hatred or personal hatred, was a thing that did not exist for him. So he looked up into the astonished, dark Assyrian face and smiled again.

She let her pitcher down into the well and brought him some water, but still she could not get over her astonishment. "How is it that thou, being a Jew, asketh drink of me, which am a woman of Samaria?" she demanded.

Our Lord said to her, "If thou knewest the gift of God, and who it is that saith to thee, Give me to drink; thou wouldest have asked of him, and he would have given thee living water."

And then he began to tell her about the water of everlasting life, speaking straight to her heart, putting his own weariness aside and fighting for the soul of this poor woman as he had fought for the soul of the Rabbi Nicodemus upon the rooftop at Jerusalem. For he knew her desperate need. He knew she was a woman who had led a wicked life and that her soul was dry and parched. But he also knew her kindness. Another Samaritan woman, if a Jew had asked her for water, might have refused it, but she did not. As always, his glorious gratitude was out of all proportion to the little courtesy done him; she gave him water from a well to drink, but he gave her the water of everlasting life. She did not quite understand now what he was saying to her, as we see from her puzzled answers, but she would have understood later when she felt the coolness of the living water springing up within her penitent soul. For the rest of the story makes it quite clear to us that this, too, was a soul that was saved.

The psalmist cried out in his longing, "As the hart panteth after the water brooks, so panteth my soul after thee, O God, yea, even for the living God." And Our Lord said to the woman by the well, "Whosoever drinketh of the water that I shall give him shall never thirst; but the water that I shall give him shall be in him a well of water springing up into everlasting life."

This water is the grace of God, the life of God, given to the penitent soul that longs and thirsts and gasps for the beauty of God. It is poured like cool water into the dying, withering, panting spirit, and the desert places are made fresh and green and alive forevermore.

The woman did not understand yet, but she knew her own longing, and she said, "Sir, give me this water, that I thirst not, neither come hither to draw."

Then Our Lord said, "Go, call thy husband, and come hither." He knew as well as she did that the man she was living with was not her husband, but he wanted to test the truth that he knew was in her.

She did not fail him. She did not lie. She answered truthfully, "I have no husband." Then we can imagine her pausing, longing to tell him about her sin, to confess it and be forgiven, yet unable to find the words to say which she had to say.

He found them for her. He told her what she was struggling to tell him. He did not reproach her, but commending her truthfulness he quietly stated the facts, and we can imagine how they must have pierced her, hearing them as she did stated by the voice of God. Like a good surgeon, Our Lord always knew exactly how to let out the poison.

"Sir, I perceive that thou art a prophet!" she gasped. She had come very near to knowing who he was.

Then, looking up at the Temple on Mount Gerizim, they talked together about worship, and Our Lord said, "The hour cometh, and now is, when the true worshippers shall worship the Father in spirit and in truth: for the Father seeketh such to worship him. God is a Spirit, and they that worship him must worship him in spirit and in truth."

"In spirit and in truth." He was telling her that worship was not the sacrificing of animals, and services in the Temple, it was the seeking of the penitent spirit of man for the beauty of God. It was her own longing.

"For the Father seeketh such to worship him."

The wonder of this is almost past believing. It is not only the poor panting hart who seeks, it is the great God also. Lover and beloved, they seek each other.

The woman said, "I know that Messias cometh, which is called Christ: when he is come, he will tell us all things."

We can feel the questioning there. She had come nearer still; she was asking him, was *he* the Christ?

He answered her with her own truthfulness. "I that speak unto thee am he."

Then the disciples came back and were astonished to see these two talking to each other. Yet not one of them questioned Our Lord. The hart had come to the water springs and the place just then felt so holy that they dared not speak.

The woman ran off headlong, so eager to tell the men of the village that the Christ was with them that she left her precious waterpot behind her. "Come, see a man, which told me all things that ever I did!" she cried when she got there. "Is not this the Christ?"

The disciples had brought food with them, but Our Lord was too tired to eat. "I have meat to eat that ye know not of," he consoled them. "My meat is to do the will of him that sent me, and to finish his work."

God, who so loved the world, had sent him into the world to save the souls of men; and in one thirsty soul the will of God had just been accomplished. Then he looked up and saw the woman coming back with a crowd of Samaritans with her, the white turbans they wore on their heads gleaming in the sun.

"Lift up your eyes, and look on the fields," he said, "for they are white already to harvest."

When the men reached him they begged him to come back with them to Sychar and to stay with them. He stayed with them for two days and many of them believed in him, and said, "This is indeed the Christ, the Saviour of the world."

5.

We now come to an incident in the life of Our Lord in which God is no longer thirsted for, as the hart longs for the water springs, but is himself the white hart hunted down. It is an incident so terrible that one wants to turn away and not think about it. Only it is necessary to think about it because it shows what can happen when a hateful streak that is in the human nature of every one of us gets completely out of hand. Some words of Our Lord's, spoken at this time, have now become almost a proverb in our language. "No prophet is accepted in his own country." We quote the words lightly sometimes, and there is another proverb that we speak lightly too, "Familiarity breeds contempt," but this incident shows us how vile is this tendency to belittle loveliness just because you are used to it. We live with lovable people and instead of reverencing their nobility we rivet our whole attention upon their faults. The windows of our home look out upon great beauty and as time goes on we scarcely notice it. In the case of the people it is pride; we like to feel superior to, or at least on an equality with, the people about us, and if we were to start paying attention to their great and good qualities we soon should not. In the case of the beauty it is blasphemy, for God is the source of all beauty and contempt of beauty is contempt of God. The blasphemous pride of the men of Nazareth very nearly murdered God before the appointed time.

Our Lord, who knew "what was in man," knew quite well that though he had been "in favour" with his own people when he had lived among them as the carpenter's son it would be a very different story when he came among them as the Christ. Accept a man they had known as a boy, who had grown up among them, as the Holy One of Israel? He knew they would never do it. Nevertheless, knowing his danger, he came among them. He had proclaimed the good news of the kingdom up and down the Jordan valley and by the shores of the Sea of Galilee, he had taken it to Jerusalem, and he was not going to leave his own people out.

And so he came to Nazareth and, as he always did, went to the synagogue on the Sabbath day. The synagogues were simple buildings, containing a raised platform where the elders sat, a chest holding the scrolls of the Scriptures, and perhaps seats for the people. The service consisted of prayers, the singing of psalms, readings from the Scriptures, and preaching. One of the elders was elected as ruler of the synagogue, and it was he who decided who should read the lessons and who should preach. On this occasion he asked Our Lord to read one of the lessons and to preach, and when the time came the minister of the synagogue, whose office was much the same as that of a verger in an English church, took from the chest the scroll of the prophet Isaiah and gave it to him. He unrolled the scroll and came to the front of the dais, and turning to the 61st chapter read to them the wonderful words in which Isaiah, speaking as the Christ, describes his office.

"The Spirit of the Lord is upon me, because he hath anointed me to preach the gospel to the poor; he hath sent me to heal the brokenhearted, to preach deliverance to the captives, and recovering of sight to the blind, to set at liberty them that are bruised, to preach the acceptable year of the Lord."

Then he gave the scroll back to the minister and sat down "and the eyes of all them that were in the synagogue were fastened on him," and for the moment or two before he began to speak there must have been a tingling, pent-up silence. For he had spoken the words of the Christ with such a wonderful and gracious beauty, as though they were indeed his own words. What was he going to say to them, this man of their own village who was making such tremendous claims for himself? Was he going to dare to say here in Nazareth, where they knew him to be Joseph's son, and where his Mother and his brothers and sisters were well-known to them, that he was the Son of God?

He dared. He said, "This day is this scripture fulfilled in your ears."

And then with an insight as great as his courage he took the thoughts that he knew were in their minds, put them into words and answered them. They were thinking, Physician, heal thyself. We have heard you have done great things in other places. If that's true, do them here, in your own country. Show *us* what you can do.

"Verily, I say unto you," he said to them, "indeed, I tell you, no prophet is accepted in his own country."

The cry of "Verily" shows us that he was making a great appeal to them. He had told them he was indeed the Christ, and now he was begging them to remember that streak in human nature that makes it so hard for a man to see the familiar and the known in its true beauty, and to accept him as the Christ in spite of it. He could do no miracle among them if they did not believe in him, for he could not help the faithless. He reminded them of the man and woman whose faith had enabled the prophet Elisha to help them, the woman whose son he had raised from the dead and the leper whom he had cleansed;

neither of them were his own people; she had been a woman of Sidon and Naaman had been a Syrian.

The appeal failed, for proud and contemptuous men can never endure to be told the truth. They had been in an ugly mood when Our Lord started to talk to them, and now his plain speaking was like a match set to a fuse. Their suppressed rage and jealousy flared up uncontrollably, so that they were beside themselves, scarcely knowing what they were doing, only knowing that they hated him, hated his gracious beauty and wanted to destroy it. They leaped upon him, dragged him out of the synagogue, through the streets of the town, out to the flower-covered hills where he had played as a boy, and to the edge of one of the steep precipices where he had stood so often looking down upon the valley far below. They meant to fling him down headlong. He had grown up in perfect love, to perfect love, among them; he was their very own, the richest treasure that any city had ever held since the beginning of the world. Yet they would have flung him to death upon the rocks below and for a moment or two gloried in it, until the evil went out of them and they saw just exactly what they had done.

He saved them from that agony, and himself from a death that would have been much quicker than the one of which he had spoken to Nicodemus, but which coming now would have frustrated God's purpose for him. "But he, passing through the midst of them, went his way." St. Luke's quiet words leave us feeling breathless. But how? How was it possible for one unarmed man to escape from such a mad and murderous crowd? The answer probably is that he was the only man there who had kept a cool head. His strong body twisted itself out of their grip, his quick wits showed him just how, and where, he could get through the crowd. Calmly, bravely, he escaped from the men who would have murdered him, and lived to die for them another day.

GOD SO LOVED THE WORLD

O Lord our God, grant us grace to desire thee with our whole heart; that, so desiring, we may seek, and seeking find thee; and so finding thee may love thee; and loving thee, may hate those sins from which thou hast redeemed.   Amen.

—St. Anselm

Chapter 5

THE GREAT PHYSICIAN

In all their affliction he was afflicted, and the
angel of his presence saved them.
>   —Isaiah LXIII:9

1.

THE FIGHT at Nazareth over, Our Lord went back to
the Sea of Galilee, and now there begins that tremendous battle, against the devils and diseases that wrench and
wrack the minds and bodies of men, that is one of the most
thrilling things in human history. All that he did—the healing,
the teaching, the praying, the suffering, and the fighting—was
perfectly balanced; he healed as he taught and taught as he
healed, prayed all the time, suffered ceaselessly in his weary body
and compassionate spirit, and never left off fighting evil in some
form or another for a single moment. But in the early chapters
of the gospels it is the miracles of healing, each so different, each
with its own perfection, its own light showing us some new truth
of character, human or divine, that take us for ever captive to the
love of God.

For though Our Lord taught always that our mortal bodies are of little importance compared to our immortal souls, yet his love never failed to leap out in defense of a suffering body. Human suffering and death came into the world because of sin, and disease though not sin in itself is one of the results of sin, and he had come to destroy sin both root and branch. And he had come, too, to show men the love of God, and men and women who were healed by Our Lord, or whose children were healed, were left in no doubt that he loved them. When he had lifted their pain off them and taken it upon himself they gave him their hearts too, and then through their hearts he was able to capture their souls as well.

As the "Verily, verily, I say unto you" rings through Our Lord's teaching, so the word "believe" rings through all his work of healing. He could only heal where there was belief in his power to heal. "Be not afraid, only believe," he would say, and when the answer was, "Lord, I believe! Help thou mine unbelief," then he could answer, "Thy faith hath saved thee; go in peace." Faith was, and is, the door from pain to peace, from death to life, both for the body and for the soul. It was his own absolute faith in the power of God that his Father had given him that enabled him to heal. It was the faith of the sick men and women in that same power that enabled them to be healed.

As in the days when he called the disciples, so now, Our Lord preached and taught in the busy city streets, in the homes of the rich and the poor, in the quiet coves beside the Sea of Galilee and in the fields and hills and villages above them, only now wherever he went he was pressed upon by the sick and the dying and the mad. Living as we do in a country well supplied with hospitals, lunatic asylums, homes for old people, sanatoriums, ambulances and well-trained doctors and nurses, it is hard for us to imagine what life was like in a country that had none of these things. When we walk along the streets of English or American cities we do not see crippled beggars lying about in dark corners, dirty and ragged and covered with sores, sobbing and moaning perhaps because they have no one to look after them. We do not meet lunatics in the streets either. In America people don't die of starvation in the street, and the mad and those who are cruelly ill are hidden away in asylums and hospitals so that we don't hear and see them. But in Palestine in those days the sight and sound and smell of human suffering was part of the normal life of a city, and everyone except Our Lord took it for granted and did not bother about it. But Our Lord did bother about it and made his disciples do the same.

Here are some sentences from the gospels.

"And at even, when the sun did set, they brought unto him all that were sick, and them that were possessed with devils. And all the city was gathered together at the door. And he healed many that were sick with divers diseases and cast out many devils."

"They pressed upon him for to touch him, as many as had plagues."

"Whithersoever he entered, into villages or cities or country, they laid the sick in the streets, and besought him that they might touch if it were but the border of his garment: and as many as touched him were made whole."

"They had no leisure so much as to eat."

The evangelists write always with such dignity and restraint that the reality of the scene they are describing does not always come home to us, but there was neither dignity nor restraint in those crowds who thronged about Our Lord. Think what it must have meant to those poor wretched people, the crippled, blind, and starving who had no one to help them, those in pain who had no drugs to help them bear it, the sick who had no hope of getting better because no one even understood what was the matter with them, the lunatics and lepers who were pushed out of the way as though they were just so much refuse, when they discovered that there was a man among them who could deliver them from their anguish simply by laying his hands upon them, looking into their eyes, and speaking to them. Or, if they could not drag themselves as close to him as that, whose very garment, clutched in their hot hands, could stop the pain. There would not have been much restraint about those crowds. They would have fought to get near him, screamed to him not to pass them by, uncovered their sores for him to see, pushed their sick babies into his arms.

Imagine yourself one of them for a moment. Imagine yourself that leper of whom St. Matthew tells us. For years he had lived the life of an outcast. No one would speak to him or come near him except other lepers, who were a horror to him because in their dreadful faces he saw the image of his own. He slept where he could, in a cranny of the rocks or huddled up against a wall, and ate any sort of food that was flung to him. He could not get his clothes washed or mended, and they were filthy and ragged. He was always in pain and going blind. And he knew that leprosy is not a disease that kills quickly. He might live for years, with the pain getting worse and his weakness increasing and his sight going. And then one day he heard of a man called Jesus of Nazareth who was going about healing the sick just by laying his hands upon them. But he did not suppose Jesus would heal him. He knew himself to be so repulsive that no decent man could bear to look at him, let alone touch him.

Yet one day, when he was sitting huddled in the shade of a wall beside the road, he saw a crowd of people coming toward him, and called out to a small boy who was scampering past to know what was happening.

"Jesus of Nazareth has been preaching and healing up in the hills. He is coming along back to Capernaum."

The leper saw the tall figure coming down the hill, the crowd following after, and he shrank in upon himself in the shadow of the wall. He hoped they would pass by and not see him, for he did not want to have stones flung at him and be told to get out of the way. And then as they came nearer he saw the face of the young man coming toward him. He had never seen such strength in a face before, such power in a human figure. Quite unconsciously he moved a little, crawling out from the shadow of the wall. And then he saw the eyes, looking full into his, and the mouth with its pity. Only this was not the kind of pity to which he was accustomed, not a pity which turned and shrank away but a pity that increased its pace and came on. The eyes compelled him, pulling him to the sore feet that could scarcely carry him. Leaving the crutches he used lying against the wall he staggered a few steps and in all his filth and wretchedness fell at the feet of the pity and the power. "Lord, if thou wilt, thou canst make me clean!" Not for a moment did he doubt the power, but he caught his breath with a gasp of astonishment when he found hands touching him. He had forgotten what the human touch feels like. Not for years had anyone dared to touch him. He was untouchable. But this man's hands were gripping him firmly, holding his swaying figure steady. "I will; be thou clean." While he lived he would never forget the ring of love in the voice, the feel of it in the hands, the light of it in the eyes. Not a soft sort of love but something so strong and challenging that the whole of him rose up to meet it. The hands were helping him but he was raising himself, too, conscious of new strength surging through his lifted body, new life through his lifted soul. He was on his feet before he knew it, standing upright, and the pain was gone from his feet. The man was speaking again, keeping his voice low, speaking to him alone. "See thou tell no man; but go thy way, shew thyself to the priest, and offer the gift that Moses commanded, for a testimony unto them."

This was the law. A man who for some reason had become an

outcast could not be received back among the people of God
without a little service conducted in the synagogue by the priest.
When Our Lord healed anyone he almost always gave them some
command, told them to do something. He could not have them
kneeling for the rest of the day at his feet, weakening themselves
with their own emotion and keeping him from getting on with
what he had to do next, but if they were obeying him they could
feel that they were showing their gratitude by their obedience.
And the thing that he told them to do was always something
practical that brought them straight away back into normal life
again. It must have been a moment of desolation for the man
who had been a leper when the hands were taken from him, and
the voice did not speak again, but he obeyed, and joy would
have possessed him as he ran through the streets toward the
synagogue on feet that were healed and strong, stripping off his
bandages as he ran and seeing that the flesh had come again on
his hands like the clean flesh of a little child.

2.

That was what it was like for the sick. What was it like for
Our Lord? We do not know, and it is a good thing for us that
we do not. If we were to know the full cost to God of sin, and
the suffering caused by sin, we could not bear it. But two sentences in the Bible take us the little way that we can manage.

St. Mark tells us that after a sick woman had touched his
clothes, "Jesus, immediately knowing in himself that virtue had
gone out of him, turned him about in the press." The healing
power had to come from somewhere and it came from him. It
was strength, cleansing, life, the strength, holiness, and vitality

that his Father had given him, passing out of his being into the being of the person to whom he gave it. He was drained of his life by all these sick people whose suffering pierced his compassion just as a body is drained of blood when it is wounded. Again and again he had to go away by himself for a while, up into the hills at night, for the night was the only time when he could be alone, and pray to God for fresh life to give them.

And just as the healing had to come from somewhere the suffering had to go somewhere, and Isaiah tells us where it went. "Himself took our infirmities and bare our sicknesses." Just as he lifted up human sin and carried it on his own shoulders so he lifted up human suffering too. And not only did, but does. Today, whatever we may happen to be bearing, we know that it is his shoulders, not ours, that are carrying most of the weight, he is merely allowing us the honor of helping him by carrying a microscopic part of the load of human pain that he carries ceaselessly. When our pain stops we know that it has not really vanished but that he has now taken the whole weight.

His giving and his carrying are mysteries, but there is another aspect of what it cost him that involved his disciples too, and that we can understand quite well, and doctors and nurses can understand only too well, and that is the ceaseless pressure of it all. Always pressed upon by the sick bodies, clutched at by the hot hands, always the clamoring voices, the sobbing and complaining, the dirt, the smell, the heat, and the flies. Our Lord moved among it all with unfailing patience and courage, but the disciples must have got to the breaking point again and again. Gone for them were the idyllic early days of their first discipleship. They were experiencing the real thing now, and there breaks from them occasionally a sentence that shows them at the end of their tether. "Send them away.... Send her away, for she crieth after us.... Send them away." But God never sends anyone away.

Nor did Our Lord ever refuse to go to anyone who needed him. The woman who touched his clothes came to him as he was passing through the crowded streets to go to a house where a little girl twelve years old was ill. She was the daughter of Jairus, ruler of the synagogue, who came running to Our Lord to beg him to come and heal her, for she seemed dying. As a good doctor does, Our Lord went at once, and his disciples went with him. But the people thronged about him and they could not get along very fast. In the crowd was a woman who had been very ill for twelve years—for as long as the little girl to whom Our Lord was going had lived upon this earth. She had spent all that she had in trying to get better, but she had only got worse, and now she was at the end of her money, her strength, and her hope ... unless Our Lord could heal her.... She believed that he could, but a woman might not speak to a man in the streets, and she was ill and frightened and shy. But now here he was actually passing by quite close to her, and she said to herself, "If I may but touch his clothes I shall be whole." She need not speak, need not be noticed even, she only had to creep up behind him and touch his garment. Somehow she managed to do that, and immediately the divine life flowed into her sick body and she knew she was healed.

But Our Lord felt at once the familiar draining away of his vitality, the familiar exhaustion, and he stopped and turned round and said, "Who touched my clothes?"

The disciples said, "Thou seest the multitude thronging thee, and sayest thou, Who touched me?"

But Our Lord continued to look round to see who it was who had touched him, his searching eyes going from face to face. For his work was only half done. He had helped a suffering body but he had not through the body reached the soul. He never left anything half done. He was not going to move an inch further down that street until he had found that soul.

In all these stories of Our Lord's healing it is as though the light that shines from his presence illumines the people about him; we see them extraordinarily clearly, seem to know them so well. And this story is such a heavenly one because the light falls upon such fine people. Having once read about them we do not forget the unselfish patience of Jairus or the courage of the woman who was healed.

For she had taken such pains to avoid the indignity of having to speak to the Rabbi in the street, the shame of being stared at and talked about. Even now she could have slipped away in the crowd and escaped it all. But she would not do that. The Rabbi had healed her, he was standing there looking for her, and she would not be ungrateful. Terrified, and trembling all over, she came and knelt at his feet, and before all that crowd of people, reticent and shrinking woman that she was, she "told him all the truth."

And Our Lord said to her, "Daughter, be of good comfort; thy faith hath made thee whole: go in peace."

She possessed far more now than the mere healing of her body. That "be of good comfort" is the angels' "Fear not"; it is the assurance of God's love right on until the end. "Thy faith hath made thee whole"—how that must have touched her heart. Not, "*My* power hath saved thee," but "*thy* faith." He took no merit to himself, he gave it all to her. The unbelievable humility of God must have lifted her heart right out of her and made it his forever. "Go in peace." To the soul assured of his love, believing in him, giving herself to him in answering love, there comes always the gift of his peace. She had to obey him then, get up and go away from him, but as she had left her heart in his keeping, and had his peace to take home with her, it was not a real parting.

Jairus meanwhile had waited in agony. Our Lord always gave his whole attention to what he was doing at the moment, and for minutes that must have seemed like hours to Jairus he had been as absorbed in this woman as though she were the only creature existing upon God's earth. He had apparently forgotten all about the little girl of twelve years who was dying. Who would have thought the worse of Jairus if he had interrupted and said to Our Lord, "Leave this woman until later. She's not dying. My child is." Or if he had even taken Our Lord's arm and tried to pull him away, and cried out, "Come quickly while there is time. In a moment it will be too late." But he did not do this. He said nothing at all. With his heart breaking within him he simply waited. And as he waited he saw one of his servants pushing through the crowd toward him, and by the look on his face he knew what had happened. He did not need to hear the words, "Thy daughter is dead; trouble not the Master," to know that it *was* too late.

But instantly Our Lord was beside him as though he, now, were the only creature alive upon the earth. "Fear not!" He had no time to cry out, no time to despair, before the assurance of God's love gripped and steadied him. "Believe only, and she shall be made whole."

They went quickly then, and came to the house, and into the room where the little girl lay dead upon her bed with all the household and the neighbors gathered round her. The terrible Eastern wailing for the dead, like the Irish keening, had started already, and the lamentations of those who perhaps did not care very much filled the room with tumult. Our Lord silenced it sternly. "Why make ye this ado, and weep?" he said. "The damsel is not dead, but sleepeth." They laughed at him. They knew a dead body when they saw one. But when he told them all to go out, all except the father and mother of the child, and Peter and James and John, they went at once. They could not withstand his authority.

The room was very quiet now, and he knelt down on the floor beside the little mat that was the child's bed, and took her hand and called to her, saying, "Talitha cumi. Little girl, arise." Her spirit, escaping away into paradise, heard his voice, turned obediently, and came back into her body again. She opened her eyes and he lifted her up, and she was well.

"Give her something to eat," said Our Lord.

It was the same sort of practical command that he had given the leper. The sudden joy, following so quickly upon the anguish of grief, might have overwhelmed the father and mother, but preparing food for the child, watching the hungry little girl joyfully eating it, brought them all safely and gently back into the normal happiness of daily life.

3.

Back again from the quiet room to the ceaseless pressure of the crowd. It was so great one day, gathered about the house where Our Lord was living, that four men who were trying to bring a sick friend of theirs into his presence could not get near the door. The sick man could not walk, for he was paralyzed, and they were carrying him on his bed, a light pallet easy to lift. They implored the crowd to make way, they shouted, they pushed, but there is nothing so selfish as a crowd of people all wanting to get in first, and they could not get through. They could not wait their turn, for a man as ill as this one was could not be left for perhaps an hour out in the street in the boiling sun. Something had to be done, and quickly. The four were resolute men, not easily beaten, and suddenly they had a brilliant idea. The house where Our Lord was living was perhaps Peter's. It was a poor man's house and so, instead of having a stone-domed roof, as the houses of rich people had, it was thatched with branches. The four decided that rather than be beaten they'd smash the roof, and they did. They climbed up and ripped off the branches until they had made a gaping hole. Nothing delights a crowd like the sight of some sort of destruction going on, and so its mood probably changed now, and willing hands lifted the sick man on his bed up to the four on the roof, and they, lying flat on the roof, let it right down into the center of the crowded little room below, down to the feet of Our Lord. The story is partly funny, partly tragic. There were Scribes there, talking to Our Lord, and their astonishment when the roof was ripped open over their learned heads and the bed slowly descended, must have been comic; but there was nothing amusing about the man who soon lay there in the midst, with his wasted body and useless trembling limbs. Our Lord, who was always so full of enterprise himself, must have been delighted by the enterprise of the four friends; we can imagine him looking up at them through the gaping hole and smiling before he looked down at the man at his feet.

"And when he saw their faith, he said unto him, Son, thy sins are forgiven thee."

It was usually Our Lord's way to heal the body first and through the body to reach the soul, but now he ignored the desperately sick body, neither touching it nor speaking of it, and directed the power of his love straight through to the soul. For it was there, in the soul, that the cause of the illness lay. This man had led an undisciplined life and because of his sin his body had become diseased. But Our Lord's sight, burning through to the soul, saw it anguished with remorse. The man was not sorry for himself but at himself. He loathed his sin more than he loathed his pain. Could he know himself cleansed of the sin then whatever the pain of his body he would know peace.

The love of God his Father Almighty shone upon him in the

116

one word "Son," and the absolution that followed swept with its cleansing through his soul. His body ceased to tremble and lay still.

The men who disliked Our Lord, the Scribes and Pharisees and rulers of the people who at last brought him to his death, seem to have had hearts like nether millstones; we are told Our Lord was "grieved at the hardness of their hearts." Again and again they witnessed scenes that should surely have touched the most worldly and tough to compassion and joy, yet the only feeling roused in them seems to have been criticism. Now they watched this drama of the rebirth of a soul and the only thing they could say to themselves was that Jesus of Nazareth had no right at all to forgive sins. Who did he think he was? God?

He answered their unspoken, caviling thoughts. Yes, he had every right. The Son of Man, the Christ, had power on earth to forgive sins. And which was easier, to say to the sick man, "Thy sins be forgiven thee," or "Take up thy bed and walk?" The sin and its result were one thing, and the power of God was able equally to forgive and to heal. Then he turned to the forgiven man. "Arise, and take up thy bed, and go thy way into thine house."

The man whose limbs had been useless to him for so long obeyed his Lord at once. He got up, rolled up his pallet, picked it up, and went out before them all.

4.

Our Lord's power over death could terrify those who witnessed it. One day, followed by his disciples and by the crowd of people who never left him if they could help it, he walked from

Capernaum to Nain, and as they came near to the walled city they saw a little procession coming out of the gate, and heard wailing and the mournful music of the flutes that are played when a dead body is carried away for burial. The procession came nearer and they saw the body lying on the bier wrapped in white graveclothes. A woman walked by the bier and there were many people with her, and their faces showed that they were all very sorry for this death. For the body on the bier was not that of an old man glad to have done with mortal pain but of a young man dead on the threshold of life, and the woman was his mother who had lived in him and for him, for she was a widow and she had no other sons.

She was crying and her tears had blinded her. She had not seen the people coming up the hill toward them. The first she knew of them was a sudden halt. Her feet, that had been stumbling mechanically forward over the rough path, were still. Her body, which had been ice cold with her grief, was suddenly warm. They had all been sorry for her in the city, but their pity had not been able to reach her. But now something was reaching her, something that warmed and strengthened her like the compassionate sun. Her swollen eyelids strained open and she was aware of a tall man standing in the path, blocking the way between her son and his grave.

"Weep not," he said.

She wiped the tears out of her eyes, as though she had no further use for them, and then she saw him. It was as though the whole of her life up till now had been a living death, but now, seeing him, she was alive.

Standing beside her he lightly touched the bier upon which her dead son lay and the bearers immediately set it down. The wailing had ceased, and the music of the flutes. The two crowds meeting here outside the city wall were still, silent, gripped by awe. No one moved. No one spoke. There was no sound under the hot sun but the chirping of the crickets under the wall. The Son of God gathered his power to him and his voice rang out in command. ⁓

"Young man, I say unto thee, Arise!"

And the dead boy moved on his bier, sat up, and began to speak.

And there came a fear on them all. This was something right outside human experience. First the silence, then the voice of God speaking in the silence, then this thing that had happened. The crowd was shaking with fear, stupefied by it. The practical thing that must be done was done this time by Our Lord himself, for no one else was capable of it. It was he who helped the warm and living boy off his bier and delivered him to his mother, put him into her arms that she might feel his warm and pulsing life.

5.

The fame of this miracle spread far beyond Galilee; it spread right through Judea. Almost the whole nation, now, knew that a great prophet had come among them, and the devils whom Our Lord flung out of the human spirits they had entered and possessed knew more—they knew who he was. "Son of God!" they screamed at him through the mouths of the poor lunatics, "let us alone! Art thou come to destroy us?" And he commanded them to be silent because they knew him. At first sight it seems strange that these dreadful spirits should all have known him, while among men only a few knew him. But God is a Spirit and they were spirits, and though the One was all heavenly light and they were all darkness, there was for them no veil of flesh hiding what they saw. And he was their enemy, who had come to destroy them, while men he had come to save, and danger is something that strikes all living things to great awareness.

Demoniac possession was a very real thing to the men of those days, because they saw it with their own eyes, but in countries such as our own where it is hidden away from our sight many people say it does not exist at all but is just another form of mental illness. Yet every now and then some doctor, psychologist, or priest writes a very disturbing book which completely upsets this comfortable idea. They have had to do with possession and they know it to be a fact. And why not? For if the soul of a man can be possessed by the spirit of good why not by the spirit of evil too; the choice is his as to which he invites into himself. But we don't much want to believe in it because it is so terrible and so terrifying. When Our Lord faced the demons, fought with them, and threw them out, was he sometimes terrified too? Surely he was. He was a perfect man but it is not a sin to feel fear, only to show it, and give way to it. All men feel fear, and the most sensitive and highly strung feel it the most. The bravest people in the world are those who are very afraid and yet never let their fear hinder them for a single moment in what they have to do. Neither naked evil met face to face, than which there is nothing more frightening, nor the hatred of his enemies, always plotting against his life, nor the knowledge that awful pain was waiting for him just round the corner, ever caused Our Lord to show the least sign of fear; but we do not know at what cost to himself he kept this splendid front.

The sight of him at close grips with such evil had a very disturbing effect upon some of those who saw it. Their own idea of holiness was of something withdrawn, something that drew back its skirts from contamination, whereas Our Lord, who did not have ideas about holiness but just was holiness, plunged down into the middle of the evil that he might rescue its victims to be holy too. This, being contrary to their own idea, shocked them, and led them to the conclusion that he conquered evil not by the power of God but by the power of the devil. Our Lord showed them that this idea, like the other, was sheer nonsense. The devil is not so foolish as to fight against himself. "Every kingdom divided against itself is brought to desolation," he said, "and a house divided against a house falleth." And then he showed them that this fight of his against evil was just one of the aspects of the coming of the kingdom, which is the coming of the love of God into the souls of men. "If I with the finger of God cast out devils, no doubt the kingdom of God is come upon you."

And then to the crowd gathered about him he told a terrible story about a man from whose soul an evil spirit had been cast out. The man was emptied of the evil, and great must have been his joy, but the spirit that had been cast out was homeless and suffering. It wandered through dry places, seeking rest, but found none. The good earth that God has made is the home of men, not of devils. Its fresh green places are so much desert to them, and offer them no shelter. They can only feel at home curled up inside the spirit of a man. So the evil spirit went back again to the soul from which it had been cast out. It must have gone back in some trepidation, for if it had found God there then it could not have got in. But there was only emptiness there. The soul was like an unused room, swept and tidy but quite empty. In great glee the spirit went off and fetched seven more spirits, even more wicked than itself, and the eight of them took possession of the empty soul, and the last state of that man was worse than the first.

Our Lord did not need to say much more to his frightened

hearers. Their only hope, our only hope, is the coming of the kingdom of God into our souls. "Blessed are they that hear the word of God, and keep it," said Our Lord. Only when we are citizens of the kingdom of God, and God rules over us, are we safe.

6.

The man in Our Lord's story left his soul empty when the devils were cast out, but on the other side of the lake was a man who filled it with the love of God and so was safe.

Our Lord did not only heal upon the western shore of the lake, sometimes he crossed over to the other side, where the beautiful Greek cities were built among the folds of the colored hills. One day, when he was in the middle of a crowd of people, he suddenly knew that somewhere among those hills there was another soul in torment that had great need of him, and he said to his disciples, "Let us pass over unto the other side." The disciples by this time must have become used to Our Lord's quick decisions, his habit of doing things "straightway," and used to obeying him without question and without delay. They sent the crowd of people away and took him "even as he was," that is, tired and hungry, and perhaps with no cloak though night was coming on, into a boat. "Other little ships" came too, and the gallant flotilla pushed off from the shore, facing a stiff row of nine miles through the darkness to bring Our Lord to the place where his love and his strength were so desperately needed. This is the first of all the many brave missionary voyages. We think of St. Columba and his monks facing the storms of the Irish Sea to bring Our Lord to the Islands of the Hebrides, of

St. Augustine bringing him to heathen England, of the monks of Mont St. Michel sailing away in their tiny coracles to bring him to the Channel Islands, and of so many more all down the ages.

It would take a long time to cover the nine miles of rather choppy water, and Our Lord considered this a heaven-sent opportunity for going to sleep. Such opportunities did not come his way very often and thankfully he lay down in the stern of the ship "on a pillow," and immediately fell into the fathomless sleep of exhaustion. John covered him with his own cloak, and in the last of the daylight stooped to look down at the beloved face. And then turned quickly away. We all of us feel that to look too long upon a sleeping face, even the face of a child, is a thing we must not do. It is so revealing of what we are not meant to see, so defenseless against our sight, that we shut our own eyes. That one glimpse of the holiness of the sleeping face of Christ, of the defenselessness of God, must have made John's body tremble as he took his place in the boat.

They were only halfway across the lake when that treacherous wind came sweeping down from the western mountains, whipping the water into white-capped waves, driving the clouds over the friendly stars, plunging them all into darkness. The roar of the gale increased and the waves mounted higher, tossing the little boats up and down like cockleshells. The cold spray dashed in the rowers' faces, half blinding them, and the boats were filling; through the shriek of the wind they could hear the water gurgling and sucking over the planks. They were in great danger, and experienced sailors that they were, they all knew it, and the fear of death came upon them in the midnight darkness. Yet neither the tumult nor the tossing of the ships woke Our Lord; he slept peacefully on. The disciples cried out to him in their terror, but the wind took their voices and carried them away. Then as children terrified in the night roll out of bed and tumble along to their father, they stumbled to him and woke him up, their reverence for the sleep of God forgotten now in sheer panic. They were even indignant with him for sleeping so peacefully while they were so terrified. "Master! Master! Carest thou not that we perish?"

Our Lord, waking peacefully, could see no reason for all this panic. There was a bad storm raging, certainly, but they were in the care of God. If it was his will that this storm should open to them the gate of paradise, then drowned they would be, but if he had work for them to do upon the other side of the lake then he would bring them to that work, storm or no storm. It was quite simple. "Why are ye so fearful?" asked Our Lord. "How is it that ye have no faith?"

But he saw that they were indeed very frightened, and frights in the night are bad for children's nerves, so he arose to send away this storm that had scared his little ones.

"Peace, be still!" he cried to the wind and the waves, his tall figure towering up in the boat, his voice ringing out powerfully above their uproar. The wind and the waves were his creatures that he had made and they were quiet when he bade them be quiet, and lay down like good dogs at his feet, and there was a great calm. The stars came out again and were mirrored in the lake.

And a new terror gripped the disciples. Who was he, this man whom even the wind and the sea obeyed? Day by day he lived with them as their friend and brother, and then suddenly shining through the homely stuff of their daily life would come the flash of power, revealing heights and depths beyond their understanding. They were trembling as they bent to their oars again, and then that terror passed, for the strange deep calm through which they were moving was the peace of God.

7.

In the dawn the little boats came to rest in a quiet cove upon the farther shore. The rosy clouds above them were reflected in water like glass. Cranes flew over the water, and the rocky hillside beyond the cove was scattered over with bushes of pink cistus. They baled out the boats and came thankfully ashore, and then the sun leaped up, warming them through and through. Tired though they were it was good to be alive in this sunshine and this peace.

And then came a fresh terror. There were cave-tombs up above them among the rocks and from one of these appeared a terrible figure, a man naked and bleeding, with a broken chain dragging from one ankle. One glance told the disciples what he was—a dangerous maniac who had been chained in this lonely place so that he could not harm his fellow men. He had been alone here for a long time, crying out in his anguish, dragging at his chain like a wild beast, cutting himself on the sharp stones in his struggles to escape, so that his wasted body was covered with bleeding sores. But with the terrible strength of the insane he had broken his chain, and now here he was, free, able to do what harm he would to whoever got in his way.

If the disciples had a brief hope that he had not seen them it was soon gone. The man caught sight of their Master's tall figure shining in the sunlight and came leaping down over the rocks toward him; they saw his face, and it was that of a man possessed. Our Lord stood steady as a rock before what must have looked like a murderous onslaught, for to withstand it was the reason for his coming. And, when it reached him, the evil checked like a broken wave against the rock of his courage. It could not withhold the tormented human creature, struggling out and away from the darkness that possessed him toward his God, from flinging his bruised and bleeding body in worship at his feet.

The disciples can never have forgotten the strange colloquy that followed as the power of God fought the power of evil for the possession of a human soul, each using the body of a man and speaking with the voice of a man.

"Come out of the man, thou unclean spirit!"

The sharp command must have cut the silence like a sword, but the answer that came from the writhing kneeling figure was shouted defiantly back "in a loud voice."

"What have I to do with thee, Jesus, thou Son of the most high God? I adjure thee by God, that thou torment me not."

"What is thy name?"

"My name is Legion."

Not one devil, but many, had taken possession of this soul. Perhaps Our Lord now had to bend low to hear the crazy beseeching that broke from the pitiful creature at his feet. . . . "Do not send us away into the dry places, Son of God, there is no rest in the deep wilderness of the world. Son of God, there is no rest. Son of God, have pity. Son of God, send us into the swine feeding up there on the hill rather than into the dry places of the earth. Son of God, there is no rest in the wilderness of the world . . . no rest . . . no rest."

Does God pity devils? He did not send them out into the wilderness. He gave them leave to go into the poor beasts who are bodies only and have no souls to lose. The man ceased to writhe and mutter and lay still, but up on the hill the crazed beasts rushed violently down the steep slope and hurled themselves over the cliff into the sea, and their herdsmen, feeling the rush of evil possess the hillside, fled in terror from the dreadful place.

It was over. The evil that had seemed to darken the sun and made the disciples shudder was gone. The naked bleeding flesh upon the ground was now the body of a man as sane as one of themselves, harmless and pitiful, needing their care. And gladly they gave it, fetching tools from the boat to get the rusty chain off his festering ankle, and water from the spring to bathe his sores, putting their own clothes upon him, fetching food from the boat, lighting a fire and cooking breakfast. It was Our Lord himself, perhaps, who bathed the wounds and got the chain off, his hands healing the pain of the flesh, his steady voice quieting the startled and bewildered spirit. For this man would have been like a child waking up from a nightmare and Our Lord would have steadied him as a man gentles a startled horse, saying, "Peace, be still!"

The confused story that the frightened herdsmen told in the city brought its citizens hurrying down to the lakeside in great alarm to see what could possibly be happening there. But at first they saw only a few fishing boats rocking quietly at anchor and a little group of men sitting peacefully in the sun. Then the quick eyes of these Greeks saw that though all these men were Galileans from the farther shore there was one who was different; a Galilean too, a young man in the prime of life like the rest, dressed like them, tanned by sun and wind as they were, yet different with the difference which a man feels who looks from a bungled sketch of some lovely scene to the reality; or as a man might feel who looking at some rough-hewn stone statue of one of the immortals suddenly turns and sees standing beside him the radiant young god himself. Such a difference might make a man afraid, and they were afraid; the more so because sitting at the feet of this man was the dangerous maniac whom they had bound with ropes and chains, and now saw clothed, sane, quiet, and happy.

They were so afraid that they asked Our Lord to go away. It seems incredible, but they did. They could have had among them for a little while a man who, if they had let him, could have changed every single one of them as he had changed the happy man sitting at his feet. But they did not know what such a change might cost them, and they were afraid; and so obedient to their wish Our Lord went quietly down to the shore to go away. It is not such a terrible rejection as the one at Nazareth, yet to read of it frightens us all the same. For it seems that if a mere man wants to push God Almighty, eternal and glorious, his Maker and Redeemer, right out of his life, he can.

But to the man who had passed through his changing and come out made new, the thought of being separated from his Saviour was something that he could not bear. "He besought him that he might be with him." Perhaps he waded out into the water and clung to the boat, imploring Our Lord to let him come too, begging and praying him to let him be with him always. The disciples would have known how he felt, for they felt the same; that to be with Our Lord was life and light and to be away from him was death and darkness; and perhaps in their great pity for him they also begged their Master to let him come. But Our Lord knew all about him and what was best for him. Probably he was a Greek and in the beautiful city a few miles inland there was a home waiting for him, a wife who loved him, and children who needed him. He must go back to them and live out his life in the place where he belonged.

"Return to thine own house," said Our Lord, "and shew how great things God hath done unto thee."

The man obeyed. He looked his last in this life upon the face of Christ, let go of the boat, and turned away. Wearing John's coat, perhaps, and Peter's talith, clad in the garments of a disciple, he went home "and published throughout the whole city how great things Jesus had done unto him." And in so doing found he had not lost Our Lord after all, for he who praises God is filled with the love of God and there is no room in his soul for anything else.

8.

Those who were healed of their diseases were grateful to Our Lord but those who were delivered from the power of evil were passionately grateful. The misery of a sick body is very hard to bear but the misery of a diseased soul can be much worse. There seem two sorts of sinners in the world; those who want to be sinners, who aware of the glory of God and his love have yet deliberately chosen evil for their good and the devil for their master, and those who have not wanted to be sinners and yet, somehow, are. There are, thank heaven, not very many of the first sort about, for they are such terrible people that they scarcely bear thinking of, but all the rest of us fall into the second category. It includes those who are bad because they have not had the chance of being anything else, those who have had every chance to be saints, and ought to be saints, but yet are not, those who have been forced into sin through the evil of others, those whose particular virtues make them especially vulnerable to temptation, and all sorts of others. And all of us, with souls diseased by sin, are at times perfectly miserable. This sin, this filth, is not what we wanted. This person that we are is not the person that we meant to be. Somehow, somewhere, we have seen a far-off glimpse of God's love, and that is what we want. But we don't know how to get there. We are stuck fast in the mud of our sin, hopeless and despairing.

For sinners who having seen him did not want him, there was little that Our Lord could do, but for the other sort he could do everything. He loved them and longed for them, fought their devils for them, taught them how to be sorry for their sins, forgave them, cleansed them, made them his friends, and out of one of the worst of them made one of the greatest of his saints.

She was called Mary of Magdala because though her real home was at Bethany, near Jerusalem, at this time she was living at Magdala, one of the lakeside cities. Tradition says that she was a dancing girl. Perhaps she danced for Herod, and in the Greek cities on the other side of the lake. She had the reputation of being a very bad woman, but from all the descriptions of her in the Gospels we can see that she was one of those people whose good qualities make it easy for others to harm them. For she was impulsive, emotional, intensely loving, and splendidly generous. It would have been her habit to act first and think afterward, trust people who were not trustworthy and get let down, and find it almost impossible to refuse anybody anything, even though what they asked for they had no right to ask and she had no right to give. Loving and generous people are so near to God, even though they may not know it, that their sin makes them even more miserable than it makes most sinners. Mary of Magdala must have felt wretched. She was bad, she hated being bad, but she did not know how to stop being bad.

When she first saw Our Lord we do not know. The Gospels tell us that he cast seven devils out of her. This may be a pictorial way of saying that she had sinned very much, or it may mean that through her sin she had become actually possessed and insane. In any case her meeting with him saved her.

Being the sort of woman she was she had to show her gratitude in an impulsive, extravagant way, the sort of way that thoroughly upsets cautious, careful people. One day Our Lord had been invited to dinner by one of the Pharisees, called Simon. It was a decorous, dignified dinner party, with the guests reclining on a horseshoe couch about the table in the center, in the central court of the house, out in the open air, with the blue sky deepening overhead. There were the music of a fountain and the scent of flowers. The guests were all men, Scribes and Pharisees, and they must have looked forward to talk that was scholarly, urbane, and dignified. These men may have been outraged at times by the startling things Our Lord did and said, but he was a teacher of Israel as they were, and today in this gathering of Rabbis he was one of themselves and they would have been ready to delight in his fine mind and presence, his knowledge and his wit.

But the dinner party had hardly started when it was disturbed. Into this peaceful men's hour came Mary of Magdala with a gift for Our Lord, a precious and expensive gift, an elaborate box of ointment. Perhaps she had been saving up her earnings so that she could give him something, and had seen the beautiful box and bought it at once without stopping to think if it was the kind of gift that was exactly suitable for a Rabbi. Or perhaps it was a great treasure of her own, and it had come over her suddenly that she must give it to him. In any case she could not wait to give it. She must give it now, at once, wherever he was and whatever he was doing.

She came into the quiet court, and came behind Our Lord where he lay on the couch, knelt down at his feet, and began to cry—tears of sorrow for her sin and tears of sheer love. She was one of those people who laugh and cry easily, just as it comes over them, and are no more ashamed of their tears than their laughter. The weeping of such lovely childlike people is seldom ugly; it is fresh as their laughter. Our Lord's feet were wet with her tears and she wiped them away with her long hair. He did not check her or tell her to go away. He accepted the homage of her love as simply and naturally as she gave it. He who was despised and rejected of men knew how terribly it hurts when someone does not want what you bring them. Everything that was given him for love's sake he accepted gladly, from the gifts of the three kings down to the drink of vinegar on the cross.

Simon the Pharisee did not protest either, for his position as host forbade him to say what he thought of this shocking emotional exhibition. But his thoughts were contemptuous. This man is no prophet, he thought. If he were he'd know this woman is a sinner. If he knew what she is he'd never let her touch him. For Simon was one of those whose idea of holiness was of something that must draw back its skirts from contamination.

Our Lord showed at once whether he was a prophet or not by reading Simon's thoughts. "Simon, I have somewhat to say unto thee," he said.

"Master, say on," said Simon.

Quietly Our Lord told a story, and the tension was eased. The guests forgot their outraged embarrassment in listening to him, and Mary stopped sobbing and kissed Our Lord's feet and anointed them with her precious ointment. The perfume of it stole out into the quiet court and mingled with the scent of the flowers.

Our Lord told them of a certain man who had two debtors. One owed him a good deal of money and the other only a little. Neither of them could pay their debt, and so he gladly forgave them both. Which of them would have loved him most?

As Our Lord asked the question his eyes were on Simon, and Simon had to answer. "I suppose that he to whom he forgave most," he said.

"Thou hast rightly judged," said Our Lord. He had nothing more to add to that brief story. Mary loved God more than Simon loved him. Such a great burden of sin had been lifted off her, and so her love was great.

And then he looked down at Mary and spoke of her to Simon

in words so lovely that they are like a song, the song of the Lover welcoming back the Beloved who has strayed. If we listen we can hear the music of the fountain in them, and think of the fountain as the weeping of us all. We are so sorry for our sins, and we want God to look at them only through our tears.

"Seest thou this woman? I entered into thine house, thou gavest me no water for my feet: but she hath washed my feet with tears, and wiped them with the hairs of her head. Thou gavest me no kiss: but this woman, since the time I came in, hath not ceased to kiss my feet. My head with oil thou didst not anoint: but this woman hath anointed my feet with ointment. Wherefore I say unto thee, Her sins, which are many, are forgiven; for she loved much; but to whom little is forgiven, the same loveth little."

Then to Mary he spoke again the words which no sinner can ever hear too often, and which Our Lord spoke so often because he knows how we cling to them. "Thy sins are forgiven. Thy faith hath saved thee; go in peace."

Mary went home with the peace of God in her soul. She had it always, and she became at last not Mary of Magdala the sinner but Mary Magdalene the Saint.

There is a hymn which we sing sometimes in Holy Week which makes us think of Mary.

> Drop, drop, slow tears,
> And bathe those beauteous feet,
> Which brought from heaven
> The news and Prince of peace.
>
> Cease not, wet eyes,
> His mercies to entreat;
> To cry for vengeance
> Sin doth never cease.

In your deep floods
Drown all my faults and fears;
Let not His eye
See sin, but through my tears.

Chapter 6

FRIENDS AND DISCIPLES

And he stretched forth his hand toward his
disciples, and said, Behold, my mother, and my
brethren! For whosoever shall do the will of
my Father which is in heaven, the same is my
brother, and sister, and mother.
                                    —St. Matthew XII:49–50

1.

WHILE he healed and taught the multitude Our Lord
was at the same time caring for his own disciples. The
original little band had grown now to a considerable number,
and always he was teaching them and training them with infinite
care and patience, for these were the men who when his physical
body left the earth would be his body in the world, his church,
indwelt by his Spirit, his body of love that never ceased from the
labor of love, and never will cease while his church endures. Out
of this larger body of men he chose twelve who would be especially near to him, as children are near to their father. This little
family would learn to love him and understand his teaching
more deeply than the others could do, and upon their love and
understanding he could build up the body that was to be.

135

When it was necessary Our Lord would make quick decisions, but he never made careless hasty decisions, as we do. He never did anything in a hurry. Before he chose these twelve he went away by himself into the mountains and stayed there all night praying to God. When the dawn came, sleepless and tired but knowing what was the will of his Father, he called all his disciples to him and chose the twelve and named them his apostles. They included the seven whom we know already, Peter and Andrew, James and John, Philip, Matthew, and Nathanael. The others were Thomas, Jude, Simon the Canaanite, and another James. Last there was Judas Iscariot, who later betrayed the great trust and the love that Our Lord now gave him. To these twelve, his beloved children, he spoke words that must have gone with them for the rest of their lives like a lantern and a song. For they were words that showed them what they must have, how they must live, and what they must be, and they were heartening and beautiful music for pilgrims traveling a long and difficult way.

Blessed are the poor in spirit; for their's is the kingdom of heaven.

Blessed are they that mourn: for they shall be comforted.

Blessed are the meek: for they shall inherit the earth.

Blessed are they which do hunger and thirst after righteousness: for they shall be filled.

Blessed are the merciful: for they shall obtain mercy.

Blessed are the pure in heart: for they shall see God.

Blessed are the peacemakers: for they shall be called the children of God.

Blessed are they which are persecuted for righteousness' sake: for theirs is the kingdom of heaven.

Blessed are ye, when men shall revile you, and persecute you, and shall say all manner of evil against you falsely,

for my sake. Rejoice and be exceeding glad: for great
is your reward in heaven.

The Beatitudes are a complete reversal of the standard of happiness that most people set themselves in this world. They do not say happy are those who are wealthy, healthy, and comfortable, who have many pleasures and no troubles or worries. They say happy are those who do not cling to any of the pleasures and treasures of this world, who are penitent and humble, who long for God as the starving and parched long for food and water, who are holy, merciful, peaceable, and suffer bravely for Our Lord's sake. There is this great contradiction between the two standards because our idea of happiness depends entirely upon what we think of as the peak of our living, the mountaintop to which we are journeying. If we think that the death of our bodies is the end of us, then naturally achievement and well-being in this world is the peak, and everything to do with our bodies becomes tremendously important because it is only through them that we will reach either. But Our Lord put the mountaintop far beyond this world; he put it even beyond Paradise, where penitent souls who love him and long for him pass at death, and where their penitence and love and longing continue; he put it in heaven itself where the soul that is purged of all selfishness comes at last to perfect union with the Beloved. If we put the peak where he did, the only possessions that will make us happy will be those that strengthen our souls for this long journey, and they can't even be seen. Our Lord gave his disciples the list of them in the Beatitudes.

Day by day he taught them and some of the things he said are collected together, and we call them the Sermon on the Mount, and read it in the 5th chapter of St. Matthew's Gospel. If, for just one week, there were nothing at all to read in all the world but just this sermon, and all men read it, understood it, did it, then the Kingdom of God would come upon earth in the following week.

The apostles had to act as well as listen. They went with him everywhere, helping him in all that he did, and then, to teach them how it would be in the future when they could not see with their bodily eyes the God who was with them, and to prove to them that nevertheless he was there, he sent them out without him to preach and heal, and cast out devils through his power. He sent them out two by two, that they might strengthen each other, for what they had to do needed courage. For he would not let them take any money with them; he did not want them even to take a change of clothes. He wanted them to learn such faith in God that they would be able to start out to work each day not knowing where they were going to sleep that night, or what, if anything, they were going to have to eat, and yet not be anxious. He wanted them to learn that if we are trying to do God's will, to obey him, love him and seek him, then God will look after us. He had already told them in the Sermon on the Mount how stupid it is to worry.

"Behold, the fowls of the air: for they sow not, neither do they reap, nor gather into barns; yet your heavenly Father feedeth them. Are ye not much better than they? . . . And why take ye thought for raiment? Consider the lilies of the field, how they grow; they toil not, neither do they spin: And yet I say unto you, That even Solomon in all his glory was not arrayed like one of these. Wherefore if God so clothe the grass of the field, which to day is and to morrow is cast into the oven, shall he not much more clothe you, O ye of little faith? Therefore take no thought, saying, What shall we eat? or, what shall we drink? or, Wherewithal shall we be clothed? For your heavenly Father knoweth that ye have need of all these things. But seek ye first the Kingdom of God, and his righteousness; and all these things shall be added unto you. Take therefore no thought for the morrow: for the morrow shall take thought for the things of itself. Sufficient unto the day is the evil thereof."

And so two by two they went out into the countryside without their Master, calling men to repent and preaching the good news of the kingdom, fighting evil, disease, and death even as he did. And they found that when their faith was strong his power was with them, for they healed many sick people and even the devils obeyed them. They came back to him rejoicing and told him all that they had done.

2.

Into the midst of this fight against disease and pain came a message from that other fighter, John the Baptist. He was still in the fortress of Machaerus and we know how worn he was by his long imprisonment because he who had cried out, "Behold, the Lamb of God!" began now in the loneliness of his cell to wonder if it was really true that Jesus, his cousin, was indeed the Christ. It was his hour of dereliction and misery, through which it seems that every great servant of God must pass just before the end comes and the gates of Paradise open to him. Our Lord in his hour of dereliction on the cross cried out, "My God, my God, why hast thou forsaken me?" In John's soul there was much the same terrible cry. He had believed himself called by God to prepare the way for the Holy One of Israel, and he had obeyed. At the River Jordan he believed he had seen the Spirit of the Lord descending upon his cousin and heard the voice of the Lord saying, "This is my beloved Son," and again he had obeyed, giving Jesus his cousin the allegiance of the Forerunner to his Christ. Had the calling, the voice, been merely his own

139

illusion? Had he been deceived? Had Jesus himself been deceived? Day after day he paced his narrow prison like a caged lion and still no rumor reached him of a great Messiah come to judgment and a whole nation risen to acclaim him. Was the Christ still to come? If so, his life's work had been in vain. If he had believed himself called, upheld, and taught of God, and it was not so, then his conviction that God was with him here in his prison cell and would uphold him in his suffering and death was also delusion. Now he was indeed forsaken of God.

His disciples were allowed to visit him, and he sent two of them to Jesus asking, "Art thou he that should come, or do we look for another?"

It was a pitiful message, coming from so valiant a fighter as John, and it must have wrung the heart of Our Lord. The temptation that he had already met and conquered in the desert must have come upon him again now, the temptation to give John such overwhelming supernatural proof of who he was that there would be no more room for doubt—or for faith either. But he conquered again and sent John instead just a message to strengthen his faith. He told John's disciples to tell him of all that they had heard and seen, to tell him that "the blind receive their sight, and the lame walk, the lepers are cleansed, and the deaf hear, the dead are raised up, and the poor have the gospel preached to them."

In this John would instantly hear an echo of the great prophecy of Isaiah which Our Lord had read in the synagogue at Nazareth, "The Spirit of the Lord is upon me, because he hath anointed me to preach the gospel to the poor; he hath sent me to heal the brokenhearted, to preach deliverance to the captives, and recovering of sight to the blind, to set at liberty them that are bruised, to preach the acceptable year of the Lord." He would hear Our Lord's voice saying to him, "Yes, the Spirit of the Lord is upon me. You were not deceived when you saw the

Dove descend. Could a man who was not the Christ do what I am doing? I am fulfilling the prophecies. I am he."

"And tell John," said Our Lord, "blessed is he, whosoever shall not be offended in me."

This was a spur to John's constancy. Was John going to allow himself to fall away from his faith? Blessed are they who having found Christ hold to him.

Immediately, even as the two disciples turned away to go back to John, Our Lord swung round to the crowd of people who were there and had been listening and broke out into a splendid panegyric of his friend. Before the message of pitiful uncertainty had time to give the people an unfavorable impression of John he wiped it out with his glowing words. John's disciples, turning away, must have paused and listened to the first few sentences that they might tell their master what his Christ had said of him. They would not have been difficult sentences to remember, for Our Lord was a poet and all that he said was unforgettable music.

"What went ye out into the wilderness to see? A reed shaken with the wind? But what went ye out for to see? A man clothed in soft raiment? behold, they that wear soft clothing are in kings' houses. But what went ye out for to see? A prophet? yea, I say unto you, and more than a prophet. For this is he of whom it is written, Behold, I send my messenger before thy face, which shall prepare thy way before thee. Verily, I say unto you, Among them that are born of women there hath not risen a greater than John the Baptist."

John's disciples would have passed out of hearing now. They would not have heard the sad words that followed, "notwithstanding, he that is least in the kingdom of heaven is greater than he." Our Lord's own disciples, his "little ones," were still children compared with John, but their child's faith that did not doubt surpassed his.

141

Soon after this the end came for John, and he would have faced it in good heart, strengthened, confirmed, and comforted, with his Christ's words still ringing in his soul.

Herod Antipas came to Machaerus. His first wife, whom he had discarded to marry his brother's wife Herodias, had fled to her father, King Aretas of Petra, whose country lay to the south of the Dead Sea. King Aretas declared war upon Herod, and Herod with the chief officers of his army immediately occupied the fortress of Machaerus, which would have been his best base if he had to fight Aretas. Herodias and her daughter Salome were with him in Machaerus, and on his birthday he invited his officers to a supper, and after they had feasted Salome danced for them. She danced so beautifully that Herod said to her, "Ask of me whatsoever thou wilt, and I will give it thee, unto the half of my kingdom."

Salome went to her mother and said, "What shall I ask?"

Herodias hated John the Baptist for his plain speaking, and she had done her best to persuade Herod to kill him, but up till now Herod had not yielded, for he both feared and respected John. This was Herodias' chance to be revenged on her enemy, and she told her daughter to ask for John the Baptist's head. Herod was sorry, but he would not break his oath, and he gave the order. John was probably asleep when the key grated in the lock of his cell and they came to fetch him. He was still dazed when they dragged him to his feet, bound his hands, and led him away to wherever it was in that dreadful fortress that they executed their prisoners. But resolute man that he was, he would quickly have got command of himself and walked with a firm step to his death. And so, alone and by night, with no friend to say good-by to him, this great man was murdered, and his bleeding head was put in a dish and brought to Salome, and she gave it to her mother.

"What went ye out into the wilderness to see? A reed shaken

142

with the wind? But what went ye out for to see? A man clothed in soft raiment? . . . But what went ye out for to see? A prophet? yea, I say unto you, and more than a prophet. . . . Verily, I say unto you, Among them that are born of women there hath not risen a greater than John the Baptist."

3.

During the three years of his ministry Our Lord often left Galilee and journeyed with his disciples to Jerusalem to attend the feasts. Besides the great Passover feast there was the feast of Weeks, which commemorated the giving of the Law on Mount Sinai, the feast of Dedication, and the harvest festival, the feast of Tabernacles, when the pilgrims built themselves booths of green branches in memory of the wandering in the wilderness. This was a very lovely feast, the feast of water and light, of rain and sun, when water and wine were poured out upon the altar in the Temple, and the great song of praise, the Hallel, was sung to the music of the flutes. This feast must have been especially loved by Our Lord because the symbols of water and light are used by him so constantly in his teaching. Without the rain and sun all earthly life would wither and perish, without the water and the light that are his cleansing and his grace there is no life for our souls.

Wherever he was there was no rest for Our Lord; the fight against wickedness, disease, and ignorance went on just the same. The journey from one place to another was for him just a change of battleground, with skirmishes fought all along the way.

On one of these journeys up to Jerusalem Our Lord fought

another battle to save the body and soul of a Samaritan. He and his disciples came near a Samaritan village one day at evening, with the sunset light streaming over the fields and hills and the cool breath of night coming like water to refresh their weariness. We like to imagine that it was Sychar again, where he had rested by the well and given to drink of the water of life to the woman who was athirst, and that Our Lord was going to see his friends there. Surely it was Sychar, because the story makes it clear that Our Lord was not a stranger to the village; a company of ten outcast lepers, wandering about outside it, recognized him instantly as he came along the road. And they knew his name too. Standing far away from him, desolate among the thorns and stones, they lifted up their voices and cried, "Jesus, Master, have mercy on us!" And Our Lord called joyfully back to them, "Go, shew yourselves unto the priests." If this was Sychar, then beyond the village was Mount Gerizim with its Temple soaring up against the sky. The lepers, wandering in the wilderness, would have looked up at it every day of their lives. But they might not join the company of the clean and well who worshiped there, and the Temple must have been to them a symbol of the human family from which they were cast out. But now came Our Lord's ringing command, "Show yourselves to the priests!" Once more they turned their faces to Mount Gerizim, perhaps with the old hopeless weariness in their movements as they turned, and looked up at all they longed for there in the sky. They moved toward it, painfully and slowly. They moved a little quicker, and the weakness and the pain seemed to fall from them as they moved. They were moving like young men, like the boys that once they had been. They were running. They were cleansed and strong and leaping like mountain goats toward the hills.

All except one, who checked himself and turned back, and came running to Our Lord and falling at his feet praised God.

His reunion with the human family must wait. Gratitude and courtesy alike demanded that before he claimed anything for himself he must praise God for his deliverance at the feet of the man who had saved him.

"Were there not ten cleansed? but where are the nine?" asked Our Lord. "There are not found that returned to give glory to God save this stranger." His tone must have been sad, yet perhaps a little amused too, as he looked at those leaping mountain goats who couldn't stop to say thank you. Then he looked back at the man at his feet and saw his face changing as he looked at him, the blurring of disfigurement and pain slipping away, the strong clean lines of health coming back. Though he healed and saved at a cost of suffering to himself beyond our understanding, yet it must have been with a joy beyond our understanding too. We who are so clogged and weakened by sin can't even begin to know what a man feels like who is so perfectly holy, so perfectly yielded up to God to do his will, that God's love can flow through him unchecked to heal and save. Though Our Lord was a man of sorrows and acquainted with grief yet he must also have been the happiest man who ever lived. He looked at this courteous Samaritan, a stranger to him by race but his son by faith, and rejoiced in him. "Arise, go thy way," he said, "thy faith hath made thee whole."

From this village Our Lord journeyed on down into the Jordan valley and to the little town of Jericho, and rested there. From Jericho to Jerusalem the road is a dangerous one. It twists and turns beneath rocky overhanging cliffs which make a perfect hiding place for bandits, and highway robbery and murder have gone on there from then until now. There is today an inn upon this road where men and beasts can go for safety when darkness overtakes them, and it is built upon foundations so old that they must be those of an inn that existed there in Our Lord's day. Perhaps he stayed there sometimes with his disciples, and at

145

evening, sitting with other travelers about the fire, listened with amusement to tales of adventure and hair-raising escapes, that grow ever more and more marvelous in the telling. Like all good storytellers, and Our Lord was the perfect storyteller, he would have stored up these tales in his wonderful memory, just as he stored up all scenes and incidents that made up the day by day background of his life, and then when a new story was demanded of him he would dip into his memory for what he wanted, just as a great painter reaches unerringly for the colors that he needs.

It was probably at Jericho that Our Lord told the story of the Good Samaritan. We imagine him going into the Synagogue to preach, and afterward, when the service was over, standing in the center of a crowd of eager young men, all asking him questions.

"Master," cried one of them, "what shall I do to inherit eternal life?"

He knew perfectly well the answer which the Scriptures gave to that question, but he was a lawyer, skilled in argument, and St. Luke tells us he asked this question of Our Lord "tempting him." He wanted to entrap him into argument and worst him in it.

Our Lord always gave a sincere question an immediate answer, but when he was aware that his questioner already knew the answer then he would make him give it himself. Then, whether he liked it or not, the man was obliged to be sincere.

"What is written in the law? how readest thou?" he asked.

The lawyer had either to give the answer or else appear ignorant of the law that was his profession; and so he gave it. "Thou shalt love the Lord thy God with all thy heart, and with all thy soul, and with all thy strength, and with all thy mind; and thy neighbour as thyself."

"Thou hast answered right," said Our Lord. "This do, and thou shalt live."

146

But the lawyer was one of those young men who like to have the last word, and he had not had it, and so he tried again. "And who is my neighbour?" he demanded.

It was an ideal question for provoking an argument, for it raises many questions. Is our neighbor the man in the same street, or the same village, or the same district? At what exact distance does a man cease to be a neighbor? But Our Lord could not be provoked into argument just for the sake of argument, and so instead of arguing he told one of the immortal stories of the world. We can imagine him pausing a moment, as a painter pauses before his canvas, choosing what paints he will use, smiling as he remembered lovingly the courteous Samaritan who had run to him to say thank you. Courtesy and mercy are closely allied, and he had not to look far for the hero of his story. Nor for the scene of it either, with that stretch of dangerous road and the lonely inn only a few miles away.

"A certain man went down from Jerusalem to Jericho, and fell among thieves, which stripped him of his raiment, and wounded him, and departed, leaving him half dead. And by chance there came down a certain priest that way; and when he saw him, he passed by on the other side. And likewise a Levite, when he was at the place, came and looked on him, and passed by on the other side. But a certain Samaritan, as he journeyed, came where he was: and when he saw him he had compassion on him, and went to him, and bound up his wounds, pouring in oil and wine, and set him on his own beast, and brought him to an inn, and took care of him. And on the morrow when he departed, he took out two pence, and gave them to the host, and said unto him, Take care of him; and whatsoever thou spendest more, when I come again, I will repay thee. Which now of these three, thinkest thou, was neighbour unto him that fell among the thieves?"

The heavenly simplicity and beauty of the story must have broken the self-assertion of that young lawyer to pieces, for his answer has the same simplicity and beauty. "He that shewed mercy on him."

"Go, and do thou likewise," said Our Lord. And surely the man did go and do likewise. Our Lord had won him to truthfulness and simplicity and must have won him to pity, too.

4.

On the journey to Jerusalem Our Lord's last resting place would have been Bethany, a village surrounded by olive trees on a little hill about three miles from Jerusalem. In a house in the village lived three of his greatest friends, and after his Mother's house it must have been the nearest thing to a home that he had. The three friends were Mary and her brother Lazarus and her sister Martha. Today nothing remains of the village that Our Lord knew except the olive trees, a huddle of stones and a rock tomb deep in the earth, but it will always be a spot upon this earth that Christians think of often and love only a little less than they love Nazareth and Bethlehem, for it was the setting for three scenes in Our Lord's life that bring him very near to us in love and power and sorrow, as Friend and King and Saviour.

In the first scene, most lovely, gracious, and tender, it is the Friend who seems to come in to us, to sit with us by our fireside or under the trees in our garden, and talk to us. The King and Saviour are there too in this scene, implicit in the authority and compassion of Our Lord's words, but in this scene it is as though he drew a veil over his glory and his grief that they may not overwhelm us, and then comes very near. And when we think of Our Lord as Friend we think of him also as Priest, that Priest whom the three kings worshiped with the gift of frankincense, for a priest is a mediator between God and man, and often too between man and man, and there can be no more friendly office in the world than this.

"Now it came to pass, as they went, that he entered into a certain village: and a certain woman, named Martha, received him into her house."

We think of two phrases that come in the story of the Good Samaritan.

"He . . . took care of him."

"He said, Take care of him."

When Our Lord and his disciples arrived at Bethany, and tired and footsore and hungry presented themselves at Martha's door, we can imagine with what delight she took care of them. We think of her as a Good Samaritan of a woman, motherly, competent, a splendid housewife and a good nurse. With cries of delight at their presence and distress at their condition she would have brought them into her clean, cool, orderly house, fetched water to wash their feet, attended to cuts and bruises, fussed over them, delivered minute instructions as to where and how they were to rest themselves, and then left them to obey her while she hurried to the kitchen to prepare the most wonderful meal she could think of. In this scene Lazarus is in the background. In neither of the three scenes does he say anything, and so we think of him as a thoughtful man, silent and self-effacing; as men tend to be who live with women like Martha. But he must have been very lovable, because St. John tells us that "Jesus loved Martha, and her sister, and Lazarus," and though it was for the glory of God that later Lazarus had to suffer and to die, yet because he loved him so much Jesus wept for him. He loved Martha just as much; in the next scene at Bethany we shall see how much; but this first scene belongs especially to Mary, for it was Mary who came to him where he sat resting in the cool shady courtyard and "sat at Jesus' feet, and heard his word." It is always at Our Lord's feet that we find Mary; humbled and repentant from the beginning till the end.

She sat there listening and learning, while the shadows lengthened and from the house in the background came the soft hum of distant voices and the clink of pots and pans. And then perhaps Lazarus came back from some errand upon which Martha had sent him and sat down quietly near Our Lord, not interrupting the talk but listening as Mary was listening, chin on hand and intent dark eyes never leaving his friend's face. The scene is marked both by the heavenly peace that Our Lord brought with him wherever he went and by the earthly peace that always welcomed him in this home. It is a picture of human friendship lifted up out of all possibility of change or loss because its foundation was the eternal friendship of immortal God.

The sudden arrival of Martha in a state of indignation does not shadow the peace. Our Lord, Mary, and Lazarus were used to Martha's indignations, they were a part of Martha whom they loved, and probably passed as quickly as a flurry of wind upon water.

"Lord, dost thou not care that my sister hath left me to serve alone?" demanded Martha. "Bid her therefore that she help me."

We know so many people like Martha; we are probably exactly like Martha ourselves. Full of bustle and self-importance we plunge into preparations for some party or other; much too elaborate preparations subconsciously designed more to show our own skill than to give pleasure to the guests. The family offer their help but we refuse it and turn them out of the kitchen because we feel grander if we do it all ourselves. But halfway through we suddenly feel dead tired, are sure we shall never be ready in time, and are most indignant with the family for taking us at our word and leaving us to it. It was in this state of indignation that Martha, hot and flustered, arrived in the quiet courtyard, and we can imagine the smiles of tender amusement that came into the eyes of Our Lord and Mary and her brother at this characteristic Martha-like behavior. But they would have been careful that the smile should not reach their lips, for Martha would have been hurt if they had laughed at her.

"Martha, Martha," said Our Lord, "thou art careful and troubled about many things: But one thing is needful: and Mary hath chosen that good part, which shall not be taken away from her."

The rebuke, with its loving reiteration of Martha's name, is so understanding and so gentle that it is hardly a rebuke at all. That "careful and troubled" gave her grateful thanks. It was for her guests that she was so fussed and bothered, and Our Lord knew it and told her that he knew it. But why be so bothered? They must eat, of course, but in this hot weather they did not want much food; one dish only was needed. If Martha had not tried to do so many unnecessary things she could have been here with him instead of in the hot kitchen. Our souls are more important than our bodies, and when the choice lies between attending to heavenly things or the earthly we must choose the heavenly; and so he could not send Mary away from him into the house.

The story ends there, but we feel sure that Martha went back into the house, saw for herself that the food she had already prepared was more than enough, took off her apron and washed her hands, and went back to join the others in the green shade. There were four of them then, two men and two women linked together in a friendship that has never suffered change.

GOD SO LOVED THE WORLD

O merciful Redeemer, Friend and Brother,
Grant that we may
See thee more clearly,
Love thee more dearly,
Follow thee more nearly,
Day by day.

Amen.

Chapter 7

SINNERS

The sacrifices of God are a broken spirit: a broken
and a contrite heart, O God, thou wilt not despise.
—Psalm LI:17

1.

FROM Bethany and his friends there, Our Lord and his
disciples went where his enemies awaited him. The walk
from Bethany to Jerusalem is a short one and leaving the road
they would have followed the narrow path that winds through
the hills, through vineyards and olive trees, up over the Mount
of Olives, down through the Garden of Gethsemane and across
the Kedron Valley to Jerusalem. The Garden of Gethsemane is
so close to Jerusalem that at evening the shadow of the city falls
upon it and the walls can be seen through the leaves of the trees.
In those days there was a wall built round the garden so that it
was secluded and quiet, and the olive trees grew so thickly together that there was always coolness and shade. Our Lord loved
this garden. He liked to go there to pray, as he went up into the

153

hills above the Lake of Galilee, sometimes alone, sometimes with his disciples. For Christians it is another of the holy places. Nazareth, Bethlehem, Galilee, Bethany, Gethsemane, Calvary— these names are music to us when we say them over to ourselves.

Between the Mount of Olives and the city the Kedron Valley was a deep chasm savagely scored in the ground, and was spanned by a viaduct. Our Lord must have passed through the Shushan Gate of the city and across the viaduct countless times, going to the garden to pray or walking to Bethany to see his friends there. Once a year, on the Day of Atonement, the scapegoat was driven from the city across the viaduct, and then taken out into the wilderness and cast from a rock. The people believed that their sins were laid upon him and that he carried them away into the wilderness to perish with him in his death, that they might be at one with God again. The scapegoat going to his death with the sins of a nation laid upon him was a symbol of Our Lord himself; only Our Lord in his death carried the burden of the sins of the whole world.

In Jerusalem the fight was harder than it was in Galilee or upon the road. Though Our Lord healed the sick in Jerusalem just as he did in Galilee, and preached and taught without ceasing, yet we think of the fight in Jerusalem as being pre-eminently a fight against sin in the souls of men, and that was a harder fight than the one against the physical miseries that are the result of sin. In this fight the devil who in the wilderness had tempted Our Lord to worship earthly power took and used against him the very power that had been rejected. Our Lord called the devil the prince of this world and it was the power of the lesser princes, the great men of the Jewish nation whose souls had been corrupted by covetousness and pride, which Our Lord fought, and parried, and fought again in Jerusalem, until at last it destroyed his body and then was itself destroyed by his victorious spirit.

The opposition of the rulers of his people, which in Galilee was no more than a perpetual rumbling of ungracious criticism, hardened in Jerusalem to a bitter hostility. The great men of Jerusalem hated and feared Our Lord for many reasons. His gallant and courageous figure seemed to them a likely focal point for rebellion; he was a born leader of men, beloved by the people, fearless and quick-witted. And this danger was increased by his claim to be the Christ and by the belief of a great many of the people that he was indeed the Holy One of Israel come to save them. The fact that Our Lord taught constantly that the kingdom he had come to found was a spiritual and not an earthly kingdom did not allay their fears. They probably did not believe him. Being themselves without reverence for truth they could neither see in what he was truth's very image nor hear the ring of truth in every word he spoke. For reverence clears the sight as nothing else can do, while its opposite, contempt, is as bad as a rush of blood to the head for blinding the eyes to the greatest as well as the smallest beauty.

It was this claim to be the Christ that must have made them hate him most of all. They were the religious leaders of their people and as such would have expected the Messiah, when he came, to be to them what a king is to his cabinet ministers. They would have expected to be nearer to him than any, in his confidence and the delegates of his authority. But this Christ had chosen his closest friends from among the poor, the suffering, the penitent, and the meek, and his very choice was an unspoken judgment of those who were none of these things. The truth of him was in such direct contrast to what they were that it cut clean across the fact of them like that ax laid to the root of the tree of which John the Baptist had spoken. They must have known from the beginning that there could be no fusion between them. They and he were like fire and water. They must either yield to him or destroy him.

155

2.

Our Lord did nothing to propitiate his enemies, for truth cannot compromise, and not all his judgments were unspoken; some of them were thundered out with such terrible force that just to read what he said to these men, nearly two thousand years after he said it, makes one afraid. We speak of him as the friend of sinners, and to penitent and loving sinners, or ignorant sinners such as the soldiers who crucified him, he showed a heavenly gentleness that is like the gentleness of a lover. But the pride, hypocrisy, and cruelty of the great men of his time aroused in him the same terrible anger that blazed out when he saw the Temple desecrated. For they were not ignorant. They knew God's law that commanded them to love God with all their hearts and all their souls and all their minds, and their neighbor as themselves. They had studied the Scriptures and taught them. Again and again their lips had said the words, "Thou desirest truth in the inward parts. . . . A broken and a contrite heart, O God, thou will not despise. . . . Thy loving kindness is better than life." And yet with such knowledge in their minds and such words upon their lips they were hypocrites, men of pride, men without kindness, bad shepherds who for greed's sake had corrupted and oppressed the sheep in their care. That deliberate corruption of the innocent, of which the corruption of the Temple court had been a symbol, was to Our Lord the most terrible of sins. "Whoso shall offend one of these little ones which believe on me, it were better for him that a millstone were hanged about his neck and that he were drowned in the depth of the sea," he said, and there is the sound of his scourge in those words, and in many other of his terrible denunciations.

"Woe unto you, scribes and Pharisees, hypocrites! for ye shut

156

up the kingdom of heaven against men: for ye neither go in your-selves, neither suffer ye them that are entering to go in.

"Woe unto you, scribes and Pharisees, hypocrites! for ye devour widows' houses, and for a pretence make long prayer; therefore ye shall receive the greater damnation.

"Woe unto you, scribes and Pharisees, hypocrites! for ye compass sea and land to make one proselyte; and when he is made, ye make him twofold more the child of hell than your-selves.

"Woe unto you, scribes and Pharisees, hypocrites! for ye pay tithe of mint, and anise, and cummin, and have omitted the weightier matters of the law, judgment, mercy, and faith: these ought ye to have done, and not to leave the other undone.

"Ye blind guides! which strain at a gnat, and swallow a camel.

"Woe unto you scribes and Pharisees, hypocrites! for ye make clean the outside of the cup and of the platter, but within they are full of extortion and excess.

"Thou blind Pharisee! cleanse first that which is within the cup and platter, that the outside of them may be clean also.

"Woe unto you, scribes and Pharisees, hypocrites! for ye are like unto whited sepulchres, which indeed appear beautiful out-ward, but are within full of dead men's bones, and of all un-cleanliness.

"Even so ye outwardly appear righteous unto men, but within ye are full of hypocrisy and iniquity. . . .

"Ye serpents, ye generation of vipers, how can ye escape the damnation of hell?"

Yet dreadful as these denunciations are, and others like them, we can yet hear the agonizing love in them. For those men, too, Our Lord loved, and for them too he died. When he thundered at them he was fighting for them, flinging himself against their wickedness, trying to break through by fear where love seemed useless. Damnation, hell, fire, burning were words he often used. He tried to make men see that hell is not a child's nightmare but reality. It exists. It is possible to go there, and a great many of us will go there, and in his denunciations of the rulers of the nation in his day Our Lord gives us a very clear picture of the kind of people who will go there. And there is another clear picture in one of the most frightening of his parables, one that he told to the Pharisees, the story of the rich man and Lazarus, a parable that with all the other stories of death and judgment seems to belong to the battleground of Jerusalem, as the happy parables of the sower and the mustard seed and the pearl of great price seem to belong to the fields and lakeside of Galilee.

"There was a certain rich man, which was clothed in purple and fine linen, and fared sumptuously every day: And there was a certain beggar named Lazarus, which was laid at his gate, full of sores, and desiring to be fed with the crumbs which fell from the rich man's table: moreover the dogs came and licked his sores.

"And it came to pass, that the beggar died, and was carried by the angels into Abraham's bosom: the rich man also died, and was buried; and in hell he lift up his eyes, being in torments, and seeth Abraham afar off, and Lazarus in his bosom.

"And he cried and said, Father Abraham, have mercy on me, and send Lazarus, that he may dip the tip of his finger in water, and cool my tongue; for I am tormented in this flame.

"But Abraham said, Son, remember that thou in thy lifetime receivedst thy good things, and likewise Lazarus evil things: but now he is comforted, and thou art tormented. And beside all this, between us and you there is a great gulf fixed: so that they which would pass from hence to you cannot; neither can they pass to us, that would come from thence.

"Then he said, I pray thee therefore, father, that thou

wouldest send him to my father's house: For I have five brethren; that he may testify unto them, lest they also come into this place of torment.

"Abraham saith unto him, They have Moses and the prophets; let them hear them.

"And he said, Nay, father Abraham: but if one went unto them from the dead, they will repent.

"And he said unto him, If they hear not Moses and the prophets, neither will they be persuaded, though one rose from the dead."

Dives, the rich man, does not seem to have been what we are accustomed to call a bad man. He had done nothing at all to get him into prison, but what he had not done got him into hell. He had just been selfish. He had enjoyed his own good fortune without giving a thought to Lazarus lying at his gate, a man so ill that he could not work to support himself but had to lie there weak and starving, with the terrible sores of starvation breaking out on his body, and tormented by the wild pariah dogs who came to lick the sores. Dives could have saved Lazarus from suffering, but if he noticed him at all he did not think his agony was any business of his; someone else could see to it. Our Lord said in another of his parables, "Unto whom little is given little will be required, but unto whom much is given much will be required." A poor wretch who has never had a chance has only to cry out, "Lord, remember me!" in his dying, as the thief did on the cross, and into Paradise his way is sure. We who have had every chance, if we are not saints at the end of it all, then remembering Dives and Lazarus we should tremble for ourselves.

In this parable Our Lord describes Paradise and hell in very few words, yet he gives two complete pictures that for the impressions they give of loveliness and horror are matchless. The agony of hell is that from it you can see Paradise. You can actually see the blessed spirits going about their heavenly business in the light of God's love; you can see all that you might have had and been yourself if you had chosen to love God in your suffering brother instead of loving just yourself. But you can't get there. Between Paradise and hell there is a great gulf fixed. This beholding paradise awakes such a longing for it that the tormented soul is burnt up by it as though he were on fire. He who in life turned from God is now athirst for God, and tormented by his thirst. And there are two more things which you see in hell which go to make up the torment of it. Dives saw Abraham doing for Lazarus in Paradise what he should have done on earth. He saw another doing that one very simple thing that would have saved him if he had done it himself. But he can't do it now. It's too late. And then he looks back to earth and sees his brothers living exactly as he had lived himself, and in misery for them he begs that Lazarus may be sent back to earth to warn them that they are living in danger of hell. Abraham reminds Dives that his brothers are not ignorant men. They know the Scriptures, and if they paid attention to them they would know how they ought to live. If the direct command of God does not capture their attention, then the appearance of a ghost would not do it. So Dives is left in his dreadful loneliness, a great gulf not only between him and Paradise but between him and those whom he cared for on earth and is now powerless to help.

And what is Paradise like? Our Lord does not attempt to describe it in any detail, and those whom he brought back from the dead do not seem to have been able to talk about it at all. And if we think a minute we see that this is only what we should expect. For the language of this world belongs to this world and describes this world; if we wanted to describe a world utterly different from this one it would be useless to us. Even when we want to describe something supremely lovely in this world we often find it very little use. We go for a walk in the beechwoods when the bluebells are out and then we come home and try and tell someone who is ill and has had to stay at home what it was like. We want him to share our joy, but when we try to describe the sun shining through the new leaves, the pools of blue, the birds singing, the feel of the earth under our feet, the fresh spring smell of it all, we can't do it. We stumble and stutter and make a very bad job of it. But what if our friend had never seen a tree, never seen a flower, never felt the warmth of the sun or the cool breath of air, how then could we give him any idea of a beechwood in the spring? We should not even try. We could only be silent.

Yet Our Lord in his wisdom can in this parable tell us two things about Paradise which make its heavenliness very real to us. It is first of all a place where, for those who have endured bravely, the pain of this world ceases. Lazarus is "comforted." The angels have lifted him out of his misery and it is over. The Book of Revelation says of those who have passed from their earthly martyrdom, "God shall wipe away all tears from their eyes; and there shall be no more death, neither sorrow, nor crying, neither shall there be any more pain: for the former things are passed away." But there is something better even than this. Abraham, that great servant of God, is doing in Paradise what the Good Samaritan did upon earth, and "taking care" of one of God's children. And he is not only comforting Lazarus but teaching Dives. There is another verse in the Book of Revelation which describes the blessed spirits in Paradise. "These are they which follow the Lamb whithersoever he goeth." The Lamb of God in Paradise, as on earth, ceaselessly heals, comforts, and teaches, and his servants, following him, do the same. Could any servant of God ask to do anything more glorious? There is no break in the heavenliness of serving Our Lord in each other; it begins in this world and continues in the other, and it is just that which is the life of the kingdom. Endlessly the multitude of ignorant sinners leaves this world, and there in the next one the multitude of the blessed spirits receive them with their comfort and their wisdom. Those already purified by pain, like Lazarus, can be drawn into so close a union with them, and through them with God, that Our Lord describes it in the symbolical words "in Abraham's bosom," but those who cannot yet reach this union are not beyond the reach of their wisdom. In this parable, though Abraham himself cannot go to Lazarus his teaching can cross the great gulf. For this hell is not the final hell into which the souls of the eternally damned pass at the last judgment. It is the hell or hades of the intermediate state, and Our Lord does not say that the gulf between Lazarus and Dives is fixed there eternally. If only Dives through endurance of his torment can learn penitence and compassion God will fling across it one day the bridge of his love, as he flung it down before Peter on the day when Peter cried out, "I am a sinful man, O Lord," and Dives will cross over to the other side.

Over and over again, with endless patience, in story after story, in sentence after sentence, with that alarm bell of "Verily, I say unto you" ringing most of the time, Our Lord teaches us that when we say unkind things to each other, criticize each other, persecute and kill each other, when we refuse to help each other, we are doing these things to God. And when we save and love each other, are gentle and pitiful and courteous, it is God whom we love and serve. "Verily, I say unto you, inasmuch as ye have done it unto one of the least of these my brethren, ye have done it unto me." But still we cannot seem to learn that lesson, even though we know there is no hope for us until we do.

3.

As well as thundering at them and fighting for them Our Lord could mourn over the rich men and laugh at them too. One day in the streets of Jerusalem a rich young man came to him and said, "Good Master, what good thing shall I do that I may have eternal life?" It was the same question that the lawyer at Jericho had asked, but this time it was sincere, and Our Lord answered him gently, "If thou wilt enter into life, keep the commandments." The young man answered, "All these things have I kept from my youth up: what lack I yet?" And again he was sincere, he was not boasting, he was just stating a simple fact. He was a good man who had tried with all his strength to keep God's commandments. And yet he was still thirsty, a hart desiring the water brooks. He knew there was something he ought to have done that he had not done. Our Lord looked at him and loved him, as at first sight he had loved Peter and James and John, and saw in him a man capable of real discipleship, a man whom he wanted for his friend. "If thou wilt be perfect, go and sell that thou hast and give to the poor, and thou shalt have treasure in heaven," he said, "and come and follow me."

When that great challenge had sounded on the shore of the Sea of Galilee the disciples had answered it. They had left all that they had and followed Our Lord, to live for him and him only. But it was not so hard for them because they had not so very much to leave. This young man had great possessions and he loved them and clung to them. For a moment he stood fighting with himself, while Our Lord stood patiently waiting for his decision. But he could not do it. He could not make the immense sacrifice to which Our Lord called him. Very sorrowfully he turned his back on the God for whom he thirsted and went away. We think of him, as life went on, becoming more and more obsessed by his possessions, more and more imprisoned by them, until at last he became as callous as Dives and indifferent to the suffering at his gate. But his thirst would not have left him, and in hell, looking across the great gulf to the heavenly pity and compassion upon which he had turned his back, he would have cried out like Dives, "I am tormented by this thirst!"

This terrible cry is one that Our Lord himself could have uttered, and he did utter it upon the cross when he said, "I thirst." There is nothing at all that we can suffer that he did not suffer too. He, too, thirsted for the living God, and if his thirst was less agonizing than ours because, sinless, he was so close to God, yet he suffered a second thirst of which we can know nothing, the thirst of God for the souls of men. As man, he thirsted for God, as God he thirsted for man, and the double thirst must have been a torment. We hear his thirst for man in his cry of grief as the rich young man went sorrowfully away. "Verily I say unto you, That a rich man shall hardly enter into the kingdom of heaven."

Yet even in his sorrow he could see the comic side of rich men. "Again I say unto you," he said a moment later to his disciples, "it is easier for a camel to go through the eye of a needle, than for a rich man to enter into the kingdom of heaven."

We think of a camel with his expression of superiority, his look of utter boredom, as he stalks along bearing the weight of his heavy hump slung round with bags and boxes, and we think at once of many people whom we know who don't seem to get any fun at all out of their possessions but seem to find them just a boring burden. There was at that time in Jerusalem a very narrow gate called "The Needle's Eye." A camel burdened with bags and boxes could not possibly pass through it, yet were he to shed his bags and boxes he might, perhaps, with a good deal of pushing and pulling and maneuvering, be got through. So when the disciples, feeling the case of the rich man to be quite hopeless, said sadly, "Who then can be saved?", Our Lord answered, "With men this is impossible; but with God all things are possible." If we can shed the bags and boxes then God in his mercy will get us through.

4.

St. John tells us a story of a sinner who reminds us of Mary Magdalene, and in this story we swing away from the anger of God back to his gentleness again. And this gentleness enfolds not only the wretched woman who had sinned but also the men who had destined her for a cruel death. Though it is a dreadful story it is a heavenly one, too, for it shows the peace of heaven flowing out from Our Lord over the sheer noisiness of wickedness and bringing a great calm.

One morning very early he came from the peace of a night of prayer on the Mount of Olives to the Temple. The sun had only just risen and it was quiet and cool. He sat down in a patch of sunshine and gradually, by ones and twos and threes, the people who had come early to the Temple to pray came to him and gathered round him, and he taught them there. St. John does not tell us what he said to them, but this quiet early morning hour would have been a good time for telling stories, and as they were in the Temple perhaps he told them the story of the two men who went up into the Temple to pray.

"The one was a Pharisee, and the other a publican," said Our Lord. "The Pharisee stood and prayed thus with himself: God, I thank thee that I am not as other men are, extortioners, un-

165

just, adulterers, or even as this publican: I fast twice in the week, I give tithes of all that I possess. And the publican, standing afar off, would not lift up so much as his eyes unto heaven, but smote upon his breast, saying, God be merciful to me a sinner. I tell you, this man went down to his house justified rather than the other: for every one that exalteth himself shall be abased; and he that humbleth himself shall be exalted."

The publican's prayer has been loved and used by Christians ever since. The Russians call it the Jesus prayer, and there was a Russian saint, Serafim of Sarov, who for years spoke no words but just these.

When Our Lord had finished his story perhaps he told them two of those lovely parables that show us how immensely precious is the soul of just one repentant sinner in God's sight. He said that God is like a good shepherd who has a hundred sheep, and if just one is lost he leaves the ninety and nine and goes after the lost one, and never ceases looking for it until he finds it, and laying it on his shoulders brings it home rejoicing. And when he gets home he makes his friends and neighbors rejoice with him too, saying, "Rejoice with me; for I have found my sheep which was lost." And Our Lord finished that story by saying, "I say unto you, that likewise joy shall be in heaven over one sinner that repenteth, more than over ninety and nine just persons, which need no repentance."

And then he said that God is like a woman who finds at evening that she has lost one of the ten precious coins that are sewn into the headdress of a bride when she marries. Though she has nine left she is so terribly distressed at the loss of the one that she cannot even wait for daylight to find it, but lights a candle and sweeps the whole house diligently until she finds it. And when she finds it she is so happy that she calls her friends and cries out to them, "Rejoice with me; for I have found the piece which I had lost." And then she restores the precious coin to its place with the other nine, where she wears them with love and pride as a gleaming coronet above her forehead. They are her jewels, those coins, and more precious to her than words can say, so no wonder she rejoices, and her neighbors with her. And Our Lord said, "Likewise I say unto you, there is joy in the presence of the angels of God over one sinner that repenteth."

And then the sound of Our Lord's voice speaking quietly of the love of God was drowned by an ugly clamor, as a mob of angry men surged into the quiet court. Men of the Temple guard were there, scribes and Pharisees, and a crowd of those brutal people who assemble when something horrible is going to happen and gloat over the sight of suffering which they themselves have not to endure. Our Lord stood up and saw a terrified woman in the midst of the mob; she was too frightened to be able to walk properly but she was dragged along by the Temple guard. They were bringing to him one of his jewels, one of his sheep. They flung her down on the pavement at his feet, sobbing and shivering, her hands covering her shamed face, and the scribes and Pharisees gathered round to accuse her.

"Master," they said, "this woman was taken in adultery, in the very act. Now Moses in the law commanded us that such should be stoned: but what sayest thou?"

These detestable men had done a very clever thing. Hating Our Lord as they did, determined as they were to bring death upon him if they could, they had deliberately maneuvered him into a position in which whatever answer he gave to their question, and gave before a crowd of witnesses who would immediately publish his answer all over Jerusalem, it would bring down upon him the anger of at least half the city. It was indeed the brutal Jewish law that a woman taken in adultery must be stoned to death. If Our Lord were to answer that the law must be kept and she must die, then he would stand convicted of a cruelty as horrible as that of the law, and all that he had said of

167

the love and mercy of God would seem to those who had heard it just so much cant, and he himself just another of the hypocrites whom he had condemned with such flaming anger. If on the other hand he were to command them to set her free then he, a Son of Israel, would stand self-condemned as a breaker of Israel's law. Again and again his enemies set these traps for Our Lord, but only the last one of all caught him, for always the cleverness of wicked men shattered itself against his heavenly and splendid wisdom. And the last trap of all only closed upon him because he chose that it should, choosing it with the same wisdom with which he had evaded the others and making of his entry into it one of the most glorious actions of his life.

"What sayest thou?" asked his enemies.

At first he did not say anything at all. He stooped down and wrote something with his finger on the pavement. What did he write, and why? We do not know. Perhaps the sight of the poor woman's agony, and of the sly cruelty on the faces of the men who were trying to hurt her and himself at one and the same time, caused him such grief that he had to hide his face. Or perhaps he was remembering a sentence spoken by Jeremiah, "They that depart from me shall be written in the earth because they have forsaken the Lord, the fountain of living waters," and was hoping that those men, scholars of Israel as they were, would remember it too, and remember that the wicked do not drink of the living water of eternal life but pass away into desolation like the shifting desert sand. But they repeated their question and he lifted himself up and spoke just one sentence. It seems almost irreverent to speak of the genius of God, and yet for sheer genius surely this answer of Our Lord's has never been surpassed. It not only saved the woman, it saved her accusers too.

"He that is without sin among you, let him first cast a stone at her."

And again Our Lord stooped and wrote upon the ground, and we can imagine the silence, the stillness, that gripped that crowd as his words struck at their hearts. No more noise and anger now, only the peace of God reaching out from the stooping figure and creating calm about them all. Then one of the Pharisees sighed and moved. He was an old man, the oldest man there. Perhaps he was weeping; we do not know; but he turned and with bent head he went away. He must have been a very brave old man, for though he spoke no word his very action cried aloud to all that crowd, "Lord, have mercy upon me a sinner." He was no longer the Pharisee of Our Lord's story, but the publican.

Another man followed him, and another. These were the men of whom Our Lord had spoken when he cried out in grief, "How can ye escape the damnation of hell?" Yet here they were convicted of sin, acknowledging sin, escaping. "With God all things are possible." Our Lord's heart must have beaten hard with joy as with his head still bent he listened to the sound of their escaping feet upon the Temple pavement.

The last footfall died away and in the absolute silence Our Lord lifted himself up again and looked about him. There was no one there except the woman, crumpled up on the pavement. He looked at her with love and longing; a lost sheep for whom he had been searching, a jewel that had tumbled out of his crown. Perhaps she looked at him too, the penitence for which she could find no words clear in her eyes for him to see.

"Where are those thine accusers?" he asked her gently. "Hath no man condemned thee?"

She said, "No man, Lord."

"Neither do I condemn thee," he said. "Go, and sin no more."

She pulled herself up from the pavement and went away out into the sunshine as he bade her. Her footfall, too, died away into silence and Our Lord was left alone to rejoice in the lost sheep saved.

169

5.

The love of Almighty God for just one sinner's soul will always be to us one of the greatest of the mysteries. In the immense universe our earth is only a speck, and upon that speck myriad human beings have lived and died, and yet each one of them is loved by the Creator of the universe with the love of a Father. The writer of the Book of Wisdom cried out in wonder and amazement, "The whole world before thee is as ... a drop of the morning dew that falleth down upon the earth. . . . But thou sparest all, for they are thine, O Lord thou lover of souls." And he did not see, as we do, the love that upholds the universe gathered to its greatness on the cross. What would he have said if he could have seen that? He would have found nothing to say except, "Lord, have mercy upon me a sinner." But if there is next to nothing that we can say there is always something that we can do, and again and again Our Lord tries to make us understand how this thing that we can do gives joy to God. It is so hard to understand how this can be. We think, if the whole earth is only as a drop of dew in God's sight, then what am I? Less than a speck of dust. And what dust! Grimy and detestable. Yet we have got to try and grasp this fact, that we can, and do, give joy to God; and not the milk and water thing that we know as joy, either, but a flaming joy beyond our understanding. Our sense of the immensity of God's giving might crush us if we did not understand that we can give too.

"There is joy in the presence of the angels of God over one sinner that repenteth," said Our Lord, and that brings us to the most wonderful of all his parables, which describes the joy not of the angels, but of God himself.

"A certain man had two sons: And the younger of them said

to his father, Father, give me the portion of goods that falleth to me. And he divided unto them his living. And not many days after, the younger son gathered all together, and took his journey into a far country, and there wasted his substance with riotous living. And when he had spent all, there arose a mighty famine in that land; and he began to be in want. And he went and joined himself to a citizen of that country; and he sent him into his fields to feed swine. And he would fain have filled his belly with the husks that the swine did eat: and no man gave unto him.

"And when he came to himself, he said, How many hired servants of my father's have bread enough and to spare, and I perish with hunger! I will arise and go to my father, and will say unto him, Father, I have sinned against heaven, and before thee, and am no more worthy to be called thy son: make me as one of thy hired servants.

"And he arose, and came to his father. But when he was yet a great way off, his father saw him, and had compassion, and ran, and fell on his neck, and kissed him.

"And the son said unto him, Father, I have sinned against heaven, and in thy sight, and am no more worthy to be called thy son.

"But the father said to his servants, Bring forth the best robe and put it on him; and put a ring on his hand, and shoes on his feet. And bring hither the fatted calf, and kill it; and let us eat, and be merry: For this my son was dead, and is alive again; he was lost, and is found. And they began to be merry.

"Now his elder son was in the field; and as he came and drew nigh to the house, he heard music and dancing. And he called one of the servants and asked what these things meant.

"And he said unto him, Thy brother is come; and thy father hath killed the fatted calf, because he hath received him safe and sound."

"And he was angry, and would not go in: therefore came his father out, and intreated him. And he, answering, said to his father, Lo, these many years do I serve thee, neither transgressed I at any time thy commandment; and yet thou never gavest me a kid, that I might make merry with my friends: But as soon as this thy son was come, which hath devoured thy living with harlots, thou hast killed for him the fatted calf.

"And he said unto him, Son, thou art ever with me, and all that I have is thine. It was meet that we should make merry, and be glad: for this thy brother was dead, and is alive again; and was lost, and is found."

He was not worth much, this prodigal son, and though we like him much better than the other type of sinner, the self-satisfied, grudging elder brother, yet he still remains rather a poor speck of dust. But he did do the one thing that gives this great joy to God. He had a good look at himself, and saw just the sort of sinful fool he was, and then pulled himself up out of the mess that he had made of his life without God, and turned his back on it and started out on the long hard road of repentance that led back to his father's house. It must have been a terrible journey, for he was a starving beggar by this time. He did not possess a thing of his own to bring to his father except his sin and his sorrow for it. In all literature is there any description of joy as vivid as Our Lord's description of this father's joy? He can't even wait until his son gets to the house but runs to meet him while he is still a great way off. He is so happy he can scarcely contain himself; he falls on the neck of this dirty ragged scarecrow of a boy and kisses him. He pours himself out in joy; there must be music and feasting and wonderful gifts. And the words that break from him, words of sheer poetry, twice repeated, ring out like all the trumpets of heaven shouting for joy.

"For this my son was dead, and is alive again; he was lost, and is found."

O my God, I believe in thee, I hope in Thee, I trust in thee, I love thee! I desire to be truly sorry for all my many sins whereby I have so often offended thee, who hast ever been so good to me. Pardon me and help me, pity me and cleanse me, save me and deliver me, for Jesus' sake. Amen.

Chapter 8

THE LIVING BREAD

This is that bread which came down from heaven.
                                —St. John VI:58

THE LAST spring of Our Lord's life found him back in Galilee again. That was the only place where he was safe now, for the courage of his outspoken speech had aroused such hatred in his enemies that they wanted to kill him more than ever and in Judea his life was in constant danger. Remembering Herod and John the Baptist, those who loved Our Lord must have felt anxious about him even in Galilee, especially when they thought Herod wanted to see him. Herod's motive seems to have been only one of idle curiosity, for he wanted to enjoy the sensation of seeing miracles performed, but his curiosity was more than likely to turn into antagonism when confronted with the same blazing truth which had confronted him in John. But Our Lord did not visit Herod. This is only a

174

little incident in his life, yet it is important because it is the one
and only time recorded in the Gospels when he refused to go to
someone who wanted him. It shows us as nothing else could do
how utterly worthless Herod must have been. If there had been
the slightest chance that Our Lord could have saved his soul by
going to see him he would have gone. But he did not go. He had
said many hard things to, and about, the Pharisees, but he had
nothing to say to Herod, and he spoke about him only once.
"That fox!" he said curtly. He turned his back on the royal
palace on the hill and went straight off to the other side of the
lake, taking his disciples with him. Herod must have told himself that that was an insult he would not forget. Later he was
able to take his revenge.

Our Lord had another reason for wanting to escape from the
lakeside; he wanted to get away from the crowds as well as from
Herod, and that not for his own sake but because his disciples
were worn out by the ceaseless pressure of the sickness and sorrow, the dirt and ignorance, the whole weight of human misery
pressing upon them night and day, so that "they had no leisure
so much as to eat." Many great men and women who have not
spared themselves in their work for the suffering have not spared
those who worked with them either, have indeed been almost
ruthless in their anxiety to get the work done. But Our Lord was
never like that. He was infinitely tender and compassionate to
his disciples and never drove them beyond their strength. "Come
ye apart and rest a while," he said now. The crowds must wait
while he took his "little ones" away and strengthened them. He
was probably far more tired than they were, but it is one of the
penalties of the strong and great that they are always helping
the little people but seldom have anyone to help them; and Our
Lord who was the greatest of the great never had anyone to
strengthen him save God.

They slipped away and got into a boat and perhaps with something of the delight of children going off for the holidays rowed off across the lake to the quiet hills upon the other side. But the people saw them go and did not let them escape to the peace they longed for. While the boat was crossing the six or seven miles of water, a multitude of about five thousand men, with women and children, and carrying their sick with them, surged along the shore of the lake, waded through the shallow water at the northern end, and running along the eastern shore cut off the retreat of Our Lord and his exhausted disciples. Gone was their peace, their hope of getting rested. Once more they were submerged by it all, the clamorous voices and the clutching hands, the ceaseless demanding, draining away their strength. Rage and exasperation, added to exhaustion, must have surely brought the disciples near to the breaking point, but Our Lord quietly accepted the inevitable and going up the hill a little way gathered the great crowd about him. He "was moved with compassion toward them, because they were as sheep not having a shepherd." All day long he healed their sick "and taught them many things," pouring out his love and strength, until the evening came and still they were there, more than five thousand of them, with night coming on and nothing to eat. "Send them away!" implored the desperate disciples. "Send them away, that they may go into the country round about, and into the villages, and buy themselves bread."

"They need not depart," said Our Lord. "Give ye them to eat."

His disciples must have looked at him in sheer despair. How could they possibly feed this multitude? There was a boy there who had five barley loaves and two small fishes, perhaps one of the little boys called "bread boys" who to this day sell bread and strips of dried fish in the Arab villages, and that was all there was.

"Make the men sit down," said Our Lord.

So the disciples made the great crowd sit down in companies on the green grass, the men and women and the little children, and the sick who were now healed and well but very tired. Though it was high summer it was cool now at the ending of the day. The burning sun had dropped behind the western hills that they could see across the lake, turning them lilac and rose color. A great peace descended upon them and a deep silence in which they could hear the lake water lapping on the shore. The tired men and women looked up with awed expectancy at the tall white-robed Rabbi standing above them on the hillside, the sunset light shining on his face. They saw the little barefoot bread boy come to him and hold up the five loaves and the two little fishes; his livelihood, all that he had. The Rabbi smiled at the child, "looked up to heaven" and gave thanks to God, and then lifting the loaves from the basket he held them in his hands and blessed them and broke them and handed them to his disciples, and the two little fish as well. The Rabbi's voice was so clear and strong that they could all hear the words of his blessing, and he spoke as though those bits of bread were all the shining cornfields of the world, and the scraps of dry fish the silver shoals of all the seas.

And it was something like that that they became in his hands. After the disciples had passed among them with the piled baskets of good food, and all the thousands of them had eaten their fill and been strengthened, it was not only just by bread and fish that they had been made new. The love of God, which with the changing seasons renews the face of the old earth with miraculous beauty, was sweeping over them, too, like wind over the corn, bowing them down into wonder and into worship. And they knew that this was not a mere man who could so teach them, heal them, feed them, and love them. They said to each other, "This is of a truth that prophet that should come into the world." And when the moment of their awe and wonder had passed they cried out that he must be their king. They came running up the hill to him, and St. John tells us that if he had let them the whole five thousand of them would have taken him by force and made him king. But he withstood them. "Straightway Jesus constrained his disciples to get into a ship, and to go before him unto the other side, while he sent the multitudes away."

The whole of this tremendous story leaves us shaken by its revelation of the power of Our Lord. The feeding of the five thousand is no less of a miracle than his mastering of the enormous crowd and his frustration of their purpose. They must have been wild with enthusiasm, thousands of determined men against one man, and yet they did not succeed in having their way with him. It was he who "straightway" had his way with them. It was he who won. He sent them away and they obeyed him as the disciples had done, and left him and went to their homes. That space of time between the moment when he broke the bread in his hands and the moment when there was enough bread for them all, and again the space of time between the moment when the multitude came surging up the hill to take him and the moment when they turned quietly away and went home, are so beyond our understanding that they are for us filled with a sense of fear; as though there were no time there at all but we had suddenly fallen through what we call time into something else. We have to stop thinking about it because we are too ignorant and sinful to know what to think.

"And when he had sent the multitudes away he went up into a mountain apart to pray: and when the evening was come he was there alone."

Praying there in the gathering dusk did he remember the bitter dark nights of his temptation in the mountains of Moab? The scene that had just passed had been like an echo of the ending of his temptation. He had not then turned stone into bread to help his own starving body, and though he had used his great power now to feed his hungry children it is not recorded that he ate any of their bread himself. Praying on the mountainside he himself was weak and hungry. Once again the offer of a kingdom had been made to him, the temptation coming upon him with tremendous force, and once again he had refused it. Remembering the suffering in the wilderness, did he look forward now to the suffering on the cross that was coming, to facing it alone with God? The hours passed and the dew fell and the dark night gathered about him, and still he prayed, and only the poets dare speak of his prayer.

> Dear night! this world's defeat,
> The stop to busy fools, care's check and curb,
> The day of spirits; my soul's calm retreat
> Which none disturb!
> Christ's progress, and his prayer time,
> The hours to which high heaven doth chime.
>
> God's silent, searching flight,
> When my Lord's head is filled with dew, and all
> His locks are wet with the clear drops of night;
> His still, soft call,
> His knocking time, the soul's dumb watch,
> Where spirits their fair kindred catch.
>
> —Henry Vaughan

179

2.

But not even from the deep places of his prayer is the cry of his children shut out. Even there they can call to him and claim him.

One of those sudden storms from the western mountains had once more swept down upon the lake and the disciples were in trouble again. The wind was contrary, they were tossed by the waves and shipping water fast. Our Lord was not with them in the boat this time and they could not cry out to him for help. At least they thought that they could not, but as they toiled at their oars, exhausted and panic-stricken, they saw a figure walking toward them. The moon was rising and struggling through the clouds, and the white figure followed a moonlit path over the waves; but they could not see his face in the dim light and they were terrified and cried out in their fear. And "straightway" came a ringing call in the voice they knew so well.

"Be of good cheer; it is I; be not afraid."

It was the voice of their beloved, but was it truly he?

"Lord," cried Peter, "if it be thou, bid me come unto thee on the water."

The beautiful, swiftly moving, shining figure answered, "Come."

And Peter, the impetuous child, caught right out of himself with love and longing, dropped over the gunwale, set his feet bravely upon the water, and took a few buoyant steps forward. But with the cold water sucking at his feet, and the spray blinding his eyes so that he could no longer see that shining figure, second thoughts came to him and he was afraid. And as his courage left him so did his buoyancy, and he began to sink.

"Lord, save me!" he cried, and stretched out his hand into the darkness that his blinded eyes had made about him. And immediately his hand was caught and held in the warm hand of Christ and the strong human body of his Lord was close beside him.

"O thou of little faith, wherefore didst thou doubt?"

They came together into the ship and the wind ceased, and the disciples knelt at Our Lord's feet, for "they were sore amazed in themselves beyond measure, and wondered." The great miracle of the feeding of the multitude had not touched their hearts as this had done, but this compassion of their Lord, that had brought him from his prayer right across the sea to help and save them, broke them altogether.

"Of a truth thou art the Son of God," they said, and worshiped him there in the midst of the sea.

"If I take the wings of the morning, and remain in the uppermost parts of the sea, even there also shall thy hand lead me, and thy right hand shall hold me."

3.

The next day many of the men whose bodies Our Lord had healed and strengthened, and whose physical hunger he had satisfied, came to look for him, and found him teaching in the synagogue at Capernaum. He performed no miracles that day, but standing up before the crowd who had gathered about him he preached one of the greatest of his sermons, the sermon on the bread of heaven, that we find in the sixth chapter of St. John's Gospel. The day before he had fed them with earthly bread and satisfied the hunger of their bodies, but today he told them of the heavenly bread of which the earthly bread had been a symbol, the bread that would feed their souls and preserve them unto everlasting life. "The bread of God is he which cometh down from heaven and giveth life unto the world," he said to them. "I am the bread of life: he that cometh to me shall never hunger; and he that believeth in me shall never thirst.... All that the Father giveth me shall come to me; and he that cometh to me I will in no wise cast out.... Verily, verily, I say unto you, He that believeth on me hath everlasting life. I am that bread of life.... This is the bread which cometh down from heaven, that a man may eat thereof, and not die."

The miracle of the feeding of the five thousand is to us now a picture of many things. If we imagine ourselves one of the crowd sitting there on the green grass, and look up and see the little boy holding his basket out to Our Lord, and Our Lord taking from it the five loaves and two small fishes and making of them enough to feed a multitude, we see a picture of the wonderful way in which he takes the very little that we have to give him and uses it; it may be almost nothing that we have to give, yet he takes that nothing into his hands, blesses it, and makes it enough for the purpose for which he wants it. And then in the crowd of people leaving their homes and following Our Lord out into the wilderness we see a picture of the way in which he looks after us if we follow him. They had no food with them and it looked as though the feeble among them would be faint with hunger before the day was over; and many of the sick folk, dragging along in the broiling sun, must have wondered if they would survive; yet at the end of the day, all was well with them. But chiefly, when we look up and see Our Lord breaking the bread in his hands, we see in this miracle a picture of the great sacrament by which our souls are fed. It is his own body that God is breaking in his hands, his body of love given for our redemption. As we watch the disciples moving along the ranks of the hungry people carrying the bread, and hear the murmur of their voices, "Here is bread for you, little child. And here, mother, here is some for you ... and for you ... for you ...

for you ...", we see a great multitude of people in churches all over the world, all through the centuries, and see God's priests moving along the ranks of them with the bread, and hear the murmur of their voices, "For you ... given for you ... for you ... preserve thy body and soul unto everlasting life."

And so we listen to the sermon on the bread of heaven with awe and adoration but not with horror or shock. But what could the men in the synagogue at Capernaum have felt who heard these words for the first time?

"I am the living bread which came down from heaven: if any man eat of this bread, he shall live for ever: and the bread that I will give is my flesh, which I will give for the life of the world. Verily, verily, I say unto you, Except ye eat the flesh of the Son of man, and drink his blood, ye have no life in you. Whoso eateth my flesh, and drinketh my blood, hath eternal life; and I will raise him up at the last day. For my flesh is meat indeed, and my blood is drink indeed. He that eateth my flesh, and drinketh my blood, dwelleth in me, and I in him. As the living Father hath sent me, and I live by the Father: so he that eateth me, even he shall live by me."

These words come to us now from the cross of Christ, and bring us to our knees, and though they embody a mystery which makes us feel amazed and bewildered when we try to think of it, yet it is an amazement with which we have grown up. We know that that is the way it is. We look at the wonder of a ripe corn-field under the sun, and say, that is our life. We look at the far greater wonder of the cross of Christ, and say, that is our life. But these men at Capernaum had not yet seen the cross of Christ, and their unprepared minds were shocked and outraged by this first impact upon them of the central mystery of the world. St. John says, "The Jews therefore strove among themselves, saying, How can this man give us his flesh to eat?" And his own disciples said, "This is an hard saying; who can hear it?" They "murmured at it. . . . From that time many of his disciples went back, and walked no more with him."

4.

That miracle, followed by the night of prayer alone with God, and then the preaching of the sermon at Capernaum, are a turning point in Our Lord's life. In them he pictured, faced, and foretold his death, and in this desertion of so many of his disciples we see the beginning of his passion. From now onward the mystery of this story seems, if possible, grander, deeper, darker, more full of sorrow.

He had angered the men who only one day before had wanted to make him their king; he had been deserted by many whom he had thought were his friends, but the twelve were still with him. "Will ye also go away?" he asked them. Bewildered as they were by the strange things that he had said, not realizing yet what suffering lay before them all, they must yet have known that he was putting some great choice before them; would they go on with him into the darkness or would they not? Peter answered for them all. "Lord, to whom shall we go? thou hast the words of eternal life."

They did not understand the half of what he said to them, they did not know where he was taking them or what was going to happen next, but they did understand this much—now that they had been with him they did not want to be with anyone else, for he now was their life.

Their brave choice made, he took his little family of faithful children and this time did succeed in taking them right away into quietness, to a place where he could teach them and try and prepare them for the things that were coming. They left the busy lakeside towns behind them and journeyed right up into the mountains of Lebanon, to the north of Galilee. These mountains arc very lovely, covered in springtime with white narcissus and scarlet anemones, the "roses of Sharon" and the "lilies of the field." The air in these hills is cool and crystal clear. Stopping to rest at noon Our Lord and his disciples would have looked back the way they had come and seen Galilee lying far below them, the lake like blue glass enclosed in the colored hills, the busy cities about it, the villages nestling like flocks of doves in the hills, the Jordan a thread of silver winding away into the haze of heat.

The great Galilean ministry was over now, and knowing that this was the last springtime of his life, Our Lord must have looked long and lovingly at the towns and villages where he had preached and healed, at the lake that he had crossed so many times and whose waters he had quieted, at the river where John had baptized him, and at the stony paths through the fields that he had tramped so often going from village to village with the good news of the kingdom. Though he had fought so many and such great battles down there the world would have said that there was little to show for it; that wickedness and misery and pain were still so rampant that all that he had done scarcely seemed worth while; and some other great man, looking back to apparent past failure and forward to a terrible death, would perhaps have felt something like despair in his heart. But we know that Our Lord did not feel like that. Sorrow he may have felt, but not despair. Men wonder sometimes if their work and sacrifice are worth while, but God does not. If Our Lord had healed only one body and saved only one soul down there in Galilee he would have thought it well worth his labor; he would have thought it fitting to die on the cross ten times over to save just one small child. And so we imagine him getting up most cheerfully, turning his back on the piece of accomplished work behind him, and leading his disciples on up the stony path ahead. It would have been a hard climb up into those mountains, but ahead of them the glorious snows of Mount Hermon glittered in the crystal air.

The story of another miracle shows Our Lord the very reverse of a despairing man, full of humor and kindliness. He and his disciples were passing through a Greek town, and a Greek woman came running after them, calling them. Perhaps she had at some time traveled down into Galilee and seen Our Lord there, and heard of his miracles, and now seeing him pass through her own town she saw in him her last hope; for she had a lunatic daughter whom she believed to be possessed by a devil. "Have mercy on me, O Lord, thou Son of David!" she cried. "My daughter is grievously vexed with a devil."

But Our Lord walked on and did not immediately answer her, and the disciples said to him in alarm, "Send her away!" If she went on crying out like that, they thought, then hordes of other sick and sorry folk would come surging out from every street and once more the peace and quiet they longed for would be denied them.

But Our Lord stopped and turned round and looked at the woman. "I am not sent but unto the lost sheep of the house of Israel," he said to her sternly.

The disciples need not have been afraid. He had not brought them up to these mountains to teach and heal the Greeks, but to teach them, and prepare them for what was coming, and he would not turn aside from God's immediate purpose for him. And he knew it was also the will of God that during the short time of his earthly life his own people should come first. The time would come when he would say to the disciples who were to be his body in the world, "Go ye into all the world and preach the gospel to every nation." But the time was not yet. And once more he turned away.

But the woman would not let him go. She fell at his feet and held his robe and cried out, "Lord, help me!"

He answered her, "It is not meet to take the children's bread, and to cast it to the dogs."

At first sight that looks a hard, even a cruel, answer, but in the Greek version of St. Matthew's Gospel the word Our Lord used is not dogs but "little dogs." And when we know that immediately we see humor in the reply. Our Lord's face would have been stern still, but there would have been a smile in his eyes as he waited to see what she would have to say to that. He liked her perseverance. She was behaving exactly like the importunate widow in his parable.

She must have been a quick-witted woman for in spite of her distress her reply flashed out with delightful humor. "Truth, Lord: yet the dogs eat of the crumbs which fall from their masters' table."

Our Lord had liked her perseverance and now he loved her wit. How his delighted smile must have flashed out over his face as he answered her. "O woman, great is thy faith: be it unto thee even as thou wilt."

And when she got home she found her daughter quite well.

5.

Our Lord and his disciples went on and came near to the beautiful pagan city of Caesarea Philippi, with its marble pillars and temples to the Greek gods, built among the thick woods that grew upon the lower slopes of Mount Hermon. Their destination would not have been the city but the woods. Here in the cool shade was the quiet and the solitude they had come to look for, and here they made themselves a temporary home and resting place. It was late summer and the trees would have given them all the shelter they needed. They would have brought some food with them, perhaps just bread and dates, the very little that such poor and wandering men as they were would have trained themselves to live upon, and they had fresh water, for a clear stream ran through those woods. It rose in a cave behind Caesarea Philippi and was one of the sources of the Jordan.

"Whom do men say that I, the Son of man, am?" Our Lord asked his disciples as they sat together under the trees, and they told him that some men thought he was John the Baptist come back from the dead, and others Elijah or one of the other prophets.

"But whom say ye that I am?" he asked.

It was Peter who answered, Peter who with all his sin and weakness and failure had such wonderful flashes of heavenly insight. He knew now without a shadow of doubt who it was who was with them, and he answered his Master with the glorious confession of faith which is the foundation stone of the Christian Church. He made it now not only for himself but for all Christian men everywhere in every age.

"Thou art the Christ, the Son of the living God."

This must have been for Our Lord one of the greatest and happiest moments of his earthly life. Here, at last, was the flame of true faith. For so long he had been nursing the flickering sparks of belief in these children of his, only to see them go out again, but now at last the flame was truly alight. It might waver and almost fail in the darkness that was coming upon them all, but it would not quite go out; it would flare up again and light would be lit from light until the faith of the Church was a blaze that went all round the world.

Our Lord was not a man who could not express his joy; it almost blazes out in his reply to Peter.

"Blessed art thou, Simon Barjona: for flesh and blood hath not revealed it unto thee, but my Father which is in heaven. And I say also unto thee, That thou art Peter, and upon this rock I will build my church; and the gates of hell shall not prevail against it. And I will give unto thee the keys of the kingdom of heaven: and whatsoever thou shalt bind on earth, shall be bound in heaven, and whatsoever thou shalt loose on earth, shall be loosed in heaven."

And so it is the church that opens to us all the door of the kingdom of love that exists here upon earth as well as in heaven, of which Our Lord is King and Prince for ever. It is the church that binds us firmly to Our Lord in love and speaks to us his word of forgiveness that sets us free from our sins.

It seems fitting that the foundation stone of the church into which all we Gentiles have been gathered should have been laid just where it was, in those pagan woods, near the great city which stood there like a symbol of the Gentile world.

Our Lord told his disciples not to proclaim him among men as the Christ. Those five thousand down in the valley below who had wanted to make him king had shown him how real was the danger that the scribes and Pharisees feared so greatly, the danger that his people might try to make him their leader in revolt. And that was not the way in which God wished that he should save the world.

Patiently, in the days that followed, he tried to show his disciples what was this way that he must follow. He told them clearly and plainly of his passion, death, and resurrection. But in their heart of hearts they still hoped for the glory of an earthly kingdom as well as a spiritual one, and they could not endure the thought of earthly defeat and death. It seemed to

189

them, as to us all, an unbearable and impossible thing that one whom they loved so much should have to suffer greatly. As we do, they put their heads in the sand and could not face it, and Peter spoke for them all when he cried out in dismay, "Be it far from thee, Lord: this shall not be unto thee."

Our Lord's reply was stern and fierce. "Get thee behind me, Satan; thou art an offence unto me; for thou savourest not the things that be of God, but those that be of men."

For it was Satan tempting him through Peter's distress; Satan bringing out one of the most villainous of his temptations, the one that tempts a man to turn aside from the duty of martyrdom in order to spare those whom he loves from suffering. And by so sparing them he does not really do them any good, either, for the way of the cross is the only way that leads to eternal life, and there in the quiet of the woods he explained that to them.

"If any man will come after me, let him deny himself, and take up his cross, and follow me. For whosoever will save his life shall lose it: and whosoever will lose his life for my sake shall find it. For what is a man profited, if he shall gain the whole world, and lose his own soul? or what shall a man give in exchange for his soul?"

6.

About six days later Our Lord left the other disciples and taking with him only Peter, James, and John he climbed higher up the mountain to where the woods fell away and up above them were the snowfields of Hermon with the air blowing down from them keen and cold. They climbed up higher still, to where it was utterly silent and they were lifted far up from the world of men, with nothing between them and heaven but those shining and terrible snows.

Our Lord withdrew a little way and stood to pray, and the three apostles sat down to rest. Perhaps they meant to try and pray too, but they were tired out after the long hard climb and presently they fell asleep. When they woke up again, stupefied with sleep and bewildered by the huge loneliness and silence, they looked round quickly for Our Lord. He was not there. In the place where he had stood praying stood another figure, clothed in light. His garments were white and glistening, such as no fuller on earth can whiten garments, white and more glorious than the snows. In their first shock and fear they did not recognize the shining face, yet when they looked again they knew that this glorious figure was not a stranger at all. He was their Lord and their Master, only until now their shortsighted eyes had not seen him very clearly; they had seen only Jesus the man; now the scales had fallen from their eyes and they saw him as he really was, as God. Then they realized that he was not alone, for two other shining figures stood with him, talking to him, heavenly spirits only a little less glorious than was their Lord himself, and they knew them to be those two great heroes and saints of their people, Moses and Elijah; Moses who had seen the burning bush in the wilderness and Elijah who had been caught up to heaven in the fire. The fire and the light of heaven were all about them and they crouched against the earth in their terror and hid their eyes. James and John could not speak, but Peter began to talk like a man in delirium, not knowing what he said.

"Lord, it is good for us to be here," he said, "if thou wilt, let us make here three tabernacles; one for thee, and one for Moses, and one for Elijah."

The blazing light had reminded his half-crazed mind of the

autumn feast of Tabernacles that was close upon them, the feast of light, and the thought of the burning bush had made him think of the green branches with which the pilgrims to Jerusalem built themselves little tabernacles to live in. While he was still speaking one of those clouds that often sweep suddenly down a mountainside overshadowed them, and as they entered into the cloud they were terribly afraid. In the pealing of thunder that followed they heard a voice, even as John the Baptist had heard a voice in the thunder in the Jordan Valley. "This is my beloved Son, in whom I am well pleased; hear ye him." Surely they would have died of the terror had not the great "Fear not!" come to save them. One of them felt a touch on his shoulder, and they heard a warm human voice saying, "Arise, and be not afraid." Still shuddering with the anguish of their fear they looked up and saw Our Lord bending over them, and he was alone, and they saw him once more as a man like themselves, with his clothes travel-stained and shabby, and the face that had shone with such blinding light once more lined with fatigue and hard work, and tanned brown by the sun.

When he had comforted them and reassured them he led them down the mountain again, asking them not to tell anyone what they had seen until after his resurrection. And he told them that Moses and Elijah had been talking with him of the things that were going to happen very soon in Jerusalem, and that those moments when heaven had come down upon the mountain had strengthened him and nerved him to face what was coming. And perhaps he told them that this vision must nerve them too. When they saw his body tortured and killed they must remember the glorious body that they had seen; and know that they would see it again when death had been conquered. The light of heaven was always much nearer to them than they knew.

O Eternal Light, shine in our hearts,
O Eternal Goodness, deliver us from evil,
O Eternal Power, be our support,
O Eternal Wisdom, scatter our darkness,
O Eternal Pity, have mercy upon us;
    that with all our heart and mind and soul and strength
    we may seek thy face and be brought by thine infinite
    mercy to thy holy presence; through Jesus Christ
    Our Lord. Amen.

—Alevin

Chapter 9

CHRIST THE KING

My King, and my God
—Psalm V:2

1.

THEY journeyed back into Galilee and Our Lord went to Nazareth and stayed there quietly with Mary in her home for the last time. This must have been his real good-by to her, for he would not be with her again until his passion, which was her passion too, came upon them both. The feast of Tabernacles was near, the pilgrims who were going to it were preparing for the journey to Jerusalem, and some of Our Lord's relatives came to him and urged him to go too. They wanted him to do in Judea the great things he had lately been doing in Galilee. St. John says, "for neither did his brethren believe on him." But if they did not believe that this man who had grown up with them was the Christ, the attempt of the five thousand to seize him and make him a king had shown them that he could be a national hero who would bring glory to the family. "Show thyself to the world," they urged him.

But Our Lord said, "Go ye up unto this feast. I go not up yet unto this feast; for my time is not yet full come."

So the pilgrims went off without him, and he stayed quietly behind in Nazareth; and intensely relieved his disciples must have been, for they knew only too well that in Jerusalem he went in perpetual danger of his life.

But they rejoiced too soon, for once the pilgrims were well started he told them that now he would go too. It was not Our Lord's way to try and avoid danger, but neither was it his way to blunder into it without proper thought and care. To arrive at Jerusalem with the other pilgrims, in the way that he was expected to arrive, might mean arrest at the city gate, but were he to slip into the city secretly he would be in the midst of the crowds before his enemies knew he was there. And once there, his own wit and courage would keep him where it was the will of God that he should be.

In the middle of the feast, when for days men had been asking, "Where is he?" suddenly he appeared in the Temple, in the very stronghold of his enemies, and standing up in the midst of the people began to teach. It was a brave and thrilling thing to do. It is a wonderful moment to imagine, when his tall figure came striding through the crowds, that parted in delight to let him through, and then in the sudden hush his well-loved voice rang out.

It was a frontal attack that must have infuriated his enemies, and as we read the passages in St. John's Gospel that describe these days we have a feeling of tense excitement and strain. Our Lord was most deeply hated and most deeply loved. The emotions about him were strong and violent, and his own speech, too, was hard and strong. He "spake boldly." He "cried in the Temple."

195

"Why go ye about to kill me?" he demanded of his enemies, characteristically stripping away their rags of pretense that they might face their own wickedness and he his danger. And the brutal answer came back, "Thou hast a devil! Who goeth about to kill thee?"

But they were going about to kill him; only they did not dare. His flaming courage held them at bay, so that "no man laid hands on him." They sent the Temple guard to arrest him but they returned to the chief priests and Pharisees without having done it.

"Why have ye not brought him?" they were asked, and the men answered, "Never man spake like this man."

For he spoke not only with great boldness but great authority, so that it was not only his courage which protected him but his kingliness too. All through his life Jesus of Nazareth, the carpenter's son, the Galilean countryman, moved among men as a king. We who worship him now as Christ the King, Son of God most high, take that for granted, but it must sometimes have astonished the people of his own day. For he was such a humble man and, except when wickedness aroused his anger, so gentle and courteous, and he was a poor man who ate and slept where he could and owned nothing but the clothes he wore. Yet he was always promptly obeyed, hungrily listened to, followed wherever he went, and sought as a leader. And when he thundered his denunciations at the rulers of his people he moved them to hatred but not to contempt. Reading the Gospels we get the impression that they felt for him not the contemptuous dislike which one would expect an aristocrat to feel for an impetuous young artisan, but the hatred tinged with fear which a king feels for another king whose power threatens his own.

They came to him while he was teaching in the Temple and asked him, "Tell us, by what authority doest thou these things? or who is he that gave thee this authority?"

Deep in their hearts they knew that the power of the man standing before them could have no other source but the power of God, and because he could read their hearts Our Lord tried to make them give the answer themselves, as he had done when the lawyer questioned him at Jericho. He said, "I will also ask you one thing; and answer me: The baptism of John, was it from heaven, or of men?"

It was their turn now to have a trap set for them. John had declared Our Lord to be the Christ, and so to acknowledge that he was inspired by God was also to acknowledge Our Lord as Messiah. If they were to say, "from heaven," Our Lord would cry out before all the listening people, "Why then believed ye him not?" Yet if they were to say, "of men," they would infuriate the people, who all believed John to be a prophet sent from God. And to infuriate a Jewish mob was to put one's life in danger. And so, beaten, they answered that they could not tell whence it was. And Our Lord said, "Neither tell I you by what authority I do these things."

And then in words that winged their way up into prophecy he told the terrible parable of the vineyard let to wicked husbandmen, who murdered the beloved son of the king of the vineyard, sent to gather the fruit of the vineyard for his father, and of the king's vengeance upon their wickedness. They knew that he spoke to them of their own doom, and warned them of it, but hatred had hardened their hearts now even against fear, and they would not turn back from the way they had chosen.

After that they sent spies to mingle with the crowds who gathered to hear him preach, to heckle him, and to interrupt him and ask him questions most cleverly designed to provoke an answer which would get him into difficulties. But they could not match his brilliance in argument. It was they who were discomfited, not he. "After that they durst not ask him any question at all. . . . They marvelled, and held their peace."

197

And on the last day, the great day of the feast of water and light, Our Lord stood and looked down with love and longing at the great crowds gathered to hear him, and cried out, "If any man thirst, let him come unto me and drink.... I am the light of the world: he that followeth me shall not walk in darkness, but shall have the light of life."

"Who art thou?" they demanded.

And Our Lord answered, "Even the same that I said unto you from the beginning.... When ye have lifted up the Son of man, then shall ye know that I am he, and that I do nothing of myself; but as my Father hath taught me, I speak these things. And he that sent me is with me: the Father hath not left me alone; for I do always those things that please him."

To those who believed in him, and longed to be set free from their sins, he spoke words of love and encouragement. "If ye continue in my word, then are ye my disciples indeed," he cried to them. "And ye shall know the truth, and the truth shall set you free."

But to his enemies, who could not accept his truth, he spoke hard thundering words that fell like blows. "Ye seek to kill me, a man that hath told you the truth, which I have heard of God. ... If God were your Father, ye would love me: for I proceeded forth and came from God; neither came I of myself, but he sent me. Why do ye not understand my speech? even because ye cannot hear my word. Ye are of your father the devil, and the lusts of your father ye will do. He was a murderer from the beginning, and abode not in the truth, because there is no truth in him. When he speaketh a lie, he speaketh of his own: for he is a liar, and the father of it. And because I tell you the truth, ye believe me not. Which of you convinceth me of sin? And if I say the truth, why do ye not believe me? He that is of God heareth God's words: ye therefore hear them not, because ye are not of God."

Infuriated, they shouted that he had a devil in him, but he answered them, "I have not a devil; but I honour my Father, and ye do dishonour me." And then the great Verily pealed out over the crowds like a trumpet. "Verily, verily, I say unto you, If a man keep my saying he shall never see death."

The tremendous claims that he made for himself had been steadily mounting. He had said that he was the light of the world. He had called himself Son of man, one of the great titles given to the Messiah. He had claimed to speak words given to him by God himself. He had dared to say that God was always with him, and that all that he did pleased God. But this last claim must have seemed to the listening crowds the greatest of them all. To those who obeyed him he would give eternal life. For his servants, there was no death.

There was a roar of protest from the crowd, answering the trumpet call of the "Verily." "Now we know that thou hast a devil!" they shouted at him again. "Art thou greater than our father Abraham, which is dead? . . . Whom makest thou thyself?"

Our Lord answered, "Your father Abraham rejoiced to see my day: and he saw it and was glad."

"Thou art not yet fifty years old," they taunted him, "and hast thou seen Abraham?"

There must have been a moment of sudden silence now, a silence full of awe and fear, and then the glorious figure of Our Lord straightened, and the last Verily sounded.

"Verily, verily, I say unto you, Before Abraham was, I AM."

And immediately there was uproar. For to the Jews "I AM" was the great and sacred name of God that must never be uttered. When God had spoken to Moses out of the bush he had said, "I AM THAT I AM. Thus shalt thou say unto the children of Israel, I AM hath sent me unto you." To speak this great Name was blasphemy, and the punishment for blasphemy was death.

Where an Anglo-Saxon mob carries rotten eggs and vegetables to hurl at a bold man who has infuriated them the brutal Jewish mob carried stones, and stones now hurtled through the air. In this very place where he had saved the woman taken in adultery from stoning Our Lord was himself stoned. This was a repetition of the dreadful scene at Nazareth, another attempt by wicked men to murder God. But the moment for that crime had not come yet, and once again Our Lord saved himself. "Jesus hid himself, and went out of the temple, going through the midst of them, and so passed by."

After that narrow escape from a dreadful death who would have blamed Our Lord if he had stayed away from Judea? But at the winter feast, the feast of the Dedication, he was back again, and preaching in the Temple as before. Gathering the people to him with his "Verily, verily, I say unto you," he told them the lovely parable of the good shepherd. At the feast of Tabernacles he had cried, "I am the light of the world," at the feast of Dedication he cried, "I am the good shepherd: the good shepherd giveth his life for the sheep." And once again he dared to claim a closer union with God than any man had ever claimed before, once again he cried aloud that the gift of eternal life was his to give. "My sheep hear my voice, and I know them, and they follow me: And I give unto them eternal life; and they shall never perish, neither shall any man pluck them out of my hand. My Father, which gave them me, is greater than all; and no man is able to pluck them out of my Father's hand. I and my Father are one."

And again they took up stones to kill him but immovable in courage he faced them and argued with them and it seems that this time the stones dropped from their hands. That he should have repeated these two claims, at peril of his life, stresses their supreme importance. For he had come into the world to do these two things, to reveal God the Father to man in the Person of

God the Son, and to lift man out of the eternal death of sin into the eternal life of the love of God, and he who was both God and man would not die until he had made men understand that in killing him they killed God and in rejecting him they murdered themselves.

The order for his arrest was given again, and once more he left Jerusalem.

2.

He spent the rest of that winter with his disciples in the valley of the Jordan, in the place where John had baptized. Waiting there for the last great battle of his life he must have felt very close to his beloved John. The spirit of John was undoubtedly there with him, for the thought of John came even into the minds of those who came out into the wilderness to see Our Lord. "John did no miracle," they said, "but all things that John spake of this man were true."

The winter passed and the spring came again, with green shoots on the vines and the voices of the birds, and a message was brought to Our Lord from Martha and Mary to tell him that Lazarus was ill. "Lord, behold, he whom thou lovest is sick."

"This sickness is not unto death," Our Lord told his disciples, "but for the glory of God, that the Son of God might be glorified thereby." For two days he stayed where he was in the Jordan Valley, and then he said to his disciples, "Our friend Lazarus sleepeth; but I go, that I may awake him out of sleep."

The disciples thought he spoke of natural sleep, but he knew that Lazarus had died. He knew that it was the will of God, part of the pattern that God is weaving out of the lives of his children, that Lazarus should die and be brought again from the dead, and so he had waited those two days, but they must have been for him days of sorrow. His three friends were suffering greatly, and he had to withhold his help. It must have been with intense joy, now that he might go to them, that he prepared for the journey.

"Lazarus is dead," he said, "and I am glad for your sakes that I was not there, to the intent ye may believe; nevertheless let us go unto him."

The disciples were dismayed, because to go back into the neighborhood of Jerusalem was to go back into danger. But they were faithful, and though later their courage failed them it is good to remember that they had it now. "Let us also go," said Thomas to the others, "that we may die with him."

Lazarus had been dead for four days when Our Lord reached Bethany. Martha and Mary were in their house and many friends from Jerusalem were with them, trying to comfort them, when they heard that he was coming along the road beyond the village. Mary was too stricken to leave the house but Martha got up at once and went to meet him.

"Lord, if thou hadst been here, my brother had not died," she cried out in her grief when she reached him. And then she looked up in his face and saw there a strength and majesty that both awed and calmed her. When Our Lord had visited Bethany before, he had come as their human friend who loved them, but now he had come not only in love but in power, not only as friend but as king. She knew, suddenly, that there was nothing he could not do if it was the will of God that he should do it, and humbly and steadily she made her confession of faith in the power of God.

"I know," she said, "that even now, whatsoever thou wilt ask of God, God will give it thee."

"Thy brother shall rise again," said Our Lord.

And Martha said, "I know that he shall rise again in the

resurrection at the last day." It is almost as though she were reciting the creed, our creed that begins, "I believe in God," and ends, "I believe in the resurrection from the dead and the life everlasting." This is the hour when Martha shows her greatness. Gone is the difficult, querulous woman of the first scene, and in her place is a woman of courage, strength, and faith. Mary had been too overwhelmed by tears and desolation to leave the house, but Martha had walked steadily through the village, braving the stares of the villagers, putting aside the convention that forbade women to speak to men out of doors, so that she might greet as soon as possible the good friend who had put his life in danger that he might come and comfort her. And she had the strength to rise up out of her grief, to affirm her faith in him, to lay hold of the comfort he brought her. Our Lord must have loved her and reverenced her most deeply at this moment, because he chose her out of all the women in the world to hear for the first time those great and ringing words to which those in grief have clung ever since.

"I am the resurrection, and the life: he that believeth in me, though he were dead, yet shall he live: And whosoever liveth and believeth in me shall never die."

Our Lord honored all women, forever, by speaking these words to a woman, and just as Peter spoke for all Christian men when he said upon Mount Hermon, "Thou art the Christ, the Son of the living God," so Martha affirmed the faith of all Christian women in every age when to Our Lord's question, "Believest thou this?" she answered, "Yea, Lord: I believe that thou art the Christ, the Son of God, which should come into the world."

And then she hurried back to the house and whispered to Mary, "The Master is come, and calleth for thee."

Our Lord had known just how to rouse Mary from the indulgence of her grief that was so weakening her. He had sent

203

her a message, just for her, for Mary, from Jesus her friend. Immediately she "arose quickly," gathered up her skirts, and ran, and we cannot doubt that when she reached Our Lord she fell weeping at his feet, where she had knelt to weep in Galilee, as she sobbed out the words that Martha had used, "Lord, if thou hadst been here, my brother had not died."

The fact that both sisters said the same thing to Our Lord shows how often they had said it to each other. "If the Master had been here it would not have happened. If only he had been here." That is always what people say when someone they love has died. "If only this had not happened, or the other. If only we had not done this or that." And the fact that it is too late now to do things differently is half the bitterness of grief.

While Mary knelt sobbing at his feet her friends who had followed her took up once more the wailing and lamenting for the dead. The very air throbbed with grief, and Our Lord "groaned in the spirit and was troubled." He must have wondered if his human children would ever learn that the death of God's servants is not the irretrievable disaster that it seems.

"Where have ye laid him?" he asked, and they answered, "Lord, come and see," and brought him to the cave in the hillside where they had laid the body, the mouth of the cave closed by a great stone.

Surrounded by the wailing people, facing that closed grave, Our Lord wept.

He wept for the sorrow of Mary and Martha, and in this moment he bore also the weight of the grief of the world and wept for the grief of every one of us when we suffer in parting from those we love. And he wept too for the dreadfulness of this death that the sin of man has brought into the world. For though the mercy of God has enabled us if we will to make of it the gateway to life, yet nothing can take away the terror of the

204

actual duration in time of the fact of death. And surely he wept too for his friend Lazarus, because it was the will of God that he should come back from the joy of Paradise and take up the burden of life on earth all over again; and in a few years time the burden of dying all over again. There is peace and glory in doing the will of God, but Our Lord knew better than any man that it is not easy.

"Take ye away the stone," he commanded.

There was a moment of horrified silence, and then the practical Martha came out with the brutal truth, that thing that makes death so detestable. "Lord, by this time he stinketh; for he hath been dead four days."

Our Lord answered her, "Said I not unto thee, that, if thou wouldest believe, thou shouldest see the glory of God?"

There was no more wailing now. They were all trembling. In a silence full of awe and fear the men who were there moved forward, leaned their weight against the stone, and slowly rolled it away. While they did this Our Lord was silently praying to his Father, praying that his great will might be done, praying for himself and for Lazarus that they might have the strength to perform it, to do this hard thing and obey.

When we read this story it seems to us the very greatest of Our Lord's miracles. His own passion was very near. Very soon now he would deliberately lay aside all his power and give himself into the hands of death. But before he did this he made this tremendous affirmation of his dominion over death. His glorious figure stood there before the black mouth of the grave in power and majesty, as King, Friend, Priest, and Saviour too, but now to be adored as King. And the whole of this great miracle is a picture of his own passion and death and resurrection. A man most dear to God had suffered, had died, and had been laid in the grave, with a great stone rolled across the opening of it. A few days he had lain there, but now—the stone was rolled away.

Our Lord lifted his head and prayed again to his Father, not silently now but aloud, his voice reaching to every man in the crowd, and to the dumb spirit within the cave, re-entering once more in obedience the body he had laid aside.

"Father, I thank thee that thou hast heard me. And I knew that thou hearest me always: but because of the people which stand by I said it, that they may believe that thou has sent me." And then he cried with a loud voice, "Lazarus, come forth."

And Lazarus came out of the dark tomb into the sunlight, but still bound about with the grave clothes and with a napkin about his head and face so that he could not see it.

"Loose him, and let him go," cried Our Lord, and there seems to be almost a note of anguish in his voice, as though he felt with Lazarus the hard pressure of those tightly wound grave clothes, pressing upon what must have seemed to him in these first moments of return the intolerable prison of the body. . . . Get him out. Let him see the sun. . . . The light of Paradise was fairer, but the sun of earth is still most sweet.

The story stops there abruptly, and not even in imagination can we dare to be with Our Lord and Lazarus in the days that followed. Not even John the beloved disciple can have been as near to Our Lord as Lazarus now was. Lazarus, now, shared with his Lord knowledge which not even his Mother shared. Lazarus in his endurance and obedience, in prophecy and in picture, had for a short while almost been the Christ.

And because of this the figure of this quiet self-effacing man becomes from the moment of his resurrection a figure of tremendous power. We do not know for how long, after this, he was an exile upon earth, patiently waiting to return to the place where he had been, but whether it was for a long or a short time his effect upon the people who knew him in the place where he lived must have been very great. Though, lacking words to describe it, he could not speak of what he knew, yet his knowledge was there, implicit in what he was. To this day the Arabs call Bethany "el Azariyeh," which means Lazarus.

3.

This great miracle reverberated through Jerusalem like a roll of thunder. Many of the men who had seen the stone rolled away, and heard the voice of God calling the dead to life again, could believe nothing else but that Jesus of Nazareth was the Christ of God. They believed that no mere man could have such power over life and over death, and they went back to Jerusalem and proclaimed what they believed. Others who had been there, puzzled and bewildered, went to the Pharisees and told them all that had happened.

The chief priests called a meeting of the Sanhedrin to decide what was to be done. The great figure of Jesus of Nazareth now dominated all men's thinking. No man who had seen him, heard him, or even heard about him, could forget his power and beauty and blazing truth. The constant speculation as to whether he was, or was not, the Christ, kept men perpetually talking about him; and now this great miracle had strengthened the faith of those who believed and added to their number. The chief priests had no doubts as to what the outcome of it all would be; an uprising of the Jewish people with Jesus of Nazareth as their leader. And revolution against the immense power of Rome was quite useless. The subject peoples had tried it many times before, with the only result their own extinction with great cruelty.

Only a short while before some hotheaded Galilean peasants, some of them perhaps friends of Our Lord, had rioted in Jerusalem. Pilate the Roman governor had had them all massacred and their blood mingled with the Temple sacrifices. If that was the kind of thing the Romans did when dealing with a small riot, what would they do faced with revolt on a large scale? The Sanhedrin knew. They said to each other at this meeting, "The Romans shall come and take away both our place and our nation."

In justice to Our Lord's enemies we have to remember that they did indeed face this great fear, and the fact that Our Lord had until now resolutely refused to have anything to do with worldly power of any sort or kind would not have delivered them from it, because in their experience a man of power, living in the world, was always in the end forced by the world to take power. Facing this fear Caiaphas, the high priest, said then to the Sanhedrin, "It is expedient for us, that one man should die for the people, and that the whole nation perish not." It was better, in his opinion, that one innocent man should be murdered, rather than that a whole nation should run the risk of extermination. He belonged to that vast company who persuade themselves that the end justifies the means, because they lack the courage and faith to do the right but dangerous thing and leave the outcome of it all to God. So the Sanhedrin took the final decision over which they had been hesitating for so long. Jesus of Nazareth was to be put to death. And from that day they watched and waited with that dreadful patience of wicked men that is like the patience of a cat at a mousehole, a thing so horrible in its parody of the patience of the saints that one cannot bear to look at it.

4.

And Our Lord went back into the Jordan Valley again, to the little town of Ephraim, and waited there until it should be time to go up to Jerusalem for the Passover feast.

It was very soon time, and he set out with his disciples upon his last journey. He knew it was the last journey and said to them, "Behold, we go up to Jerusalem, and all things that are written by the prophets concerning the Son of man shall be accomplished. For he shall be delivered unto the Gentiles, and shall be mocked, and spitefully entreated, and spitted on. And they shall scourge him and put him to death: and the third day he shall rise again." But still they could not or would not face what was coming. The thing for which he was trying to prepare them was so terrible that their minds refused it. They were like a man who thinks that by shutting and bolting his door on a windy darkness he makes it nonexistent.

But Our Lord faced it, and we ask ourselves, how did he manage to live as he did, knowing what he did? We, facing some test of courage, do not know the details. A soldier knows he must fight a battle, but he has no idea what will happen to him in that battle; he may be wounded, he may be killed, but on the other hand he may come through safely. When we go into hospital for an operation we know it will probably be horrid but we don't know how horrid. But Our Lord knew in all its dreadful detail exactly what was going to happen to him. He had known it for a long while. And yet he lived each day serenely absorbed in the work of that day, as though that were the only day there was, as though all eternity existed in that day. And he made of this last journey a king's progress, happy all the way, mounting up into the final joy of the triumphal entry into Jerusalem. St. Luke has a glorious sentence, describing the journey. "He went before, ascending up to Jerusalem." He was eager, pressing on, mounting up as though upon wings, as though for God to die for the wicked men who had rebelled against him was the crowning joy of his life. And so, for his supreme love, it was.

The first joyous happening of this journey was the healing of the blind Bartimaeus. Coming from Ephraim Our Lord and his disciples were approaching Jericho and the people came crowding out to welcome him. They must have had a special love for him in Jericho. He had told the story of the Good Samaritan there and they had it as their possession forever, to tell to their children and their children's children, for as long as their lives should last. Bartimaeus heard the tramp of the passing feet, the voices and the laughter, and asked what was happening, and he was told, "Jesus of Nazareth passeth by." There is a royal ring about those words, as though they said, "The king passeth by."

And immediately Bartimaeus began to cry out, "Jesus, thou son of David, have mercy on me." And when they told him to be quiet he went on crying out, louder than before.

The moment he heard the cry of distress Our Lord stopped and commanded that the beggar should be brought to him. "What wilt thou that I should do unto thee?" he asked, and Bartimaeus, his blinded face turned toward the golden voice, said, "Lord, that I may receive my sight!"

And Our Lord said, "Receive thy sight: thy faith hath saved thee."

Upon the darkness of so many years a faint light glowed. Bartimaeus shaded his straining eyes and gazed, his whole being struggling forward as must the spirits of those who fight their way through the darkness of death to the light beyond; and the light grew, took form and beauty, and became the face of God, smiling upon him. Then Our Lord turned and walked on, and Bartimaeus "followed him in the way," the joyous way of the cross, stumbling sometimes but recovering himself and going on

again, never taking his opened eyes from the figure going on
ahead, uttering cries of happiness, glorifying God, nearly beside
himself with delight. The crowd caught up his praises and
echoed them, and so on a wave of joy Jesus of Nazareth was
swept into the town.

Passing in the midst of the crowd beneath a sycamore tree,
Our Lord looked up and saw a little bright-eyed man perched
up there like a squirrel, and he stopped and laughed and called
out gaily, "Zacchaeus, make haste, and come down; for today I
must abide at thy house."

Zacchaeus was a taxcollector with a strong sense of humor but
rather weak morals. Upon that other visit to Jericho he had not
managed to see the great Rabbi, because he was a little man,
short in the leg, and always had his view blocked by stouter,
long-legged men. But this time he had been determined to see
for himself what sort of man the Rabbi was, and so when no one
was looking this wealthy citizen, a man of considerable age and
importance, had scrambled like any grubby little urchin into the
sycamore tree that grew so conveniently in his garden, and swung
there well hidden by the green leaves.

But not from the eyes of God, who had found the sinner Adam
skulking among the leaves of the garden of Eden, and called,
"Adam, where art thou?"

"Zacchaeus, come down," called Our Lord.

And the sinner Zacchaeus made haste and dropped down out
of the tree. Humorous men are not easily disconcerted and once
on his short legs again he joyfully and courteously made his
guest welcome, and then standing with his little figure sturdily
braced before the tall Rabbi he spoke up for himself. They
thought him rather a bad lot in the town, and they were saying
that he was in audible murmurs behind the Rabbi's back. That,
he thought, was not fair. "Behold, Lord," he said, "the half of

my goods I give to the poor: and if I have taken anything from any man by false accusation, I restore him fourfold."

Our Lord knew that already. He knew this man's generosity and loved him for it, and he knew also that if Zacchaeus' ideas of honesty were a little confused, yet he tried to do right according to the light that he had. He smiled and said gently, "This day is salvation come to this house, forsomuch as he also is a son of Abraham. For the Son of man is come to seek and to save that which was lost."

And Our Lord went with Zacchaeus into his house and lodged there, and Zacchaeus made a happy feast for him. He had always been good to the poor and now he was rewarded, for this poor man whom he entertained was the King of Heaven.

In the sunshine of the next morning Our Lord and his disciples continued their journey, along the narrow winding road that led past the Good Samaritan's inn and down over the hill to Bethany. For a little while after they left Jericho a crowd of happy people accompanied them; then they were left behind, and the twelve were alone with their Lord and King. But still they did not understand what kind of a throne it was to which this royal progress was leading, and they were full of exultant thoughts about the greatness of the earthly kingdom which they still believed would be established when they reached Jerusalem. James and John came to Our Lord like a couple of little boys asking their father for a treat and said, "Master, we would that thou shouldest do for us whatsoever we shall desire."

Knowing as he did the terrible testing time that awaited his "little ones" Our Lord's heart must have sunk at the childishness of the question, but he answered gently, "What would ye that I should do for you?"

And they said, "Grant unto us that we may sit, one on thy right hand, and the other on thy left hand, in thy glory."

And Our Lord said, "Ye know not what ye ask. Can ye drink

of the cup that I drink of? And be baptized with the baptism that I am baptized with?"

And they, unaware that he spoke of the cup of suffering and the baptism of death, answered cheerfully, "We can."

Though they did not know it they spoke prophetically and truly. James would die a martyr's death and John suffer great things through his long life for his Master.

"Ye shall indeed drink of the cup that I shall drink of," said Our Lord, "and with the baptism that I am baptized withal, shall ye be baptized. But to sit on my right hand and on my left hand, is not mine to give; but it shall be given to them for whom it is prepared."

What they considered the conceit of James and John angered the other disciples and they all tramped along the road arguing like so many children as to who should be greatest in the kingdom that was so soon to be established. Our Lord never lost patience with them, never grew weary of telling them the same thing over and over again; just as he never loses patience with us, who are equally slow and stupid in learning the lessons that he would teach us. He had told them so many times that his kingdom was not an earthly kingdom, that he was going up to Jerusalem to suffer and die there, and that only the truly humble are the truly great. Yet patiently he said it all over again. "Whosoever will be great among you," he said, "shall be your minister: And whosoever of you will be the chiefest, shall be servant of all. For even the son of man came not to be ministered unto, but to minister, and to give his life a ransom for many."

5.

They came to Bethany and rested there. Was it at Bethany that there occurred one of the loveliest incidents of Our Lord's life, an incident which artists love so much and have painted so many times? The happiness of it seems to fall into place here, upon this happy journey.

Our Lord was sitting in the courtyard of Martha's house, resting in the shade, when some village mothers brought their children to him that the great Rabbi who had raised Lazarus from the dead might bless them. The mothers would have been shy, but bright-eyed and eager, with that glowing softness on their faces which mothers have when they are bringing their baby to someone who agrees with them that this child is the wonder of the world. The newest babies would have been in their arms, the ex-babies, who had had their faces scrubbed, would have been staggering along clutching their mothers' skirts; or if they were too young to stagger reposing themselves regally in the aching arms of little elder sisters. The older boys and girls would have been as happy and bright-eyed as their mothers. For Our Lord was no stranger to them. He had come so often to Bethany and they knew him so well. He was the man who told such wonderful stories, who was always so pleased to see them and with whom they felt so safe. And so they all came tumbling gladly into the courtyard, gay as a lot of bright-plumaged little birds, some of them carrying wilting bunches of spring flowers they had picked for him, or some treasure they wanted to show him clutched in a hot fist.

But the disciples who were with Our Lord, their heads full of the glories that were coming, saw no reason why their Master, so soon to be a great king, should be bothered with a lot of little village urchins, and they rebuked the mothers who were bringing them, only to be sternly rebuked themselves by their Lord. Had he not just told them that he had come not to be ministered unto but to minister? And he held out his arms to the children and cried, "Suffer the little children to come unto me and forbid them not; for of such is the kingdom of God."

Strait is the gate and narrow is the way that leads to the kingdom of heaven. The path is narrow as the needle's eye, the kind of little path that children love, the gate small and easy for them to unlatch, the lintel above it adjusted to the height of a child. The path is too narrow for covetous men burdened with possessions, the gate so small that the self-engrossed walk past it without even noticing it, the lintel so low that no proud head can bend itself low enough to get underneath. Worldly growth is an expanding process, a building up and a swelling out, but the paradox of spiritual growth is a refining process; we have to shed one layer of useless and grubby accretion after another until there is nothing left at all but the golden kernel of a child's humble, loving, and contrite heart.

"Verily I say unto you," said Our Lord, "indeed and indeed I say unto you, Whosoever shall not receive the kingdom of God as a little child, he shall not enter therein."

He was reminding his disciples of something that he had said upon another day. "The kingdom of God is within you." It is not only something which we enter but something which we receive. That life of love that is the kingdom is an atmosphere. It is like the glorious air we breathe; it must be both about us and within us or we die. And we cannot receive it into us, any more than we can enter into it, until all the useless dirt has been scoured out of our souls and they are pure and receptive as the souls of little children.

Our Lord took the children into his arms one by one; the

babies and the ex-babies, and the older children with their gifts and treasures. Each one he held and blessed as though it were his greatest treasure; and to him, as to its mother, indeed it was. For the mother had suffered and risked death to give it physical life, and he was about to suffer and die to give it spiritual life; and to men and women made after the likeness of God no one is so precious as the one for whom they suffer, and there is no joy to equal the joy of suffering for another. "Greater love hath no man than this," said Our Lord, "that a man lay down his life for his friend," or his brother or his child. And talking about mothers he said, "A woman remembers no more the anguish for joy that a man is born into the world."

6.

Before Our Lord left Bethany for Jerusalem Martha and Mary and Lazarus made a feast for him. There were many guests there, from Jerusalem as well as Bethany, but the guest of honor was Our Lord, and he sat among them all that night not only as their Friend and King but as their Saviour too. The thought of death and of salvation would have been in all their minds, for Lazarus whom the great Rabbi had saved from death sat there among them and many of the guests had come as much to see him as to see Our Lord, but only Our Lord knew that in a few days' time he would die for them all, and that this was the last time that Martha would make a feast for him. He would have felt the sorrow of parting but he would not have shown it, for this good-by feast was part of the journey up to Jerusalem that from beginning to end was such a happy journey, happy because for his supreme love it was a greater thing to be a Saviour

than a King, or even a Friend. Friendship and majesty do not
necessarily bear the stamp of death but salvation must be marked
with the cross or it is not salvation.

Martha waited upon the guests, serving them with the de-
licious food which she had cooked for them, and Lazarus sat with
the guests as their host, but it was Mary who gave to that feast a
richness of beauty that has made it memorable for all time. She
got up from her seat and went and knelt in her accustomed place
at Our Lord's feet. In her hands she carried a box of spikenard,
an aromatic and very costly ointment, and with it she anointed
her Master's feet and wiped them with her hair, as she had done
nearly three years ago in Galilee, and the lovely spicy scent of
the spikenard filled the room. She did it perhaps to remind Our
Lord of the days when their friendship had first begun, and to
show him by the costliness of the gift at what tremendous price
she valued it, but her action had a symbolism that went far
deeper than that. As at the beginning of his life the three kings
had knelt at Our Lord's feet for all of us, so now at the ending
of it Mary knelt there for us all. They had given their gold
and frankincense and myrrh, their wealth, their prayer, their
pain, to the King, to the Priest who is also Friend and Mediator,
and to the Saviour, and Mary now did the same. The gold of the
gift was its costliness, the aromatic scent filling the room was the
incense of prayer, and spikenard, like myrrh, was used to embalm
the dead, and must have brought to many there the thought of
death. They must have been all silent a little while watching
the kneeling figure, identifying themselves with her as we do,
caught up for one moment into the eternal worship of heaven of
which moments like these upon earth are the foretaste and the
pledge.

The heavenly moment passed, snapped off and broken by the
intrusion of sin. Judas sat among the guests as one of the twelve

apostles, for he still took his part in the life of the brotherhood, doing their business for them and keeping for them what money they had, but since the day in Galilee when Our Lord had chosen him to be one of his special children he had turned away from the light and traveled along some path of darkness in which he had lost himself. With his eyes blinded by his darkness he could see no beauty in Mary's act of worship.

"Why was not this ointment sold for three hundred pence, and given to the poor?" he asked, and St. John in his Gospel writes bitterly, "This he said, not that he cared for the poor; but because he was a thief, and had the bag, and bare what was put therein."

But Our Lord with gentleness and love banished the darkness and brought back the light of heaven.

"Let her alone," he said over Mary's bent head: "against the day of my burying hath she kept this."

Our Lord's words to Mary have been called the loveliest sentence in all literature. Certainly they are the perfect expression of a gratitude which few men are selfless enough ever to think of expressing. A dead body must be looked after, made clean and tidy and wrapped in linen, and who among the dying say thank you to those whom they know will perform this service? But Our Lord knew that Mary would be one of those who would do this for him and so now while he could he said, "Thank you." Mary would have remembered this later, and like Peter on the Sea of Galilee her heart would have been almost broken by the splendor of God's gratitude for the least service done him.

The feast ended in peace and happiness and the guests went home under the stars, but when Judas left the house he went out into a darkness deeper than that of the night. He went to the chief priests and said, "What will ye give me, and I will deliver him unto you?"

They bargained with him, and promised to give him thirty pieces of silver, if he would betray his Friend and Master. He accepted the bribe, and from that moment sought opportunity to deliver the Saviour of the world to death.

7.

We have thought of Our Lord's life as being like the three movements of a great symphony, with its first movement gentle and tender, the second a slow powerful mounting into tragedy, and the third a song of victory. But now, just before the fear and darkness descend, there comes a foretaste of the victory. The triumphal entry into Jerusalem, the happy ending of a happy journey, is like the gleam of light that comes sometimes before a storm, that one carries in memory through the hours of darkness until the greater glory breaks.

The day after the supper Our Lord told his disciples to go to the next village, where they would find a white ass's colt, an unbroken colt that had never been ridden before, tied outside a house that stood where two ways met. They were to untie the colt and bring it to him, and if anyone protested they were to say, "The Lord hath need of him."

The disciples did as they were told and found the colt where Our Lord had told them they would find it, and as they were untying it some men standing by asked, "What do ye, loosing the colt?" And they replied as they had been bidden, "The Lord hath need of him," and the men let them take it.

There is something mysterious here, that we do not understand. For Our Lord knew that the colt would be found at the place where two ways met, and it is evident that the taking of the colt and the words, "the Lord hath need of him," conveyed some message to the men waiting there. It has been suggested that the underground movement was once more trying to force Our Lord to be their leader in rebellion and that this choosing of the colt was Our Lord's way of saying no. Long ago, in Eastern countries, when some conqueror came riding to a city bent upon war he rode a dark war horse, but if he came in peace he rode a white ass. Those watching upon the battlements would know if it was peace or war by the color of the king's mount. Perhaps some message like this had been sent to Our Lord by the underground, "In such and such a place you will find a dark horse, at such and such a place a white ass. Choose which you will." And he chose peace.

And so he rode out from Bethany to fight his last great battle against sin and death with no weapon in his hands. They held nothing but the bit of rope with which he guided the colt, and presently even the power of guiding his own movements would be taken from him. Rope would bind his hands, not lie in them. Yet he would conquer by the power of the peace of God in which he now rode, and his victory would be the greatest the world has ever known.

Every detail of the triumphal ride in the spring sunshine is a joy for Christians to think about. Some pictures show Our Lord riding upon a gentle little white donkey, but what he actually rode was not a donkey but a Syrian ass, a creature difficult enough to ride at any time, but when unsaddled and unbroken a proposition that the most daring horseman would have tackled with misgiving. But Our Lord mastered the wild young creature, mounted it, and rode it in the midst of a crowd of excited people into the noisy streets of a city. It is an act of daring that makes one want to cheer, and perhaps it was the sheer courage of it that started the cheering in the first place, as his disciples and the people of Bethany followed Our Lord up over the Mount of Olives and down across the valley to Jerusalem. As they went their numbers would have increased, for the pilgrims encamped outside Jerusalem would surely have joined them. And then the character of the cheering would have changed, for they would have remembered the prophecy of the Psalmist, "Blessed is he that cometh in the name of the Lord," and the prophecy of Zechariah, "Rejoice greatly, O daughter of Sion, shout, O daughter of Jerusalem; behold, thy King cometh unto thee: he is just and having salvation; lowly and riding upon a colt, the foal of an ass," and have cheered because this was their Saviour come at last, their king riding forth in majesty to deliver them from their enemies. It may be that among the crowd of pilgrims was some man who had been a shepherd boy in the fields of Bethlehem, and had heard the great "Fear not," and the angels singing, "Glory to God in the highest, peace among men." But whether he was there or not this riding forth of Our Lord and our God to his death takes our thoughts back to his birth, for it is the angels' song that we hear again in the shouts of the happy people. "Peace in heaven and glory in the highest," they cried. "Hosanna! Blessed is the King of Israel that cometh in the name of the Lord."

And they broke off branches from the palm trees and the olive trees, and strewed them in the way, and they spread their own bright clothes on the path, and perhaps the children who had followed from Bethany, some of them children Our Lord had held in his arms and blessed, picked the flowers in the grass and flung them down too before the feet of the white colt, and others waved palm branches like royal banners.

And so the King came to Jerusalem and entered in at the gate of the city, and the people there who loved him came to meet him and added their number to "the great multitude" that were there already, crying, "Blessed is he that cometh in the name of the Lord; Hosanna in the highest." And all the city was moved, saying, "Who is this?" and the multitude shouted back, "This is Jesus, the prophet of Nazareth of Galilee."

There were Pharisees among the crowds in the streets and they looked upon the scene with dismay. The city was packed with people, the pilgrims who had come up for the great feast and the Roman soldiers who had been drafted in to keep order among them; and the hated Roman governor, who had massacred other pilgrims and mingled their blood with their sacrifices, was in residence. Passions were running high and the atmosphere was tense with excitement and rebellion; and here came Jesus of Nazareth, this born leader of men, riding in among the acclamations of the people like a king come to his own. They must have expected that in another hour, if the excitement was not checked, that which they feared would have come upon them and the blood of their people would be flowing in the streets.

It is one more flashing revelation of the kingliness of Our Lord that in their fear they appealed not to the Roman officials among the crowd but to Our Lord himself. "Master, rebuke thy disciples!" they cried to him. By their instinctive turning to him, by the cry of "Master," they revealed what they knew about him in their hearts. They might hate him, but they knew his power. He could, if he would, master the crowds as easily as he had mastered the unbroken colt.

But he answered them, "I tell you, that, if these should hold their peace, the stones would immediately cry out."

His royal progress was the will of God, and he would not check it. When he had brought Lazarus back to life he had shown himself greater than death, now he showed himself a greater king than the representative of Caesar, whose progress through the streets could command no acclamations. In a few days, of his own will, he would yield his body to death and to the power of Caesar; and afterward men would remember that all through he had been greater than either.

CHRIST THE KING

Ride on! ride on in majesty!
In lowly pomp ride on to die;
Bow thy meek head to mortal pain,
Then take, O God, Thy power, and reign.

Chapter 10

GETHSEMANE

Reproach hath broken my heart; and I am full of
heaviness: and I looked for some to take pity, but there
was none; and for comforters, but I found none.
—Psalm LXIX:20

1.

THE days passed and while his enemies watched and
waited for Judas to fulfill his promise and betray his
Master to them, Our Lord also watched and waited. By day he
taught in the Temple, as he was accustomed to do, using each
last hour that was left to him in the service of his people, and at
night he went out to the Mount of Olives and lodged there.
Perhaps he did not sleep much, knowing his death so near. He
saw the moon rise, silvering the olive trees, and prayed under
the canopy of the bright stars, and he heard the cocks crow and
the trumpets calling at dawn from the Temple walls, and
watched the sun rise over the beloved city of Jerusalem. There is
so much for a man to watch who knows his death is near. The
beauty of earth is not lost for those who die, for all beauty

exists in God, and God is never lost, but the dying know that they will never again see it in just this way, out of these eyes, touched with this hand that will soon be dust, the warm air soft upon this body. They watch each fall of a leaf and want to hear the song of the birds just once more. Our Lord was true man. All that the dying feel he felt during those nights of waiting.

During these days and nights he thought ceaselessly, and with agony, not of himself but of his people, not of his approaching passion but of theirs. Only forty years after his death the rebellion he had refused to lead would break out, and be crushed with great cruelty. Jerusalem would be destroyed, his people massacred and taken into slavery. The whole story would be one of the most dreadful in the world's history. And if his people had listened to him while he was among them, had chosen to give themselves to love instead of hatred, to seek peace instead of power, none of it would have happened. But they had not listened, and now it was too late. Looking out over the lovely city he lamented over it, the words wrung out of him by a grief for the suffering of men that has never been staunched, and never will be until the work of redemption begun upon the cross is finally finished and he has gathered every one of his children to himself.

"O Jerusalem, Jerusalem, thou that killest the prophets, and stonest them which are sent unto thee, how often would I have gathered thy children together, even as a hen gathereth her chickens under her wings, and ye would not! Behold, your house is left unto you desolate."

And he wept over the beloved city, saying, "If thou hadst known, even thou, at least in this thy day, the things which belong unto thy peace! But now they are hid from thine eyes."

Our Lord could not save the city but he could save his own followers, and he told them exactly what they must do to save themselves when the troubles started. They must leave the city

225

and fly into the hills. They must go at once. "Let him which is on the housetop not come down to take anything out of his house: Neither let him which is in the field return back to take his clothes." And when the time came they obeyed him, they fled secretly from the city to the north, where they hid themselves and kept their faith alive.

Only twice in the Gospels is it recorded that Our Lord wept, for only the most intense grief could have wrung tears from so strong a man. He wept at the grave of Lazarus over the grief of the world and the hatefulness of death, and he wept now over the terror and agony of war and destruction; and we can believe that he wept not only over this particular war that would destroy the beloved city of Jerusalem, but over the passion of the whole world until the end of time. "For nation shall rise against nation, and kingdom against kingdom," he said to his disciples, "and there shall be famines, and pestilences, and earthquakes. All these are the beginning of sorrows. . . . And because iniquity shall abound, the love of many shall wax cold." God has given man the gift of free will, and without destroying our manhood he cannot take it back again to save us from the results of what we have chosen. Choosing sin we choose also grief and war and death; but while we endure what we have chosen we can remember that God weeps.

He did not only weep for his children who must live and suffer through these later horrors, he thought and planned for them too. His martyrs today have his instructions, delivered to his disciples in this last week of his life and handed down from generation to generation of his saints. They must expect "distress of nations, with perplexity . . . men's hearts failing them for fear, and for looking after those things which are coming on the earth." He cannot save them from suffering; they must expect to be hated, persecuted and killed; but he tells them what to do. They must trust in him; when delivered to trial he will teach them what to say. "Whatsoever shall be given you in that hour, that speak ye; for it is not ye that speak, but the Holy Ghost." They must be patient. "In your patience possess your souls." They must endure. "He that shall endure to the end, the same shall be saved." And they must be joyful. "When these things begin to come to pass, then look up and lift up your heads; for your redemption draweth nigh."

The redemption will be a double one. Their own private agony will bring them through the death of the body to everlasting life, and through the agony of the world will break at last the end of all things and the new heaven and the new earth. They are to look upon both agonies as men look upon the fresh green leaves of spring. "Behold the fig tree, and all the trees; when they now shoot forth, ye see and know of your own selves that summer is now nigh at hand. So likewise ye, when ye see these things come to pass, know ye that the kingdom of God is nigh at hand."

Turning to leave the world Our Lord thought much of the end of the world, and to these days belong the great parables of the final judgment with their terrifying imagery of death and hell, the pealing trumpets, the avenging angels and the darkening of the lights of heaven. "Take heed," he said, "watch and pray, for ye know not when the time is. And what I say unto you, I say unto all, watch."

Watch and fear not, for every end is a beginning and every death a birth. "Verily, verily I say unto you, except a corn of wheat fall into the ground and die, it abideth alone; but if it die it bringeth forth much fruit."

And then his thought came back for one brief moment from the passion of his people, of the world, and of his saints, to his own, and like every true man he shrank from the thought of death.

"Now is my soul troubled," he said, "and what shall I say?

Father, save me from this hour? But for this cause came I into the world. Father, glorify thy name."

There came a peal of thunder then and those who stood near Our Lord thought that they heard words in the thunder. "I have glorified it, and will glorify it again."

The splendor of the world speaks the glory of God, and the heavens tell it, but chiefly in the suffering of his Son and of his saints is God glorified, for through it the whole universe will be lifted up to its redemption, and as the moment of his shrinking passed, Our Lord rejoiced in the thought of that final consummation. "I, if I be lifted up from the earth, will draw all men unto me."

2.

There is a day which is as holy to Christians as Good Friday or Easter, Christmas or Whitsun, and that is the day before Good Friday, when Our Lord upon the last night of his life upon earth gave us the Holy Eucharist, the sacrament of his body and his blood, which is the life of Christians.

For the Jews it was the day when they gathered in families to eat the Passover feast, in memory of that night when God delivered them from their enemies and they ate their last meal in Egypt before setting out on their long journey to the promised land. Upon that night plague struck the Egyptians, but the sickness passed over every house where the children of Israel were gathered, each man with his loins girded, his shoes on his feet, and his staff in his hand, standing to eat in haste of the meat and unleavened bread and bitter herbs that would strengthen him for the journey. Before they had eaten their meal each householder had splashed the blood of the lamb he had killed for meat upon the posts of the doors, as a sign that the plague should "pass over" that house. We see in the first Passover supper a picture of what was to come. As God delivered the children of Israel from their enemies so Our Lord saves us from our sins. As the blood of the lamb saved them then, so the blood of Our Lord, his life poured out upon the cross, is our salvation now. As they ate of this meal as pilgrims setting out on a long journey so the Holy Eucharist is our strengthening for the journey to heaven.

When the day came the disciples asked Our Lord, as the father of their little homeless family and the head of their household that had no house, where they could make ready the feast, and Our Lord told two of them to go into the city and watch for a man bearing a pitcher of water, to follow him to the house where he would lead them, where the owner of the house had put an upper room at their disposal. From this it would seem that Our Lord had made preparations to eat this supper with his children in some hidden place, where no enemies could break in upon them and where their last hours together would be quiet and undisturbed. In Palestine women, not men, are the water carriers, so the unusual sight of a man carrying a pitcher of water would be a signal that his disciples would not miss. Tradition tells us that this upper room was in the house of Mary, the mother of Mark, and the spot where the house stood has always been holy ground for Christians. They believe that the upper room where Our Lord gave us the Holy Eucharist is the same room where he appeared to his disciples after his resurrection, and where he gave them the gift of the Holy Spirit after his ascension. To this house Peter fled when he escaped from prison, and upon the ruins of it the Christians built the first Christian church when they returned to Jerusalem after its destruction.

In the quiet upper room the two disciples prepared the simple feast. There was a U-shaped cushioned divan about a low table and upon this they would rest, leaning upon their left side, to symbolize their freedom from bondage. Upon the table they put the roasted lamb, the bitter herbs that symbolized the years of slavery in Egypt, and the unleavened bread, which was baked crisp and flat, like biscuit, and was easy to break. They lit the lamp, but perhaps they hardly needed its light, for the paschal moon would have been at the full and shining into the room.

Our Lord and his disciples, the twelve whom he called apostles, arrived two by two, so as not to attract attention, coming quietly up the outside staircase to the upper room. Our Lord surely came in last and said as he always said when he came to his waiting children, "Peace be unto you." The scene which follows is steeped in quietness. The whole moonlit city was hushed now, all the families gathered together in their homes, the streets deserted, but in the upper room the peace was the peace of God which passeth understanding.

They took their places round the table, Our Lord taking the place of the father of the family. They were wearing the white festal clothes that were always worn at this feast. Our Lord wore his long white seamless robe all through his passion. Mary had woven it on her loom at Nazareth and it must have been a great treasure. It was the custom for the eldest son to sit upon his father's right hand, and St. John the beloved disciple took this place, and it would seem from what followed that Judas sat upon Our Lord's other side. Perhaps Our Lord asked him to sit next to him, for up till the very last he was trying to save Judas. Then the first cup of wine was poured, Our Lord pronounced the blessing, and the supper began.

There must have been a great royalty about Our Lord that night, for he had come to the steps of his throne and the eve of his crowning, and the apostles must have felt it, for they began to talk about his kingdom. But still they did not understand what kind of a throne it was from which their Lord would reign, and they started arguing as to "which of them should be accounted the greatest" in the kingdom. The stupid altercation must have rent the peace of that quiet hour and torn Our Lord's heart also. This was the same argument that he had silenced upon the road to Bethany only a short while before. Would they never understand?

He got up from his seat and took off his outer coat and girded himself with a towel, as servants do who are about to serve their masters, and pouring water into a basin he went round behind his disciples and began to wash their feet. From man to man he went, kneeling at the feet of each of these sinful, stupid, blundering children who loved him, lifting their hot grimy feet in his cool and strong hands, bathing them gently and drying them with the towel. In all the glorious story of the unbelievable humbling of the Incarnation there is no more heavenly instance of the humility of God than this. The Lord God Almighty, Creator of heaven and earth, King of men and angels, eternal, most glorious, kneeling on the floor to wash his children's feet. For a few moments they were silent and still, stupefied by love, wonder, and shame, and then Our Lord came to Peter and Peter spoke. "Lord, dost thou wash my feet?" he whispered.

And Our Lord said, "What I do thou knowest not now; but thou shalt know hereafter." Later, when his children had seen the throne of the cross and the crown of thorns, had seen and known the bitterness of the passion and the glory to which it led, this action of their Lord's would fall into place in the pattern of things. This would be their way too, and the way of all the saints from that day to this. They would strive for humility as other men strove for power, turn from the easy way of life to the hardest they could find, and so pass from the discipline of these things to their strong endurance of the cross and their joyful resurrection.

As God knelt at his feet Peter felt himself once more at the

231

edge of that abyss that is the difference between the holiness of God and the sin of man, and he could not bear it. "Thou shalt never wash my feet!" he cried.

And Our Lord, reaching for his dirty feet, holding them and cleansing them, said, "If I wash thee not, thou hast no part with me."

And then Peter understood. Our Lord was bringing into being now a way of union with his children deeper than any that had gone before, and how could that union be unless the children were cleansed? God and sin cannot be together in the same small soul. God must bend low in his glorious humility and cleanse the house with his forgiveness before he can come into it. And Peter said, "Lord, not my feet only, but also my hands, and my head."

When we read this story of the Last Supper which was also the first Eucharist we feel always that we are in two places at once. We are in the upper room and we are wherever, at the moment when we read, the Eucharist is being offered. Behind the words spoken by Our Lord and his disciples we hear other words. Peter's cry has behind it our own words of penitence when we confess our sins at that most holy service, and behind the sound of the water that cleansed him we hear the words of absolution that cleanse us then. And so it is all the way through until the end.

As he passed on to the next man Our Lord said, "He that is washed needeth not save to wash his feet, but is clean every whit." He meant that his children who are living all their lives in penitence are also living always in the joy of his forgiveness, and need only to be cleansed from the soiling that comes between one act of penitence and the next. And then, as he knelt at the feet of the next man he said, "And ye are clean, but not all."

We can guess at whose feet he knelt then. How could Judas have endured it when Our Lord reached so humbly for his feet and gently washed them? How could he have resisted that appeal to him not to spoil the perfection of the family, not to be the one foulness that marred it? His heart broke later. It is past understanding why it did not break then. The whole problem of Judas is beyond understanding. So much has been written about him, so many explanations of his conduct have been hammered out, yet none of them satisfy, and still he remains a dark and frightening mystery. When Our Lord chose the twelve apostles from among the multitude of his disciples Judas was one of them and must at the time have been capable of great things, or Our Lord would not have chosen him. He managed the business affairs of the brotherhood and so must have been a competent man, but beyond that we seem to know nothing about him. He does not emerge from the Gospel narratives a living character as do Peter, James, and John, Nathanael, Matthew, and Thomas. Beyond stating the bare and dreadful facts of the betrayal the evangelists say nothing about him; probably because they could not endure even to think of him. We see him chosen by Our Lord to be one of his special children; we see him for three years in day by day companionship with the wisest and most loving man who has ever lived, the most loyal, the holiest, the most magnanimous and brave, and this man called him friend, loved him, and served him, and yet at the end of the three years he betrayed this friend to death by means so despicable and horrible that they have shocked and sickened every man or woman who has heard or read of them from that day to this. It seems impossible that he could fall from such light to such a depth of darkness. We shrink from acknowledging that such a thing could happen. Yet it happened, and it could happen again. It could happen to any of us. It is possible to live near to Our Lord for a long time and yet at last to fall away from him into hell. Nothing can keep us safe except a clinging to Our Lord that is like the clinging of a limpet to a rock, with a humility and penitence and love that are renewed with every breath we take.

233

Our Lord gently wiped the feet of Judas, and straightened himself, and put on his coat, and sat down again. "Know ye what I have done to you?" he asked. "Ye call me Master and Lord: and ye say well; for so I am. If I then, your Lord and Master, have washed your feet; ye also ought to wash one another's feet. For I have given you an example, that ye should do as I have done to you."

And then Our Lord began to be most terribly distressed, and "troubled in spirit," and cried out in his trouble, "Verily, verily I say unto you, that one of you shall betray me." Whatever his suffering it was not Our Lord's way to let others know of it, but now he showed it. He was trying every way he could to save Judas. As step by step, as far as we are able, we follow Our Lord along the way of the cross, we find him thinking not of himself but of those who are killing him, by their weakness, their hatred, their ignorance, or their fear, fighting not to save himself but to save them. And always the greatest of his saints have been like him in their martyrdom. It was an English saint, Sir Thomas More, who cried out at his trial to the man whose lies had helped to deliver him to death, in words that Our Lord himself might have used to Judas, "I am sorrier for your perjury than for my peril!"

There was no response from Judas, but the other disciples looked at each other in doubt and distress. John, leaning upon his left arm as tradition required that he should do, moved a little closer to his Master, and leaned back so that his strong young shoulder touched Our Lord's breast. It was the action of a loving son who moves quietly and quickly to stand shoulder to shoulder with his father to confront the trouble. Peter beckoned to him that he should ask who it was who should do this dreadful thing, and John said in a low voice, "Lord, who is it?"

Our Lord answered, "He it is, to whom I shall give a sop,

234

when I have dipped it." The sop was a portion of the paschal lamb, tied together with unleavened bread and bitter herbs. If there were guests present at the feast the father of the family dipped it in gravy and passed it to the one whom he most wished to honor. Our Lord now dipped the sop and with a gesture of courtesy turned and gave it to Judas. They were sitting next to each other. Had Judas looked at Our Lord he must have seen the grief and love in his face as he made yet one more attempt to win back his erring son. Had he looked he must have pushed the sop from him and knelt at Our Lord's feet and sobbed out his penitence there. But it seems that he did not look, for he accepted the sop. The words which Our Lord speaks now are the only ones recorded in the Gospels in which we seem to hear the utter weariness of defeat and failure. "That thou doest, do quickly," he said briefly to Judas. It was no good. It seemed there was no more he could do. Let them both get the hideous betrayal over and done with as soon as possible. St. John says, "He then, having received the sop went immediately out: and it was night." Certainly it was night, but a night of full moon and stars almost as bright as day. St. John would seem to mean by those four last words that Judas went away into the darkness of the soul that has refused the love of God.

We can imagine how the disciples now shifted their positions to fill the gap, closing the ranks of the faithful about their Lord, and how they cried out that they would always be faithful. "Though all men shall be offended because of thee, yet will I never be offended," said Peter.

Our Lord answered sadly, "Verily I say unto thee, That this night, before the cock crow, thou shalt deny me thrice."

But Peter cried out, "Though I should die with thee, yet will I not deny thee." And the other disciples promised too that they would die rather than forsake him.

Their protestations died away into silence and in a deepening stillness and peace the feast went on. Our Lord said to them, "A new commandment I give unto you, That ye love one another; as I have loved you, that ye also love one another. By this shall all men know that ye are my disciples, if ye have love one to another."

And then for the first time upon earth the Eucharist was celebrated. The time had come for the father of the family to take the crisp Passover bread in his hands, to bless and break it and give it to his children, and the disciples waited for the familiar words of the blessing. They came unaltered, and spoken by Our Lord they were music in the quiet room. "Blessed art thou, O Eternal, our God, King of the universe, who bringeth forth bread from the earth." And then came words they had not heard before.

"Take, eat; this is my Body, which is given for you. Do this in remembrance of me."

They must have looked up, startled. What did he mean? They must have looked at his body, and remembered how ceaselessly it had been spent and given in the toil of love ever since they had known him. How his body would be given for them on the cross, broken for his children at every Eucharist until the world's end, they could not know yet, but as they took the bread that he gave them, and ate it in wonder and reverence, there must have been a confused prayer in their hearts that their bodies too might become bodies of love to live and die for him.

It was time for the pouring of the second cup of wine and the blessing of it, and Our Lord said, "Blessed art thou, O Eternal, our God, King of the universe, creator of the fruit of the vine." And then again came words they had never heard before.

"Drink ye all of this; for this is my Blood of the new testament, which is shed for you and for many for the remission of sins. Do this as oft as ye shall drink it in remembrance of me."

Obediently they took the cup and drank. A man's life, the

Jews believed, is in his blood, and is poured away when his blood is shed. As they drank, it was the very life of God that was poured into their life, reconciling them anew to God their Father and washing away their sins.

They handed back the empty cup, and sang a hymn of thanksgiving. But they did not yet leave the upper room for Our Lord had so much that he wanted to say to them. For three years now he had been teaching them with unwearied wisdom and patience, but still they were such children and had understood so little, and now his time was very short. He gathered them about him and spoke as men speak sometimes upon their deathbeds, or as they speak when they are going on a long journey from which they think they may never return, words of such intensity that they are hardly words at all but a sort of distilling of the soul of the man, a precious essence pressed out drop by drop and word by word, an utmost giving of himself in love to those he leaves. St. John, the beloved disciple, gathered this distilling of the spirit of Our Lord; every word burned into his memory, and kept it safe. To read the 14th, 15th, and 16th chapters of St. John's Gospel for the first time is one of the greatest experiences that can ever come to a man or a woman in this world. To read it for the hundredth time is an experience just as great. One can only read them kneeling. From the words "Let not your heart be troubled," to the words "I have overcome the world," we do not know where we are except that we are with Our Lord.

It was in this hour of their parting that Our Lord promised his children that when he left this world they would not be alone. The third Person of the Blessed Trinity, the Holy Spirit, that love between the Father and the Son who is both the Father and the Son, would come to them and would comfort them. "And I will pray the Father, and he shall give you another Comforter, that he may abide for you forever; even the Spirit of truth; whom the world cannot receive, because it seeth him not, neither knoweth him: but ye know him; for he dwelleth with you and shall be in you. I will not leave you comfortless: I will come to you."

When Our Lord had spoken to his children he prayed for them, and not only for them but for all of us who have loved him from then until now, for all who ever will love him, and that great prayer St. John remembered also word by word, and kept it safe. That, too, one must read upon one's knees. In that prayer Our Lord, praying for us, lifts us all up into the presence of his Father and ours. To read his prayer gives one a sense of utter safety. His prayer for us goes on night and day forever. It is like arms about us, and while we choose to be his children and cling to him it will never let us go.

This first celebration of the Eucharist began with the command, "Love one another," and with the last words of Our Lord's prayer it came round full circle to love again as he prayed for us to his father, "that the love wherewith thou hast loved me may be in them, and I in them."

3.

They sang a last hymn together and the Passover supper was ended. In a few hours Our Lord would be arrested and his children would be left without him. He reminded them that his prayer would be holding them fast. "Simon, Simon," he said, "behold, Satan hath desired to have you, that he may sift you as wheat: But I have prayed for thee, that thy faith fail not: and when thou art converted, strengthen thy brethren." And then he reminded them of that other time when they had been without him, when he sent them out alone to preach the gospel without money, or even a change of clothes, and they had been kept safe. "Lacked ye any thing?" he asked, and they said, "Nothing." But he knew that they had not yet learned the lesson of utter dependence upon God that he had tried to teach them; even now they had their purses with them, and two swords; but like a father who lets his children go off upon some journey carrying their toys with them he let them keep their purses and their swords. "Here are two swords," they said proudly. Two swords against the power of Rome? Our Lord was never bitter, but there is irony in his reply, "It is enough."

They went down the outside staircase from the upper room and walked together through the quiet moonlit streets. They went out of the gate of the city and across the viaduct over the brook Kedron, and came to the garden of Gethsemane. Here it was peaceful and still, and the leaves of the olive trees were silver in the moonlight. As he stood under the trees, with his children gathered about him for the last time before his death, Our Lord saw in a flash of vision both their parting and their reunion again. He said, "All ye shall be offended because of me this night: for it is written, I will smite the shepherd, and the sheep of the flock shall be scattered abroad. But after I am risen again, I will go before you into Galilee."

Then he told his disciples to rest there under the trees, and taking with him only the beloved three, Peter and James and John, he went deeper into the garden. He "began to be amazed, and to be very heavy," and he who had prayed for them with all the strength of his being now begged his children to pray for him. "My soul is exceeding sorrowful, even unto death," he said to them. "Tarry ye here, and watch with me."

Our Lord went away from them about a stone's throw and this time he did not stand to pray, as was the custom, but fell upon his knees with his face to the ground. And as he knelt there among the stones the first agony of the passion came upon him. This is the beginning, now, of the appalling suffering that he bore for the salvation of the world. All suffering is a mystery, and when we come near to one who is suffering greatly, we feel the mystery of it and feel too a sense of great love and reverence, so that the one who is suffering becomes for the time being almost holy to us. And we feel too a sense of guilt, because we know that suffering is the result of sin, and that every smallest sin of ours has added to the great weight of pain crushing the world. But what can we feel when we know that the man who is suffering is God, holy and sinless, suffering because of our sin, bearing the whole weight of our sin, and that not because he has to but because he has chosen to? It is all intensified now; the mystery, the sense of love and reverence, of holiness, of guilt; and added to it all there is a feeling of terror because this had to happen, because the only absolutely sinless man who has ever lived had to suffer more than the greatest sinner who has ever lived, because God Almighty had to die, and we—every one of us—caused his death. We feel we would like to shrink away and not have to watch God die. And perhaps this is partly a feeling of which we need not be ashamed, because the ground here is so holy that we know we cannot and dare not come too near, and reverence holds us back. But partly also it is cowardice and that we must conquer. It has been truly said that we must all of us, if only once in our lives, as far as we are capable, face the Cross of Christ. Sheer gratitude demands it of us. It is a thing that we can only do by ourselves. Neither the written nor the spoken word, nor the painted picture dare say too much. They can only map out the way for a journey that we must take alone.

Spiritual or physical agony can be endured in silence only up to a point; beyond that point if some sort of sound is not torn from the body the mind cracks. It is typical of Our Lord that whenever during his passion he reached this point he did not groan, or cry out as sinners do, but prayed. Anyone who has ever tried, in the midst of any sort of pain, to turn from self to God, knows how hard it is to do, how the effort to do it seems to wrench one's whole being. Yet Our Lord did it every time. He prayed now, "Abba, Father, all things are possible unto thee; take away this cup from me: nevertheless not what I will, but what thou wilt."

This cry of Our Lord's is unspeakably precious to us, showing us as nothing else does how exactly like ourselves he was in all but sin. He dreaded the ordeal of pain, the fear and agony of death, just as we do. He shrank from standing up before all those crowds, being stared at, mocked, humiliated. He felt he could not bear it, could not face it, could not go through with it. What he was facing now was what he had chosen, and he had come to Jerusalem to die with joy and gladness, but martyrdom at some distance away is one thing, and martyrdom when it has actually got its teeth into your mind and flesh is quite another. We have to think now of something of which we do not like to think. Doctors tell us that the capacity for suffering varies to an almost unbelievable degree between one person and another. A mental or physical trouble which causes great pain to one man is just an ache or worry to the next. There is no criterion for suffering. We can none of us judge of the pain of another. But we do know that a man who has great sensitiveness and awareness of mind and spirit has a far greater capacity for suffering than a man who has not. And Our Lord had all his faculties developed to the very highest and most perfect point of sensitiveness, and had therefore a power of suffering greater than any man has ever had. The piercing of the nails and thorns hurt him a good deal more than it would have hurt us. The mental suffering that he had to bear was far worse for him than it would have been for us. And as he knelt in the garden he knew exactly how bad it was all going to be with an intensity of knowledge that we could never have. And so he prayed, "O my Father, if it be possible, let this cup pass. . . ." But just as he was able to wrench himself out of his pain into prayer so he was able to wrench the prayer itself from self to selflessness. "If it be possible." He was not going to turn aside from his passion if it meant turning aside from our salvation; but he asked the Father if it would not be possible for him to save us in some way that would not be so impossibly hard. Then he wrenched his selfless prayer a step higher still, from us to God. "Nevertheless not what I will, but what thou wilt." His prayer could mount no higher. There was no more to say. He got to his feet and came back to his faithful three. That awful loneliness of suffering, that makes a man feel cut off from the rest of humankind, imprisoned in his pain, had come upon him. He wanted the reassurance of their presence, the sound of their voices and the comfort of their love.

But when he came to them he found them asleep. It had been a long hard day, and the deep experience through which they had passed in the upper room had exhausted them. They were asleep like children and could not give him the help he had come to seek from them. "What! could ye not watch with me one hour?" he asked Peter as he roused them. But he would not reproach them, for he knew they had tried to pray, only they were not disciplined enough yet for their spirits to be able to triumph over their tired bodies. But he was in anxiety for them, seeing them with their vigilance relaxed and knowing the testing time so near. "Watch, and pray, that ye enter not into temptation," he said. "The spirit indeed is willing, but the flesh is weak."

He went away again. Physical movement can ease great mental suffering just for the moment, but when he knelt to pray again the agony came back once more. We cannot know, but perhaps what he faced now was no longer the physical ordeal of his passion but something infinitely worse. Upon the cross he bore the weight of the sin of the world, and the punishment of it. The inevitable result of sin, and its punishment, is separation from God. We know what we feel like when we have sinned; the sense of a weight pressing on us, the wretchedness of feeling that by our own act we have put a dark curtain between ourselves and God's light. We are utterly miserable until we have repented of our sin, prayed to God for forgiveness, and been forgiven by his mercy, until the weight is lifted and the barrier down. That every sinner who has ever lived, and ever will live, might claim this forgiveness and this freedom, Our Lord bore the weight of every sin that every one of us has ever committed, and endured every moment of every sinner's isolation. That means that upon the cross he who was utterly sinless endured the torment of the damned, that conviction of being eternally separated from God that is called the second death. No man could have endured this. Only Almighty God could have endured it. But when he knelt in the garden it was with his man's mind that Our Lord knew he would have to endure this darkness, and the agony of his mind, passing to his body, forced great drops of blood to sweat from his body. Yet once again he wrenched himself up into prayer and up to God. "O my Father, if this cup may not pass away from me, except I drink it, thy will be done."

He went back to his friends but for the second time they had failed him and were asleep again. Silently he turned away from them and went back to the terrible place under the trees where the stones were stained with his blood. Perhaps the agony now was chiefly that of waiting through the slow minutes that seemed like endless hours for the thing to happen, waiting alone in the darkness, and the cold that could be severe at night in the month Nisan, with his sweat-drenched garments clinging to his shivering body. But he managed to pray the same prayer again. "Not my will. Thine." He had reached complete acceptance, both of the physical death of his body and of the second death, and death accepted became the angel of death strengthening him.

While Our Lord prayed, and the disciples slept, something was happening beyond the brook Kedron. Through the gate in the city wall through which they had passed another company of men was passing, taking the same way toward the garden. They were led by a Roman tribune, and behind him tramped men of the Twelfth Legion, in Jerusalem to keep order through the feast, and a detachment of the Temple guard. Beside the tribune walked Judas. When he left the upper room he had gone straight to the chief priests. He had known Our Lord would go to the garden of Gethsemane and pray there and had told his enemies where they would find him unarmed and undefended, except by a few easily scared disciples. Nevertheless the chief priests were taking no chances, and must have appealed to Pilate for a detachment of legionaries to strengthen their own men. With the moonlight glistening on their swords and helmets, carrying torches and lanterns, they tramped across the viaduct and wound up the hill toward the garden, so many of them to confront so few.

Our Lord meanwhile had risen from his knees and come to Peter and James and John for the last time. He looked down upon their sleeping faces as a father looks at his dreaming children, and there was no reproach in his heart, only love and pity. "Sleep on now, and take your rest," he said gently. Then he heard something—the tramp of feet, a sharp command, and a cry of fear as the eight disciples near the entrance to the garden woke suddenly to find armed men about them. He saw lights moving among the trees, and the gleam of steel. The relief must have been intense and overwhelming. The waiting was over. Now, splendid man of action that he was, he could go into action. There is almost a ring of joy in the quick words he addressed to Peter and James and John as he shook them awake. "Behold, the hour is at hand, and the Son of man is betrayed into the hands of sinners. Rise, let us be going: behold, he is at hand that doth betray me."

All that happens next is a confusion of fear, flight, doubt, and hesitation. But in the tumult of it all there is one completely calm and competent man present, and he is Our Lord. It was he who gave the orders and quieted the confusion. Almost we get the feeling that he arrested himself. He stood straight and steady beneath the olive trees, calming and controlling his terrified disciples, confronting the traitor Judas, and the tribune with his men behind him. Judas had told the tribune, "Whomsoever I shall kiss, that same is he: hold him fast." Now he came forward in the flickering light of the torches, crossed the few yards of stony earth that separated him from the greatest friend he had, came to him, greeted him, and kissed him. It is past understanding how his feet carried him across that bit of earth, or how he did not die where he stood when his lips touched the face of God.

"Friend," said Our Lord, "wherefore art thou come?"

The unutterable depth of the love of God shines out in that quiet question. At the moment when Judas' face touched his Our Lord felt not anger at this vile act of treachery but intense longing to try yet once more to save this son whom still he loved. "Friend, you whom I love, what are you doing?"

But it seems that Judas was past knowing what he was doing. He was falling so headlong into damnation that even the shining out upon him of that perfect love could not help him now.

But it halted the men who had come to make the arrest. Though Judas had given the signal they stood where they were and could not come forward. There were probably many decent men among them, and the love and courage of the man who had been betrayed, contrasted with the foul treachery and the hateful manner of the betrayal, stunned them. Judas had been able to cross those few feet of ground, but they could not. Our Lord himself had to help them to do what they had come to do.

It is St. John who gives us this picture of the splendor of his bearing as he came forward from among the terrified disciples into the torchlight.

"Jesus therefore, knowing all things that should come upon him, went forth, and said unto them, Whom seek ye? They answered him, Jesus of Nazareth. Jesus saith unto them, I AM he. . . . As soon then as he had said unto them, I AM he, they went backward, and fell to the ground."

The great Name of God must have shone out from his last sentence like the sudden flash of a sword, in much the same way as the great love of God had shone out in his words to Judas. Because of his kingliness they had not been able to arrest him in the Temple. Because of his kingliness they could not arrest him now. They could only fall back from him in fear and awe and kneel before him.

He asked them again, "Whom seek ye?" And the tribune answered again, "Jesus of Nazareth."

Our Lord replied patiently, "I have told you that I am he: if therefore ye seek me, let these go their way."

His thought for them must have roused the disciples from their shock and bewilderment and to their everlasting credit they showed fight. That brought the soldiers back to their normal frame of mind. A rabble of excited Jews in a nasty temper was a state of affairs they were accustomed to, and they were on their feet in a moment and dealing with it. It would seem that now there was a sudden brief scrimmage. Peter the impetuous had possessed himself of one of the two pitiful swords, but he was a fisherman, not a soldier, and he did not use it expertly. All he did with it was to cut off the ear of Malchus, one of the servants of the high priest who had come with the Temple guard. Perhaps there would have been more bloodshed, for apart from the two swords the disciples had only their fists to fight with, but Our Lord was concerned now that his children, his church that must live on in the world after he had left it, should escape imprisonment and death, and he stopped the fight with a ringing command. "Put up thy sword into the sheath!" he called to Peter. "The cup which my Father hath given me, shall I not drink it?"

Peter obeyed and the fight was over. The legionaries and the Temple guard, with the hot blood pounding in their veins after the excitement of the scrimmage, had lost that true vision of Our Lord that they had had a moment before. They dared at last to close upon him and seize hold of him. He showed now just one flash of indignation, a spark of that glorious anger of God that had cleansed the Temple and started the hatred that had brought him now to this desperate pass.

"Are ye come out, as against a thief with swords and staves for to take me?" he asked them. "I sat daily with you teaching in the temple, and ye laid no hold on me."

Then he saw Malchus, bleeding and cursing quite close to him, and pity took the place of indignation. He must have said to the men who were holding his arms, "Leave my hands free one moment, please," and stretching out his right hand he touched the wounded man and healed him.

Our Lord's passion was one great act of love, wrought for the whole of mankind, the depth of its mystery so unfathomable that it is to us a darkness and a silence. But just as stars in the night sky both reveal to us its depth and make it bearable, so his acts and words of love break like light through the darkness of his passion. They come one by one, a shining chain of them, his words of love to Judas, his prayer for the disciples, "Let these go their way," the healing of Malchus, all the words of love from the cross; we hold to them one by one as they come, and learn from them all that we can learn of the depth of the silent mystery beneath.

The healing of Malchus was the last of Our Lord's miracles of healing. After that they put his hands behind his back and bound them with rope, and he was not able to use them again. Then the armed band closed about him, the tribune gave the word of command, and with the prisoner in the midst of them they left Gethsemane. Our Lord looked for the last time upon the olive trees of the garden, saw for the last time the splendid pile of Jerusalem upon Mount Sion standing up against the night sky, with the lights of the city twinkling and the Temple walls like mother-of-pearl in the moonlight. He knew that by this time tomorrow he would have suffered death by torture, but he would have entered the beloved city gladly, as he always did, his strong easy stride matching that of the marching men about him, his shoulders braced and his head held high. Malchus was without doubt marching as close to him as he could get, and they were both of them captives, the one to the hate of man and the other to the love of God.

4.

Meanwhile the disciples "forsook him, and fled." The shame of that must have been with them until they died. They had been with Our Lord in the upper room, they had seen him kneel before them to wash their feet, they had received the bread and the wine at his hands, they had listened while he spoke to them the words of eternal life, they had heard his great prayer for them, and they had vowed that though they died with him they would not forsake him. And yet they did forsake him. If it seems incredible we have to remember the circumstances of their testing. All that had happened in the upper room must have moved them to an intensity of love for Our Lord that they had never felt before, but it must also have confused them. Their dreams of an earthly kingdom had been brought tumbling down. The behavior of Judas had shocked them. The meaning of the words that Our Lord spoke when he blessed the bread and wine would not have been clear to them until much later; at the time when they were spoken they must have aroused in them bewilderment as well as awe. And confusion and bewilderment are very close to fear. And then they were probably physically worn out at the ending of the day. When they fell asleep in the garden it would have been into the deep sleep of the very tired, and the last thought in their minds would have been one of fear. With this fear they would have been wakened suddenly by the tramp of armed men and the gleam of steel. Everyone knows what it is like to be awakened suddenly in the early hours of the night from the first deep sleep of exhaustion. We feel disintegrated, "all to pieces," often physically ill. It takes several moments before we can pull ourselves together. And the disciples were given no time at all to pull themselves together. Before they had got the sleep out of their eyes the thing was on them like a wild beast pouncing. And they were most of them simple, kindly countrymen, used to peaceful country days, to boats and the sea, sowing and reaping, not conspiracy and betrayal and the tramp of armed men in the night. They must have awakened to sheer terror, that black terror of the moment that seems to wipe out past and future. It surely shows us how much they must have loved Our Lord that they did not immediately run away but mastered that first dreadful fear, rallied round him, and put up some sort of a fight. It was not until they saw him with his hands bound, with the Temple guard and the legionaries closing about him, all the might of the high priests and of Rome, that they despaired and fled.

All but two of them. Peter and John followed their Master at a little distance. They followed the marching men through the moonlit streets to the palace of Caiaphas, built on the slope of a hill not far from the house of the last supper. The gates were unlocked and Our Lord was taken inside by the men of the Temple guard, while the legionaries marched back to their barracks. John, who had come here so often on business for his father, and knew the servants and his way about the house, pushed his way through the crowd of men in the outer courtyard and came to the inner court, where steps led up to a gallery leading to the chief rooms of the house. He must have seen Our Lord go up the steps and along the gallery and pass out of his sight. Heartsick, he turned back to look for Peter but could not see him. He went back to the door of the court and found him waiting desolately there, and persuaded the portress to let him in. It must have been after midnight now, that hour of the night when a man's vitality is at its lowest and those who are miserable in any case fall into a veritable abyss of misery. It was very cold in the roofless court and the servants had lit a fire to warm themselves and had gathered round it with some of the men who had come with Our Lord from the garden. Peter, shivering as much with exhaustion and wretchedness as with the cold, drew timidly near to warm himself. John, we think, would have gone to the foot of the steps up which his Lord had been taken, and stood leaning against them, listening. But he would not have heard anything, for the door of the upstairs room would have been shut.

Our Lord stood with bound hands before a few hastily summoned members of the Sanhedrin, to be questioned by Annas, the father-in-law of Caiaphas, the high priest, who a few years before had been high priest himself and was the head of the high priestly house. The Sanhedrin were in a difficult position. They could not themselves put Our Lord to death. They might sentence him, but the death sentence had to be ratified by Pilate, the Roman governor, and carried out by Rome, and Rome would only crucify murderers, brigands, pirates, rebels, and conspirators. Murder and robbery ruled out, the Sanhedrin's only hope lay in persuading Pilate that their prisoner was a rebel and conspirator. Annas therefore set himself to question Our Lord, trying to trap him into making answers which could be used as evidence of conspiracy. But Our Lord was not to be intimidated. Throughout all the weary hours of the trials that followed one upon another he was steady and serene, refusing to yield one inch to the demands of injustice. This first trial was unjust, and he knew it, and so did the men who were sitting in judgment on him. By Jewish law it was illegal to question the prisoner himself. It was the law that witnesses to the prisoner's guilt must appear before the court and that the questions should be addressed to them. Our Lord, looking round, saw no witnesses, knew that Annas had no right to question him, and did not answer the questions. But at this first trial he did not remain silent. Injustice always roused his anger. He had never said anything in secret, had had nothing to do with conspiracy, but this unjust trial *was* conspiracy, a secret conspiracy against him, and he made his protest against it. As he had always spoken openly, so he demanded of them fair and open trial, and the presence of the witnesses.

"I spake openly to the world," he said. "I ever taught in the synagogue, and in the temple, whither the Jews always resort; and in secret have I said nothing. Why askest thou me? ask them which heard me, what I have said unto them: behold, they know what I said."

One of the men standing by struck Our Lord upon the face, saying, "Answerest thou the high priest so?"

It was not the law, either, that prisoners should be struck while the trial was going on, and Our Lord made his protest against this too. "If I have spoken evil, bear witness of the evil," he said. "But if well, why smitest thou me?"

His enemies saw that they were accomplishing nothing by this trial except the wasting of time. They might go on with the questioning and the blows for hours, but neither the clearheadedness nor the courage of this man would give way. It was they who must give way. They must give him what he demanded, the legal trial before the full Sanhedrin, with Caiaphas as his judge and the witnesses present. They must have been infuriated, for this would take time and there was need for the most desperate haste, for at six o'clock on the evening of the day that would soon be breaking the Sabbath of paschal week began, and everything must be over by then. There could be no sleep or rest now for anyone until the prisoner was dead. Caiaphas commanded that he should be sent down to the prison in the cellar below the house while the preparations for the second trial were made.

While Peter warmed himself the men about the fire were talking of the prisoner and his arrest in the garden. The portress who had seen Peter with John glanced round now and saw Peter standing there, and said, "Thou also wast with Jesus of Galilee."

Peter, cold and wretched, with his life and courage at their lowest ebb, was taken off his guard and startled nearly out of his wits. "I know not what thou sayest," he said, and moved hastily away toward the porch. And while he stood there the cock crew. It could not have been yet the cock-crowing of dawn. It was that queer time between two and three in the morning that we call the false dawn, when the cocks start a short but eerie crowing, and the animals stir and wake up for no reason that a man knows of, and then go to sleep again. Among men, too, if they are awake at this time, there is a feeling of silence, of strange fear. The moment passed and the taunting of Peter began again.

Several of the men about the fire had seen him in the garden, and one of them called out, "Did not I see thee in the garden with him?"

Peter was in a panic now, and cried out, "I do not know the man," and he swore it with one of the oaths of his Galilean lakeside, in his Galilean dialect. Then they began to laugh and jeer at him, for the Galilean men were always laughed at for their speech. "Surely thou art one of them," they cried, "for thy speech betrayeth thee."

Peter began to curse and to swear, shouting out, "I know not the man!"

And for the second time the cock crew. Startled, Peter looked up. Our Lord was being brought along the gallery on his way to his prison cell, and "the Lord turned, and looked upon Peter. And Peter remembered the word of the Lord, how he had said unto him, Before the cock crow, thou shalt deny me thrice. And Peter went out, and wept bitterly."

He wept for his own betrayal, but John must have been in a misery too deep for tears. Not knowing what had happened upstairs he would have seen Our Lord taken through a door in the wall and would have known that it led to the prison below. He would have heard the heavy door clang shut. There is something horrible, something irrevocable about the shutting of a prison door. It is like a sort of death for those who leave the world of free men, and for those who love them and see them go.

Tradition has made holy a few worn flagstones, still to be seen in Jerusalem, which are believed to be all that is left now of the cellar below the house of Caiaphas, and many lovers of Our Lord have knelt to pray upon those flagstones. Prison has always been a place where God's saints, as well as his sinners, spend a good deal of their time, and surely one of the things that must often keep them from madness must be the thought of him in his cell. Between his various trials there may have been more than one of them, and though he was not in them for very long it would have been long enough for him to know all about being in prison. He experienced the darkness and the clammy cold, the waiting, the boredom, and the fear. He probably was hungry and thirsty and perhaps they had forgotten to bring him bread and water. He was tired out, with nowhere to lie down. He prayed, and praised God in his prison, as his disciples did, and do, after him, and if there were other prisoners with him he would have talked to them, and one or two to whom he talked were born again. Were Our Lord and the penitent thief at any time during the day in a cell together? There is so much that must have happened during those crowded hours that we would give anything to know, and can never know. These hours are so typical of Our Lord's crowded life. He died so young, and when we think of the short space of time in which so much had to be done and suffered we understand better St. Paul's words, "I fill up that which is behind of the afflictions of Christ." Though in one sense Our Lord's life was a completely perfect and finished thing, yet in another sense the redemptive suffering that has its fount in him is continued through the centuries by his servants who are his church, his body in the world. Just as he himself lives in them and through them so his imprisonment, his pain, continue in them and through them for the salvation of the world.

The time of waiting dragged away, and he was fetched from his prison and taken upstairs again to confront the full Sanhedrin with Caiaphas as judge, and the witnesses who had been summoned to give evidence against him. They were witnesses who had been suborned to give false evidence. One by one they stood up and, questioned by Caiaphas, poured forth their lies and their half lies. Our Lord stood silent. He knew, and the Sanhedrin knew, that no prisoner could be convicted unless two witnesses could give identical evidence, and this none of these perjured men were able to do. Had Our Lord answered them they would have got on better. It is much easier to go on telling lies if you are answered back than it is if you meet only silence. To a liar silence is the most damping thing possible. The nearest they came to saying something true about him was their assertion that he had said he would destroy the Temple and in three days build another made without hands—words that could be taken as the words of a rebel, and something like this he had said in speaking of the death and resurrection of the temple of his body. But even so the witnesses could not agree as to his actual words. And still Our Lord stood silent and quite still. It is hard enough for most men to remain silent when they hear obvious lies told about them, but harder still when there is some truth in what is said, and when with just a few words they could justify themselves. But Our Lord stood there in divine silence, in heavenly patience, his dignity and peace unbroken. By this time he was probably the one man in the judgment hall retaining calmness and control, and his kingliness brought Caiaphas to his feet in rage. "Answerest thou nothing?" he demanded. "What is it which these witness against thee?"

But still Caiaphas was confronted by the silence and the peace of God. And also by his own failure, for no two witnesses had agreed together. There remained only one way in which he could condemn his prisoner to death. It was the Jewish law that a man could be put to death for blasphemy. If he could induce Our Lord to say in his presence words which to a Jew were blasphemy he could sentence him to death. He knew how he could do it and he set the trap. Yet we know that he set this trap only because Our Lord permitted him to do it. Our Lord's silence, his peace, had led Caiaphas to this, the only step left to him to take. What happens now is terrible and yet holy, glorious, and most fitting, for the words of Our Lord that condemned him

255

to death and took him out of this world proclaimed to the world who he was and why he came.

There was a pause and then the high priest, standing, spoke the words of the oath of testimony, "I adjure thee by the living God." No pious Jew could refuse to answer to this oath. If he refused to answer he was no true son of Abraham. Our Lord had been born a Jew, had lived a Jew, and as a Jew he chose to die.

"I adjure thee by the living God, that thou tell us whether thou be the Christ, the Son of God?"

That was the question of Caiaphas, and this was God's answer.

"I AM: and ye shall see the Son of man sitting on the right hand of power, and coming in the clouds of heaven."

He had spoken the great Name of God, identifying himself with God. He had given himself the title of Son of man, the Messiah, the Redeemer. He had claimed for himself immortal power. He had come to the world to reveal God, to redeem man, to reign forever.

The scene that followed must have been most terrible. Every man was on his feet crying out against the blasphemy, and the high priest rent his garment from the top to the bottom as a sign that blasphemy had been spoken. "What further need have we of witnesses?" he cried. "Behold, now ye have heard his blasphemy. What think ye?" And the Sanhedrin answered, "He is guilty of death."

That was the signal for the rough men who stood about the prisoner to treat him as they would. He was cast out now, condemned, deserted, and they were about him like baying hounds about the white hart. They blindfolded him, spit in his face, struck him, and jeered at him, saying, "Prophesy unto us, thou Christ, Who is he that smote thee?" He endured the blows and jeers, as he had endured the lies, in silence, but a French writer, Père Perraud, has said that if he had answered the question he would have said to them, as to each one of us when we strike him with our sins, "The one I love."

"Lord, by thy divine silence, by thy wondrous patience, by thine adorable humility, keep me quiet and still, and possess me with thy peace." Amen.

—Father Andrew

Chapter 11

CALVARY

Is it nothing to you, all ye that pass by? behold, and
see if there be any sorrow like unto my sorrow.
—Lamentations I:12

1.

BUT still it was necessary for Pilate to ratify the death sentence, and it was only Jewish law, not Roman law, that
could condemn a man to death for blasphemy. Our Lord must
be brought to Pilate as a rebel as well as a blasphemer. But his
enemies were in a stronger position now. They could bring to
Pilate a man already condemned by their own law and with the
flavor of guilt about him, and they had had, during the night,
good practice in the bringing of false accusation.

In the early hours of the dawn Our Lord was taken from the
palace of Caiaphas to the Castle of Antonia where the Roman
troops were garrisoned. The praetorium (the judgment hall)
was inside the castle, but it had a balcony or portico overlooking
the street. Caiaphas, and the members of the Sanhedrin who

were with him, could not go into the castle, for to go beneath a Gentile roof during the Passover feast would have been to defile themselves; so they stayed outside on the balcony while Our Lord was taken to Pilate in the praetorium, where the governor sat with his secretaries and interpreter and helmeted legionaries on guard.

Pilate was presented with the written indictment, a fabrication of lies declaring the prisoner to be a rebel and blasphemer and worthy of death under the Roman law, and also the death warrant for him to sign. Caiaphas and the men with him must have hoped that Pilate would simply read through the indictment, believe the lies it contained, and sign the warrant without further investigation. But they were disappointed. Pilate was no fool. His record shows that he could be a hard and cruel man, but he would not have been a Roman governor if he had not been a shrewd judge of men and affairs. He had, too, the Roman reverence for law and justice. He was not taken in by that indictment. He saw it for what it was. Then he looked at the prisoner, standing before him with bound hands. Our Lord's white festal garment, which had been so clean and fresh at the last supper, was now stained with the blood of his sweat and the dirt of his prison, and his face was bruised from the blows he had endured. Nevertheless, Pilate knew a great man when he saw him. He put the unsigned warrant back on the table, got up, and went out to the balcony. Caiaphas and the Sanhedrin were waiting. From now on we get a sense of crowds gathering, of steadily increasing noise and tumult. City crowds are quick to know when anything unusual is going on, and early though it was, they were probably already gathering in the street below the balcony. And they would have been an ugly crowd, for there was nearly always trouble in Jerusalem at the time of the great feast. Pilate, feeling the hatred and animosity of the men about him, looking down at the crowd below, must have been aware that a dangerous day was before him, the kind of day in which anything might happen, from riot to revolution, before the sun went down. Though he was a weak man he was a fighter up to a point, and his spirit must have leaped up to meet the danger.

"What accusation bring ye against this man?" he demanded of the Sanhedrin. He had already read the indictment, and his curt question showed them clearly that he did not believe a word of it.

"If he were not a malefactor, we would not have delivered him up unto thee," they replied. "We found this fellow perverting the nation, and forbidding to give tribute to Caesar, saying that he himself is Christ a king."

Christ, the Messiah. Pilate had heard of their crazy ideas about their Christ. This, then, was simply a religious question. "Take ye him, and judge him according to your law," he said contemptuously.

"It is not lawful for us to put any man to death," they reminded him. They had come here to get him to sign the death warrant and here they would stay until he had done it.

Christ—a king. Pilate turned abruptly and went back into the praetorium. If the prisoner had indeed claimed to be a king of his people then that was treason against Rome, and treason was punishable with death. He must talk to him again. Once more he sat upon the judgment seat, looking at the young man standing before him. He had recognized his greatness before, now he saw the stamp of his kingliness very clearly on his bruised face. St. John records the conversation that followed between the two. It is so deep, so intimate a conversation, that it is hard to realize that the two men were not alone together, for there were soldiers on guard beside them and a secretary writing down what each man said. Pilate knew no Hebrew, but Our Lord would probably have been able to talk to him in either Latin or Greek without the aid of the interpreter.

"Then Pilate entered into the judgement hall again, and called Jesus, and said unto him, Art thou the king of the Jews?

"Jesus answered him, Sayest thou this thing of thyself, or did others tell it thee of me?

"Pilate answered, Am I a Jew? Thine own nation and the chief priests have delivered thee unto me: what hast thou done?

"Jesus answered, My kingdom is not of this world: if my kingdom were of this world, then would my servants fight, that I should not be delivered to the Jews: but now is my kingdom not from hence.

"Pilate therefore said unto him, Art thou a king then?

"Jesus answered, Thou sayest that I am a king. To this end was I born, and for this cause came I into the world, that I should bear witness unto the truth. Every one that is of the truth heareth my voice.

"Pilate saith unto him, What is truth?"

To the treacherous questions of Annas and the lies of the false witnesses Our Lord had returned no answer, but Pilate was putting his questions in all sincerity, he really wanted to get at the truth, and to sincere questions Our Lord always gave a full answer. He told Pilate all that he needed to know. It was true that he was a king, but his kingdom was not of this world, he had no earthly army to fight for him and Rome had nothing to fear. Then having satisfied Pilate the governor, whose duty it was to maintain peace and order in his province, he went further still, and drawing very near in the splendor of his truth to the truth of this man, he stood before him for one instant as truth itself, demanding the obedience of his son.

But Pilate swerved away. "What *is* truth?" he asked, and though there is in that question the cry of the whole tormented heathen world, blindly seeking truth, yet this time it must have been an insincere question because it was not answered. Pilate did not really want to know. He was a fighter, but he was also a coward, and he was afraid of what the result of his knowledge might be. There was silence. Our Lord had fought for the soul of this man, as he had fought for Judas, but Pilate had swerved away and just now there was no more that he could do.

A messenger entered and handed Pilate a note from his wife. He took it and read it. "Have thou nothing to do with that just man; for I have suffered many things this day in a dream because of him." Pilate's wife Claudia was a granddaughter of Caesar Augustus. Pilate must have loved her greatly for he had obtained permission to bring her with him to Jerusalem, although the Roman governors were as a rule forbidden to take their wives with them to their provinces. She must have been a very great lady, sensitive to all goodness, for she had been aware even in her dreams that a good man nearby was in danger. The peremptory tone of the message tells us that Pilate was accustomed to trust her judgment and obey it. He had read her message in silence and it backed him now in his decision not to sign the death warrant of this innocent man. He brought Our Lord out to the balcony and said to the men there, "I find in him no fault at all."

But he had not, as he hoped, settled the matter. The sight of the man who had been already so much hurt by them stirred them to fresh hatred and they burst out into vehement and cruel accusations. Our Lord was silent. "Answerest thou nothing?" Pilate asked him. "Behold how many things they witness against thee." But Our Lord made no defense, and the lies spent themselves against his dignity, so that Pilate marveled. But he was stunned and bewildered by the fierce hatred of these Jews and did not know how to save the prisoner from it. Then in the flood of accusation he heard something that gave him a valuable piece of knowledge. The prisoner came from Galilee. He did not come from Judea, the province of which he was governor, but from Galilee, the province of the Tetrarch Herod Antipas. As a weak man will, he clutched eagerly at this chance of shifting the responsibility on to someone else. Herod was in Jerusalem now. Herod should judge the case. Weary beyond words now, Our Lord was once more marched through the streets of Jerusalem for the fourth of his trials.

In the beautiful white marble Asmonaean Palace he stood before Herod. The Tetrarch was delighted to see him. His wish that Jesus of Nazareth should appear before him and perform some miracle for his amusement had been ignored in Galilee. Now he had the chance of revenge. This scene is brief but terrible. Our Lord stood in his silence while his enemies accused him and Herod pestered him with questions, then silently he endured Herod's revenge.

"And Herod with his men of war set him at nought, and mocked him, and arrayed him in a gorgeous robe, and sent him again to Pilate."

Once more Our Lord stood in the praetorium and once again the responsibility was Pilate's. He accepted it, for he was a long way from being beaten yet. Once more he went out to Caiaphas and the chief priests, waiting again on the balcony. If he was not beaten neither were they. With each rebuff their hatred grew. By this time they must have looked at Pilate, as he at them, with loathing. Cruel though Pilate himself could be, their determination to hand over one of their own countrymen to a dreadful death at the hands of an alien power must have seemed to him one of the most detestable things he had ever met. He looked from them to the crowd in the street below, which had increased greatly in numbers during the last hour and was now an ugly crowd. Pilate hated the Jews, and looked at the crowd, too, with loathing. Then he remembered the chief reason why it was there. It was the custom that the Roman governor should release one Jewish prisoner at each Passover feast, and the crowd had the right to choose its man. It was collecting now to demand its rights. The cruelty on the faces of the leaders of this people, the mob below, gave Pilate an idea. If these detested priests wanted blood and suffering they should have it, and if the mob wanted the release of a prisoner they should have that too. He would have Jesus of Nazareth flogged and then release him. Then everyone would, he hoped, be satisfied. He spoke what he hoped was the last word on the subject loudly so that the people in the street could hear.

"Ye have brought this man unto me, as one that perverteth the people; and behold, I, having examined him before you, have found no fault in this man, touching those things whereof ye accuse him: No, nor yet Herod: for I sent you to him; and, lo, nothing worthy of death is done unto him I will therefore chastise him and release him."

Then he turned to the centurion standing by and gave the command for the flogging, and Our Lord was taken away to endure the punishment. But turning back to the chief priests he saw no satisfaction on their faces. The Roman flogging, so hard to endure that it was called "the intermediate death," was not enough. They wanted crucifixion and nothing less. Nor was the crowd satisfied. It became more and more restless, angrier, more dangerous. Shouts of "Barabbas!" came up to Pilate. "Away with this man and release unto us Barabbas." A revolutionary and a murderer, Barabbas was imprisoned in the castle, perhaps shut up in a cell opening onto the courtyard where the soldiers were at this moment stripping Our Lord for the flogging. His ordeal, and Pilate's fight for him, took place at the same time. Pilate, with one part of his mind, would have visualized the scourging within the prison even as he stood at the balustrade of the balcony and fought with the Jewish mob for the life of his prisoner, and the yelling of the mob perhaps reached Our Lord as the soldiers bound him with ropes to the flogging post.

"Will ye that I release unto you the King of the Jews?"

Pilate cried to the crowd below him. But again they yelled, "Barabbas! Barabbas!" Pilate said, "What shall I do then with Jesus, which is called Christ?" And they shouted back at him, "Crucify! Crucify!" The chief priests had sent their spies among the mob to inflame the shouting and the tumult, to infuriate them with lies and taunts, to rouse their anger against Jesus of Nazareth and their determination to have Barabbas. We need not think that this mob that was now demanding the death of Our Lord was the same crowd that had cried "Hosanna!" on Palm Sunday. It was the dreadful mob that goes down through history, a thing scarcely human, with the collective mind of a savage beast, wanting only blood, no matter whose, and as easily swayed by the lies of wicked men as a cornfield is swayed by the wind. This mob was composed of the riffraff of the city, of ignorant pilgrims to whom Jesus and Barabbas were mere names, of rebels and malcontents, and all those idle, mindless, sadistic creatures who collect at any street corner to gloat over an accident, or an arrest, or any form of suffering. If Our Lord heard them, in the brief moment of quiet while the ropes were knotted, he would have prayed as he prayed in the moment before the nails went through his hands, "Father, forgive them, for they know not what they do."

A Roman flogging was a terrible thing to endure. It was delivered by soldiers with the flagellum, a short whip with leather thongs weighted with fragments of metal. Men had been known to die under it. When it was over Our Lord was not able to stand. The soldiers helped him to a stone seat set against the wall, and put the purple cloak which Herod had given him in mockery over his shoulders until he had recovered enough strength to put on his clothes again. It would seem that these soldiers, so accustomed to the sight of suffering that one flogging more or less was all in the day's work to them, were yet stirred and shaken by the silent courage of the man they had scourged, because they did what cruel men always do when they have been made to feel uncomfortable; they took refuge brutally in what was to them a joke. The purple cloak gave them their clue and they continued Herod's mockery. A thorn tree must have grown in that yard, like a symbol of all the suffering that so many men had endured there, and they cut off a spiked branch and bent it into the shape of a crown and put it on Our Lord's head, pushing it down hard so that the thorns pierced his skin and the blood ran down his face. They picked up a hollow reed that lay there and hit him on the head with it, and then gave it to him to hold like the parody of a king's scepter. They spat in his face and jeered at him and went down on their knees in mockery. They said, "Hail, King of the Jews!" and smote his face with their hands. And this, too, he endured, for this was what he had willed. He had refused the gold crown that men had offered him once that he might have this crown. In the wilderness he had refused the scepter of power and now they gave him a broken reed to hold, the symbol of helplessness. Yet it was a real royal cloak that he wore, the royal robe of suffering. St. Hilary says that it was woven for him by all his martyrs, who gave their blood to make a cloak for him, to cover him in the hour of his shame.

The brutal scene came to an abrupt end, for Pilate had sent for the prisoner. All through the scourging and the mockery Pilate had fought. Three times he had asked the crowd, "Why, what evil hath he done?" He had stood between the hatred of the chief priests behind him and the fury of the mob below like a man caught between two converging floods of danger, and then his courage began to fail. It is hard to know what passed in his mind and prompted his movements now, as he turned back into the praetorium to meet Our Lord who was being brought up from the flogging. He thought, perhaps, that if he showed him to the crowd the sight of him would stir their pity—for a mindless mob can be as easily stirred to sudden pity as to sudden fury, and Pilate knew all about mobs. He was used to seeing men who had been scourged but he must have been shocked and stunned by what he saw when he entered the praetorium. The soldiers in their haste to obey the governor had brought Our Lord just as he was, still wearing the purple robe and the crown of thorns. "Art thou a king then?" Pilate had asked earlier in the morning, and Our Lord had replied, "Thou sayest...." Now he stood before him crowned.

Pilate rose now to the height of his short-lived greatness. He took Our Lord out to the front of the balcony and showed him to all the people, just as he was, in that terrible and piteous condition, yet a man of such courage and such power that he could walk unaided to the balustrade and stand there a king before them. "Behold, I bring him forth to you, that ye may know that I find no fault in him," Pilate cried. "Ecce homo! Behold the man!"

That is a cry that has sounded in every age. There has only been one man in the history of the world who supremely matters to the world. This one man made man, was man, saved man, and is man to all eternity, and apart from him no other man has any manhood at all. And to Pilate in the moment of his greatness it was given to cry, "Look!" God let him do that for him. And men have always looked, sometimes to their salvation and sometimes to their damnation, but there has never been an age in which men have not looked at God made man and crowned with thorns for man. But the men in the street below were blind to the glory of what they saw. A little earlier they might have been moved to pity, but Pilate had misjudged his moment. Once cruelty gets hold of a crowd it spreads from mind to mind with terrible speed, and now it was too late. They were blind and drunk with it. "Crucify him! Crucify him!" It was a great roar of hate that beat up into the face of Our Lord. It is not possible to begin to think what his suffering must have been at this moment as he stood there confronting man his child, whom he loved, and heard that cry. All through his short life on earth he had toiled for man and prayed for him with love that was never tired, but that love and work and prayer had only been a flowering in space and time of an eternal love and work and prayer. And now he was despised and rejected of men.

For Pilate the tumult meant fear. That detestable mob down there had gone mad. The thing had got out of hand and there would be a dangerous riot soon. It was his duty to administer justice but it was also his duty to maintain peace and order in this country. He began to step back from the difficult heights; back to the state of mind in which he had been when he sent Our Lord to Herod, and once again he tried to shift the responsibility, this time upon the shoulders of the chief priests. "Take ye him and crucify him," he said, "for I find no fault in him."

It seems that Pilate hardly knew what he was saying now, that he was losing his head, because he knew they had no power to execute a man themselves; only he could do that. The cries of "Crucify! Crucify!" were still deafening, and through them the chief priests shouted out the fault in him. "We have a law and by that law he ought to die, because he made himself the Son of God."

Pilate was more afraid than ever, this time with a superstitious fear. Son of God? The Romans believed that the gods did sometimes walk this earth in human form. Who *was* Jesus of Nazareth? At first he had seemed a very great man. Then a king. Was he something even more than a king? He beckoned Our Lord to follow him and went back to the comparative quiet of the praetorium, and for the last time the two men faced each other.

"Whence art thou?" demanded Pilate.

Our Lord did not reply, for the answer to that question had

been given last time they talked together. "My kingdom is not of this world," he had said. He had come into the world from beyond the world and so was indeed divine.

Pilate, fearful and unnerved, began to bluster. "Speakest thou not unto me? knowest thou not that I have power to crucify thee, and have power to release thee?"

Our Lord answered, "Thou couldest have no power at all against me, except it were given thee from above: therefore he that delivered me unto thee hath the greater sin."

God's stern rebuke to the blustering arrogance of man is accompanied here, as is the way of God, by such tenderness, as though he were looking for excuses for his son. The reply so touched Pilate that for the last time he went back to the balcony and tried just once more. But still he could do nothing. "Crucify him!" was the only answer he could get from the crowd, and turning in a last appeal to the chief priests he was suddenly confronted with blackmail.

"If thou let this man go, thou art not Caesar's friend: whosoever maketh himself a king, speaketh against Caesar." They would tell Caesar that Pilate had backed the pretensions of a man who had dared to call himself King of the Jews. Pilate's very career was in danger now, and from two directions at once. A dangerous riot might be fatal to him and so might lies told behind his back to the Emperor. When a weak man once gives way he gives way suddenly and badly, as Pilate did now. He was tired out, worn down, finished. He capitulated. But he would punish these priests who had beaten him. "Shall I crucify your King?" he demanded savagely.

Since they had repudiated a king of their own to this they could make only one reply. "We have no king but Caesar." They hated Caesar, but Pilate had made them admit that Caesar was their king. He sat down and the death warrant was brought to him and he signed it. Then for the third and last time he tried to shift the responsibility. He sent for a bowl of water and washed his hands before them all, so that the mob could see what he was doing. "I am innocent of the blood of this just person," he said. "See ye to it."

And the mob shouted back, "His blood be on us, and on our children."

But Pilate must have known, even as he washed his hands, that it was on him too. Like Caiaphas he had taken the coward's way, the way of expediency, and for fear of what might come condemned an innocent man to death. He could not shift the responsibility, but there was one more bit of revenge that he could take against the men who had forced him to this. It was the custom to nail an inscription to the cross, above the head of the man who hung there, with his name written upon it and the crime for which he had been condemned; and the parchment was brought to Pilate that he should do this. He wrote upon it, "Jesus of Nazareth the King of the Jews." And he wrote it three times over, in the three languages of the country, Hebrew, Greek, and Latin. Just as he had cried, "Ecce Homo!" for all the world to hear, so he wrote this that every man who looked upon the cross that day, Jew or Greek or Roman, would know he looked upon a king. Grimly he showed the chief priests what he had written and saw by their faces that he had infuriated them as much as he had hoped he would.

"Write not, The King of the Jews; but that he said, I am King of the Jews," they implored him.

"What I have written I have written," said Pilate, and turning his back on them all he went away.

The soldiers took Our Lord down into the castle courtyard again and made him ready for his death. They took off the purple robe and put his own clothes on him. Two thieves who were to be crucified with him were brought out from their cells and made ready too. The three crosses that they had to carry through the streets of the city to the place of execution were dragged out from the place where they were kept. And the door of Barabbas' cell was unlocked and he was set free.

In this glorious and terrible story all that we need to know has been told us, yet there remain so many questions that we cannot help asking ourselves. Had Barabbas watched the scourging through the grill of his cell? As he went out into freedom did he speak to the man who was dying that he might live? Freedom and life are gifts to every one of us from Our Lord, won for us by his death, but Barabbas was the first of us to take the freedom and the life from his hands. They must have greeted each other in the castle courtyard, Our Lord with such joy that he could die for his son, Barabbas with shame and gratitude that would deepen later into penitence and bring him at last to Paradise.

2.

There is another sinner whom we have to look at now for a moment, hateful though it is to look at him. When Judas knew that Our Lord was condemned the darkness that had blinded him was lifted and he saw the truth. He saw the holiness, the beauty, the light and love of Our Lord, and over against this loveliness he saw himself. And he, this thing that he was, this hideous thing, had with his darkness put out the light.

He ran through the streets, panting, sweating, half-crazed with remorse, and came to the Temple, to the court where the Sanhedrin were accustomed to meet and where they were probably waiting until it was time for the crucifixion. "I have sinned," he said, "in that I have betrayed the innocent blood," and we do not know if he shrieked it out, or sobbed it, or whispered it. They did not care. The sight of his agony was nothing to them. "What is that to us?" they said. And he took the thirty pieces of silver and flung them on the ground and turned and rushed out into the street again. But there was nowhere he could go. He had no home and no friend, for he had destroyed the man who was both his home and his friend. And wherever he went he would have with him this thing that was himself, this filthy thing that he loathed with a sick loathing that was killing him.

He came at last to some lonely place, some yard or field where there was a tree or a beam jutting out of a wall, something that provided a man with the means of doing away with himself. He had lost sight of Our Lord now, he did not see him any longer, but only himself, this thing that he could not endure, that at all costs he must get rid of. Yet it was not too late even now. If now he could have cried out to Our Lord for forgiveness he would have been forgiven. But he could not do that. Despair is not penitence. It is the self-disgust of the proud, the sort of misery that a vain woman feels who looks in the glass, and sees her beauty gone, and weeps for rage. He was too proud a man to take himself humbly and lay that self down at the feet of Our Lord in penitence, and too self-absorbed a man to wrench his sight away from himself and look up to God, and for utter love of what he saw struggle up out of himself to the light. Cutting himself off from Our Lord he was alone with what he was, and that is hell. He took his girdle from about his waist, fitted a noose round his neck, hanged himself, and "went to his own place."

3.

Just outside one of the city gates, the Gate Genath, beside the main road that led into Jerusalem from the north, was a piece of deserted ground where the executions took place. It was called Golgotha, the Place of a Skull, and tradition has always called it the rock, or hill, of Golgotha, or Calvary. The way through the streets from the castle of Antonia to the Gate Genath, the Via Dolorosa along which condemned men carried their crosses, was only a short distance but it must have seemed a very long way to them because it led uphill, and the crosses weighed so heavily on bodies weakened by torture and imprisonment, and the narrow streets were packed with a brutal mob come to stare and jeer, to make coarse jokes and fling filth and insults at the prisoners. For the cross was the gallows of that day and crucifixion a death of disgrace as well as torture. The Romans had adopted it from the Carthaginians, the most cruel of the ancient peoples, but they never insulted a Roman citizen by putting him to death in such a way, they kept it for slaves and subject peoples. So when God chose this way to die he went right down into the very depths of misery and degradation and made himself one with all the enslaved and persecuted wretches who have ever lived.

The procession made its way out of the gates of the castle, out into the crowded street. A centurion on horseback, leading troops of the Twelfth Legion, came first, clearing a way through the mob. Behind him came a legionary bearing a placard on a pole with the crimes of the prisoners written upon it. He was followed by the prisoners carrying their crosses, and then by more troops carrying whips to scourge on the prisoners and keep back the crowd. It is thought that Our Lord was not wearing the crown of thorns now but that one of the soldiers carried it that he might be crowned with it upon his throne, the cross.

We Christians speak glibly sometimes of "bearing the cross" when we are putting up with a few aches and pains and some inconveniences, but one glance at this bearing of the cross should strike us silent and ashamed. The man who is bearing the cross now, Our Lord and Our God, yet true man, with the flesh and nerves and mind and spirit of a man, and in the perfection of his being more sensitive to suffering than any man has ever been, had already endured hours of torment—spiritual, mental, and physical. It had gone on all night. He had had no sleep, no rest. He had been hurried from one place to another, pushed about, shouted at, insulted, and beaten. If he had eaten at all it had only been prison fare, coarse bread and little of it. He had lost blood in the scourging and upon his wounded back they had laid the weight of the cross. He must have been almost too weak to move, in too much pain to get his breath, yet he had to lift up his arms and hold it and then move forward beneath the weight of it. That a man so weakened should carry that cross uphill through shouting jeering crowds, under the heat of the sun, was a thing impossible. Yet it was done. There is a courage that does the impossible thing and endures the unendurable suffering. And there is also a courage that does not refuse help.

Our Lord must have been down several times, and up again, and on, before he fainted, and Longinus the centurion realized that though the courage of this man was undefeatable his physical strength could come to an end. Getting off his horse to deal with this dilemma he saw a strong-looking man in the crowd and shouted to him to help the prisoner bear his cross. Simon of Cyrene refused. Perhaps he swore and refused in fury. Why should he touch the accursed cross? Why should he help a fainting criminal? He had to be compelled—perhaps with the whips. Cyrene is in Africa, and if Simon was an African the centurion would have had no compunction in using the whips. Flogging and lynching have been the lot of black men through much of their history, and it was fitting that one of them should lift some of the weight of the cross off God's torn shoulders and help him carry it to Calvary. Our Lord, as he came back to consciousness again, would have felt what any brave young man would feel; ashamed and sorry that he had not been able to keep on his feet, hating the fuss and commotion. Yet he had the courage to accept the unwilling, grudging help humbly and gratefully, so that he might get to Calvary and die there. It would have been a great deal easier to refuse help and die in the street, but it would not have saved us from our sins. By the time they reached the end of that terrible journey Simon was no longer unwilling. We know this because his two sons, Alexander and Rufus, later became Christians. And so did Longinus the centurion.

Sometimes, when we think that there is no suffering that can come to us that Our Lord has not endured before us, we make one reservation. We say, "He did not have to be old." But in this falling beneath the cross Our Lord endured all that is miserable in old age. It is not being old in itself that hurts; it is becoming weak and unable to go on any more, and falling down ignominiously beneath burdens that you have carried successfully up till now, and then on top of all that having to be helped along the way to death by somebody who perhaps does not want to help and only does it because he is ordered to. Our Lord may have died young, but there is nothing about old age that he does not know. Upon the Via Dolorosa he began in his own person the redemptive suffering of it, and the old, everywhere, throughout time, carry on his work and "fill up that which is behind in the afflictions of Christ."

Mary the Mother of God stood in the crowd and saw her son go by. She had need now of all her long years of training in fortitude. We can believe that she stood erect and watched him, silent and tearless, exactly like him in her quiet acceptance of something that would have been too terrible to bear if it had not been that it had to be borne. She had brought him into the world, and as a little boy he had had great need of her to love him and look after him, and he would need her again now, to comfort him in his dying and care for his body when he was dead. So she turned and followed him uphill to Calvary. John the beloved disciple, Mary Magdalene, and her sister Mary Cleophas were with her; but they were nearer the breaking point than she was. Her heart did not break because he had need of her heart. He had always needed her. Even when they had been separated in body she had been with him, suffering with him and working with him, and so his passion was her passion too and she would be with him wherever she could. Father Andrew in his book *God's Adventure* suggests that even at Gethsemane she was with him. She had followed him at a distance to the garden and knelt there watching him. She could not go near him, for this was something that he must pass through alone with his Father, but she could watch and pray as the disciples had failed to do. If that is so it is she who recorded what happened then, who saw the vision of the angel strengthening him. The vision would have strengthened her too, carrying her back to the angel of the Annunciation and the great "Fear not." She would have known that in the power of God they would come through this, her son and she, for underneath are the Everlasting Arms.

Amongst the crowd of people that pressed about the prisoners were those who grieved and were sorry as well as those who mocked. There is a story told of a woman called Veronica who, seeing Our Lord half blinded by the sweat pouring down his face, came forward and wiped it away. And afterward she found the outline of his face upon her handkerchief. And there were many women who wailed and lamented, perhaps mothers whose children Our Lord had healed, and to them Our Lord spoke the only words he uttered on this journey. Simon was helping him now, and by this time with a will, taking the weight of the cross, and he had strength to speak. His words show us what was in his mind upon this journey—not his own agony but the agony of his people that had been haunting him in the days before his arrest.

"Daughters of Jerusalem, weep not for me, but weep for yourselves, and for your children. For, behold, the days are coming, in the which they shall say, Blessed are the barren, and the wombs that never bare, and the paps which never gave suck. Then shall they begin to say to the mountains, Fall on us; and to the hills, Cover us. For if they do these things in a green tree, what shall be done in the dry?"

The procession of death wound its way out of the city gate and came in sight of the hill of Calvary.

4.

Even the most selfless people, when they are suffering, find it hard to think of anything but their own pain, but throughout his passion Our Lord was thinking of the people about him and praying for them. He was still praying for his own people as they climbed up the hill to the place of execution, and then these same people were forced back by the Roman spears so that the legionaries might get on with their work in the open space at the top of the hill. It was terrible work that they had to do and though it was part of the routine of their life they must have hated doing it, especially when their prisoners fought and struggled. Before they started they offered each man a drink of wine mingled with myrrh and other drugs. The effect would not last long but it would just deaden the beginning of the pain. The two thieves gulped their drink thankfully but Our Lord refused his. He wanted to keep his mind as clear as he could that he might go on praying. It was of these other sons of his, these

Romans, that he was thinking now, and for them he was praying as they stripped his clothes off him and laid him on the ground upon the cross—of them and of all wretched men everywhere and always who are forced by a brutal system not of their own devising to do brutal things and be brutalized by what they do, through no fault of their own.

"Father, forgive them; for they know not what they do."

When the one man was nailed on his cross and the other two tied, the crosses were raised and lowered into the pits in the ground prepared for them. Then the legionaries took up their stations to keep guard until the end, and the crowd was allowed to come nearer and pass by the crosses and look upon the torment of these three men. The sight of such pain did not silence them and they mocked as they passed by. "Thou that destroyest the temple, and buildest it in three days, save thyself," they shouted at Our Lord. "If thou be the Son of God, come down from the cross." And the chief priests, passing by, had their revenge for that inscription that Pilate had written for the cross. "If he be the King of Israel, let him now come down from the cross, and we will believe him," they said. They followed that by the most cruel jibe of which they were capable. Our Lord's trust in God his Father had always been unshakable, and they knew it, and now they taunted him with the fact that God had deserted him. "He trusted in God; let him deliver him now, if he will have him: for he said, I am the Son of God."

And then unknown to themselves, thinking only that they were tormenting Our Lord, they spoke the great truth about redemption. "He saved others; himself he cannot save."

The sun was high now, and the heat was adding the misery of thirst to the other torments of the crucified men. The hours would be very long and some of the soldiers sat down on the ground to pass the time as best they could. They divided the prisoners' clothes among them, as was the custom. Our Lord's white festal robe, that Mary had woven without seam, was left over. In spite of the blood and dirt that stained it they could see what a beautiful garment it was, and they did not tear it up and divide it among them but cast lots as to who should have it. In doing this they fulfilled the Psalmist's prophecy of the suffering Christ, "They parted my raiment among them, and for my vesture they did cast lots."

The crosses of the two thieves stood one on each side of Our Lord's cross, and his arms and bleeding hands were stretched out toward them, in prayer for them and for all rogues and vaga- bonds everywhere and always. Half-crazed with their pain they too jeered at Our Lord. They had heard the taunt of the priests, that Our Lord had trusted in God his Father and that God had deserted him, and they echoed it. In the bitter words of the Gospel, they "cast the same in his teeth." They could have thought of no more cruel jibe to fling at him, and it must have caused him piercing grief even though he did not, yet, believe it. Even in his pain he still believed that his Father was with him and prayed to his Father for these two suffering men on either side of him. For one of them the pain became more than he could bear and he cried out, "If thou be Christ, save thyself and us," and then railed at Our Lord because the pain went on. Yet the silence of God's prayer reached out to these two and held them, saving them in ways they did not understand. One of them, Dismas by name, as the minutes that were like hours dragged by, did begin to understand something, and what he understood was the difference between himself and the man beside him. He had come now to the place where Peter had been when he cried, "Depart from me, for I am a sinful man, O Lord," and Judas when he said, "I have sinned in that I have betrayed the innocent blood." He and the other thief were criminals who had risked and deserved the gallows, and got their just deserts. But not this man between them. He had done nothing to merit this pain and death. The cursing and muttering of the other man was suddenly intolerable to this thief, an insult to some splendor that he had caught a glimpse of here between them, and he told the other man to be quiet. "Dost thou not fear God, seeing thou art in the same condemnation? And we indeed justly; for we receive the due reward of our deeds: but this man hath done nothing amiss." But he did not, as Judas had done, stay bogged in the filth of his own sin, helpless and despairing, he wrenched himself out of it toward the splendor beside him, just as perhaps he turned his head on the cross, though the movement was an added torture, to look at Jesus. We do not know for how long he looked, but during the silence between this cry of penitence and the cry of love that followed he traveled a long way. Men do sometimes travel quickly and far when they are suffering, further perhaps in ten minutes of great pain than ten years of ease. Looking at Our Lord he knew at last what he wanted, and had always wanted. He wanted just this very splendor of love that was beside him and upholding him, this man whom they called the King of the Jews. He wanted to be with him always.

"Lord, remember me when thou comest into thy kingdom."

Perhaps Dismas scarcely knew what he was saying, but he knew the royalty of this man, and Our Lord's prayer for him was the very air of the kingdom of love breathed upon him, and so the right words came. Though all the words that the soul speaks as the prayer of Christ draws her up to him are the right words. "Like as the hart panteth after the water brooks . . . I will arise and go to my Father . . . Lord, remember me." And sometimes there are no words, only that abandonment of the soul in love that gives such joy to God.

Before the thief had moved to look at him Our Lord had turned his head in pain upon the cross toward his son. He was ready, waiting with that humble waiting of Almighty God that breaks to pieces the pride of sinners when they think of it. The moment the love was offered he accepted it with an outpouring of his own, with joy and gratitude.

"Verily I say unto thee, To day shalt thou be with me in paradise."

This "Verily I say unto thee," which we love so much as we hear it chiming like a bell again and again through the Gospels, is spoken here for the last time while Our Lord was still in a human body like our own. We do not hear it again until after the Resurrection, when his body was no longer like ours. And so it makes of this promise something of supreme importance, a particular bright star among the promises, the leader of them all. Indeed and indeed I say unto you. It is true. It is real. Hold on to it. The lover and beloved will meet. Every sinner who loves me and longs for me will find me. One day you will see me and be with me. However long you may wait, however desperate the struggle, there will come a day that is "today."

Although Our Lord's prayer on the cross was for every man and woman and child who has ever lived, from the beginning of time until the end of time, he did not forget his own family. His Mother stood by his cross with Mary Cleophas and John and Mary Magdalene. The courage of those four, in being there, is the measure of their love. His love, the love of God, upheld them then and made them able to bear it, while their human love upheld him, Jesus the man, and helped him, too, to bear it. Looking down at his Mother and John, his two best beloved, he thought about them and planned for them. They would be lonely without him. The time would seem long until it was "today" for them. But he thought of a way to comfort them.

"Woman, behold thy son. . . . Behold thy mother."

And from that hour John was a son to Mary, and she was a mother to him.

Dark clouds had come up and hidden the burning sun. It grew

darker and darker, and by midday it was like night. But there was none of the kindly coolness of night for it was stifling and hot. The breathless heat and stillness, the darkness at midday when it should have been bright and shining and clear with all the crickets chirping, must have been terrifying, and many of the people who had only come to mock and stare hurried away, smiting their breasts in fear. When things are frightening and uncanny, and that deep unexplainable fear of something or other that is always at the back of one's mind comes forward and captures the whole mind, men go home if they can. They feel safer there. And so we can feel sure that the only people who remained close to the cross now were the centurion and his men, whom discipline and obedience to duty kept there, afraid or not afraid, and those to whom home was wherever Our Lord was, even though that might be on a lonely hill in the darkness beneath the cross. As Our Lord passes now into the deepest and most dreadful part of his agony it is comforting to think that hatred and mockery had drawn back, leaving only obedience, courage, and love to watch with him.

In the darkness the watchers would no longer have been able to see the faces of the three men on their crosses. They would have heard the two thieves sobbing, and perhaps muttering in delirium as the high fever of great pain muddled their minds, but from the central cross came only silence. Mary the Mother of Our Lord, and John, would have known that he whom they loved had passed away from them into some depth and darkness of suffering where they could not follow. With the physical pain they had had some comradeship of understanding, and when they could speak to Our Lord and hear him speak to them the unbearable was bearable, but now they were shut out and separated from the beloved and had to bear a pain that, though not to be compared with his in intensity, was the same in essence.

For his agony was the torment of separation from God, the

torment of the damned that he was enduring to save us from damnation. It was the knowledge that he would have to endure this that had made him sweat blood in the garden. How this agony came upon him we cannot know. The taunt of the chief priests, "He trusted in God; let him deliver him now, if he will have him," had been quoted from the terrible 22nd psalm, in which the suffering servant of God feels that God has forsaken him. The thought of God's desertion had perhaps come into his mind then, taking firmer and firmer hold of it as his weakness increased, and was the gate through which his spirit passed into the final darkness. This darkness and Our Lord's silence lasted for three hours. No word of love came to break it, no star shining for us in the night. The depth of the mystery of the love of God can never be for us anything but silence and darkness.

At the end of the three hours the silence was broken and the darkness rent by that most terrible cry from the cross.

"Eloi, eloi, lama sabachthani? My God, my God, why hast thou forsaken me?"

Our Lord's heart broke with that cry. He had borne all that even he could bear. But though that cry must have nearly broken Mary's heart too she knew by it that her son had come back to her. His cry was from the 22nd psalm. He had come back through the same gate by which he had gone away. His next words, though deep beneath their human meaning is God's great thirst for the souls of men and man's thirst for God, were yet simple as those of a child, words that she must have heard so often when he was a little boy. It was as the human son of Mary that he said,

"I thirst."

The light was coming back and the soldiers, looking up at him, could see his face again and realized that he was dying. Strong men lived sometimes for days upon the cross and it must have astonished them to see this strong young man at the end after

283

only several hours of it. Even the most brutal of men are pitiful to the dying, and one of the soldiers filled a sponge with vinegar and put it on a reed and held it up to him. He had refused the drug offered him before the crucifixion, offered as a mere matter of routine without much pity, but he did not refuse the vinegar. He was never known to refuse a free gift of love. When he had received the vinegar he cried out,

"It is finished!"

It was a cry of victory. He had finished the work that his Father had given him to do. He had accomplished the will of God. His last thought was that his Father had not forsaken him after all. He said gently and peacefully,

"Father, into thy hands I commend my spirit."

And then he bowed his head and died.

5.

Longinus the centurion was standing very close to Our Lord when he died. St. Mark says he "stood over against him." He had seen courage often enough but never until today the perfection of it. He had seen innumerable men die, but never a death like this. Like the penitent thief he had traveled a long way in the hours that had passed since he rode his horse up the Via Dolorosa at the head of the procession of death. Now, as the light came back, he stood beneath the cross and made his confession of faith. "Truly, this man was the Son of God," he said. It was exactly the same as Peter's, "Thou art the Christ, the Son of the living God," and Martha's, "I believe that thou art the Christ, the Son of God." That men and women should say that was the reason why Jesus of Nazareth lived and died. When we can truly say that we have seen God revealed in Christ, then on that foundation stone Our Lord can build up our salvation.

His confession made and his obedience offered up the centurion went on with his work. The Roman practice of leaving the victims on the cross until they died, or until their executioners got tired of seeing them there and in mercy killed them, had to be modified at Jerusalem, where the Jewish law forbade a victim to hang on the cross all night. If the men had not died by the late afternoon they had to be dispatched by the crucifragium, the breaking of the legs. It was after three o'clock, and the two thieves were still living, and the Romans killed them in this way. They had seen Our Lord die and so they did not have to do that to him, but one of them, to make quite sure, pierced his heart with a spear and from the wound there flowed blood and water. St. John, who saw it, writes, "he that saw it bare record, and his record is true; and he knoweth that he saith true, that ye might believe." We speak easily of breaking hearts, but doctors say that when a heart has in very truth actually broken a liquid resembling water flows out from it with the blood. It is therefore absolutely impossible for us ever to doubt the love of God when we know that upon a certain day in time, on a certain rocky hill upon this earth, God's heart actually broke for us.

The legionaries took the bodies down from the crosses and we can believe that they handled them gently, glad that the pain was over. With the bodies of the two thieves they did whatever they were accustomed to do with the bodies of criminals, which were the property of Rome, but Our Lord's friends were not going to have his body left to the care of Roman executioners if they could help it. Two of them worked hard for his honor and the comfort of his mother. These two were Nicodemus, who had come by night to Jesus so long ago, and had heard him say, "God so loved the world . . . ," and Joseph of Arimathea, a secret disciple of Our Lord's, who was also a member of the Sanhedrin.

285

These two must have fought hard to save Our Lord, but two against so many would have had no chance. St. Luke gives us a splendid word picture of Joseph. "And, behold, there was a man named Joseph, a counsellor; and he was a good man and a just: (The same had not consented to the council and deed of them;) he was of Arimathea, a city of the Jews: who also himself waited for the kingdom of God. This man went unto Pilate, and begged the body of Jesus."

That was a brave action of Joseph's, for he might have been put in prison for it. But Pilate gave his permission at once, thankful perhaps that there was one thing he could do for the just man he had condemned to death. Nicodemus meanwhile had collected the spices with which the Jewish people embalmed the bodies of their dead, myrrh and aloes, about a hundred-pound weight, which would have cost a great deal, but he did not care what he spent if only he could honor his Lord. These two men came together to the cross, and the body of their Master was given into their keeping. In a garden close to Calvary was a new rock-hewn tomb which belonged to Joseph of Arimathea. Like so many rich men with orderly, forward-looking minds he must have made preparations for his own dignified burial and purchased this fine tomb for himself. But his own burial mattered nothing to him now, in comparison with Our Lord's, and gladly he gave up his tomb. Members of the Sanhedrin had increased Our Lord's pain upon the cross by their hatred and mockery, but these two did what they could now to atone for that by their generosity and love and care.

Joseph had bought fine new linen for a shroud and in this they carried the body of Our Lord to the tomb in the quiet garden. There went with them the faithful ones who had watched by the cross, and other women who had ministered to him and the disciples in Galilee. It was getting late and they could not now perform the full Eastern ritual of the embalming of the body. That must wait until the morrow of the Sabbath was over, and the third day had come. But they did what they could, washing the beloved body and wrapping it closely in the winding sheet, with a napkin folded about the head, and putting little bunches of spices between the folds of the linen. Then they laid their Lord's body gently on the slab of rock within the tomb, as though sleeping on a bed, and were comforted a little, as are all mourners always, by the splendor of a good man's face in death, and the peace of the knowledge that no pain could wrack him or evil touch him ever again. They came away, and the men rolled a great stone across the opening of the tomb, and they left the quiet garden and went home to rest through the Sabbath until the third day dawned and they could come again to the tomb. As John took Mary the Mother of Our Lord, and his mother too now, through the quiet streets to his home, his arm about her because she was almost too tired to walk, did they say to each other, "Do you remember what he said? 'After three days I will rise again.'" If they said that to each other, if they remembered, there would have been a hope in their hearts which would have kept them from weeping.

The next day the chief priests also remembered something Our Lord had said about rising again on the third day, and they were uneasy. Perhaps their uneasiness was increased by the strange ending to that Friday of darkness and fear. There had been an earthquake and the curtain that hung in the Temple between the Holy of Holies and the outer court, symbolizing the separation of the Holy God from his sinful people, had been torn in half from the top to the bottom, just as though the separation had vanished and God and man were made at one. And rocks had been rent and tombs flung open and good people in the city of Jerusalem were saying that they had seen visions of saints who had left this world. It was almost as though something tremendous had happened in Paradise, as though that life

287

was invading this one, as though a great wave of joy was breaking against the curtain between that life and this and sending it billowing in. The chief priests did not like it and they went to Pilate and said, "Sir, we remember that that deceiver said, while he was yet alive, After three days I will rise again. Command therefore that the sepulchre be made sure until the third day, lest his disciples come by night and steal him away, and say unto the people, He is risen from the dead: so the last error shall be worse than the first."

Pilate said, "Ye have a watch: go your way, make it as sure as ye can."

He spoke surely with sarcasm. He was aware of the billowing of that curtain and knew that against a certain power that is sometimes abroad in the world men are quite helpless. Nevertheless, what could be done was done. A great seal was put on the stone that had been rolled before the tomb, and soldiers of the Temple guard kept watch in the garden through the quiet Sabbath and through the long still night of moon and stars that followed. It was the holiest night the world has known, except that night when Christ was born.

Almighty and everlasting God, who of thy tender love towards mankind, hath sent thy Son, our Saviour Jesus Christ, to take upon him our flesh, and to suffer death upon the cross, that all mankind should follow the example of his great humility; mercifully grant, that we may both follow the example of his patience, and also be made partakers of his resurrection; through the same Jesus Christ Our Lord. Amen.

—Collect for the Sunday before Easter

Chapter 12

VICTORY

Death is swallowed up in victory. O death, where is thy sting? O grave, where is thy victory?

—1 Corinthians XV:54–55

1.

T IS all joy now, the greatest joy that this earth has ever known, or ever will know until Our Lord and Saviour Jesus Christ comes again and raises her up from her old bondage to sin and death to share his resurrection life with him. Even now she shares it, in each new spring with its bird song and budding leaves; she shared his joy before it came to him on earth and in time, shares it now, shares it in all the springtimes that will ever be, because with God there is no time but only the eternal now of his everlasting joy. And we share it too. Every baby's birth, every death that is the birth of a soul in Paradise, every fresh beginning in our bodily life, every repentance and new birth of the spirit, every waking up to a new morning, every birth of a picture or a poem or a friendship, all laughter, all song spring from this one fount of the life of God triumphant over death. This is the third movement of the symphony of this life, only it is unlike any other music that the world has ever heard because it has no ending. God lives.

The next day very early in the morning, when the light was just creeping into the sky and the cocks were crowing, Mary Magdalene, Mary Cleophas, and Salome, the mother of James and John, walked quickly and quietly through the deserted streets of Jerusalem. They were going to embalm the body of their Lord and they carried with them more precious spices, ointments, and fresh linen. Mary the Mother of Our Lord was not with them. Though her spirit was unbroken her body had by this time borne all it could. The two Marys and Salome, their eyelids swollen with their weeping and their faces drawn and tired, felt a little less wretched now that there was something they could do for their Lord, and they talked a little about the trivial things that one does talk about when one is unhappy, just to turn one's mind away from the grief for a moment or two. Had they got everything they wanted, they asked each other; they wondered if the gate in the city wall would be open and if the earthquake shock that had come at the ending of the night had done much damage.

The gate was open and they came to the garden just as the sun was rising. The olive trees sparkled in the silver light and the garden was fresh and lovely. There was the scent of flowers and the birds were singing. But they stopped, and looked at each other in sudden dismay. As always happens when one is utterly worn out they had remembered everything except what mattered most. . . . That great stone rolled across the opening of the tomb —who was going to move it for them? How were they going to get in? Then one of them remembered the soldiers whom they had heard were keeping guard over the tomb. Perhaps they would be kind, remembering their own dead, and roll away the stone and let them go into the tomb. Heartened, they went on again.

But when they reached the tomb the soldiers had gone. There was no one there—only the birds, bursting their throats with joy. But the stone was rolled away.

Their hearts were beating unaccountably as they came to the door of the tomb, bent their veiled heads in reverence for their Lord who lay there, and stepped inside. Then quickly and, instinctively their eyes went to the stone slab where they had laid their beloved. He was not there. And though it was so early there was no darkness or clammy gloom inside the tomb; there was light. And such light, more glorious than the light of the rising sun outside, yet gentle as the light of the moon and the stars. And there was a fragrance and a freshness here that did not come from the dawn and the flowers in the garden but was the very breath of heaven. The freshness and the light came from two figures who sat one at the head and one at the foot where the body of Jesus had lain, keeping their guard over that bit of holy stone. And there in the midst of the light they saw smiling eyes that looked at them and lips that curved with tenderness. But they fell on their knees and hid their eyes in terror, for the smiling faces were not of this world and they could not endure to look upon their light.

"Fear not ye."

The fear died in them, for they knew that God loved them. There was nothing to be feared anywhere, in heaven or on earth or in hell, for God was alive and God loved them. But they could not look again on those smiling faces, and it was with covered eyes that they heard a voice speaking, a heavenly voice weaving in and out of the song of the birds. And words formed in their minds, words that formed a message that they could remember and repeat, so that we know it now by heart. "Ye seek

Jesus, which was crucified. He is not here; for he is risen, as he said. Come, see the place where the Lord lay. And go quickly, and tell his disciples that he is risen from the dead; and, behold, he goeth before you into Galilee; there shall ye see him: lo, I have told you."

They were outside, and in the garden again, without knowing how they had got there. And Mary Cleophas and Salome, obedient to the heavenly vision, went quickly out of the garden, through the gate into the city and through the streets to the house of grief where Peter and John were gathering their courage to face the misery of a new day.

But Mary Magdalene was not with them for she had flown on ahead of them, and not in joy but in misery and despair. Wildly impetuous, passionately loving creature that she was, she had not waited with Salome and the other Mary to breathe the air of heaven and hear the angel's voice. That one glimpse of the empty tomb had sent her nearly crazy. The agony of Good Friday had been followed by two sleepless nights and a long day of grief through which she had kept herself sane with the thought that she would see her Lord's face once more, kneel at his feet just once more, render him one more service. It was not good-by forever—not yet. She would see his face again. And then —the tomb had been empty. There was nothing there. The body of the beloved had been stolen. The shock was so dreadful for her that her bruised mind could not grasp the meaning of the light and glory in the cave. It meant nothing to her. Her Lord was gone. She burst in upon Peter and John crying out, "They have taken away the Lord out of the sepulchre, and we know not where they have laid him!" And then she was running back again through the streets, taking a different way to Mary Cleophas and Salome, back to the garden, to the place where her hope had been, but where her hope now was dead.

She stood at the entrance to the empty tomb, leaning against the cold stone, crying her heart out, and as though she were not suffering enough already she turned to look down once more into the tomb and see the empty place. The glorious two were still sitting there, one at the head and one at the foot where the body of Jesus had lain, but despair is not able to see heavenly things. Yet she heard a voice marveling at her despair with tender amazement; for all the birds were singing and the world was pulsing with light. "Woman, why weepest thou?" It must have seemed to her a voice in her own crazed mind for she just sobbed out over again what she had said to Peter and John, "Because they have taken away my Lord, and I know not where they have laid him."

She must go somewhere. She must do something. She could not go on looking at the empty tomb. She dragged herself round and heard again the same gentle question repeated, not from inside the tomb this time but from outside.

"Woman, why weepest thou?"

There was a man standing there in the garden.

"Whom seekest thou?"

She could not see who it was, for her tears blinded her, but she supposed he was the gardener, and hope was born in her again. He would know, perhaps, where her beloved lay. She spoke to him, her voice hoarse and broken with her weeping. "Sir, if thou have borne him hence, tell me where thou hast laid him, and I will take him away."

"Mary."

Their own name, spoken by a voice they love, can sometimes bring people back from unconsciousness, from near madness, even from the brink of death. With just the speaking of her name Mary's bruised mind was healed and her blind eyes were opened. She looked up and saw him who had been dead alive

293

again, young and most glorious, the body that had been tortured strong with a new strength, the face that had been "marred more than that of any man" alight with a new beauty. And yet he was the same. The change was just that his mortal youth had become immortal and his human strength and beauty had been given back to him eternally. Though he stood in light and seemed robed in it he was the same Jesus of Nazareth whom she knew, her Master and her Lord, and would be forever. Kneeling in her old place at his feet she gave him the joyous greeting of "Rabboni!" and reached out her hands to touch his shining feet, and hold the stuff of his robe of light in her hands.

"Touch me not," he said gently, "for I am not yet ascended to my Father: but go to my brethren and say unto them, I ascend unto my Father, and your Father; and to my God, and your God."

A little later his children were able to touch him, to hold his warm living hands and touch gently the scars upon them, and we do not know quite certainly why Mary was not able to do that now. Yet with Our Lord's words to help us we dare make our human conjectures. We know that Our Lord had passed from his cross to Paradise, to the place where we all go when we die, and where he had promised the penitent thief he would be with him. That visit to Paradise is for us a deep silence, but as in the other silences there is one sentence in the Bible that tells us just something. St. Peter in his epistle says that before Our Lord's resurrection "he preached to the spirits who were in prison." That is, he went among the ignorant souls who long for God and taught them and saved them in that world just as he had done in this. There, as here, there was no part of our experience that he did not share with us. For our sakes he chose to be a disembodied spirit for a little while, just as we must be, and while he preached to the souls in prison he was not yet clothed upon with his glorious resurrection body. Perhaps the body that Mary saw was not yet, if we dare put it like that, quite finished. Though she saw him clearly, perhaps if she had touched his feet she would not have felt them between her hands. It would seem from what Our Lord said to her that upon Easter Day there was some sort of ascent to the Father that completed his human experience, and that after that, when he came from the Father to visit his children on earth, his body was the perfectly completed body that Thomas touched when he cried, "My Lord and my God!" Because he is true man what he did we will do, too. For us, too, one day, when we have been purified, there will be an ascent to the Father, a union with him, that is beyond our understanding now, and we, too, shall be clothed with a resurrection body like Our Lord's. With us, it all takes so dreadfully long, because of our sin. For his perfection the journey was very short.

How lovingly he comforted Mary, because she could not touch him yet. "My Father and your Father. My God and your God." That locked them close together. Between souls in their human bodies, souls set free from them, souls clothed with the new body, there is bound to be some measure of separation. Yet what does it matter? We all meet and are one in God our Father.

2.

Our Lord went his heavenly way home to his Father, and Mary ran like the wind through the streets to tell her glorious news, and the garden was deserted for a few minutes while that lovely spring day laughed and warmed itself, and glowed there at the heart of time and breathed out its fragrance to all the years. On the grass lay a spear, perhaps, that had been flung down, or an overturned lantern among the flowers, left there when the soldiers fled at the rending of the tomb. We do not wonder that they fled when we read the brief record they have left of their experience.

"And, behold, there was a great earthquake: for the angel of the Lord descended from heaven, and came and rolled back the stone from the door, and sat upon it. His countenance was like lightning, and his raiment white as snow. And for fear of him the keepers did shake, and became as dead men."

There is no terror for us, only exultation as we picture that great angel rolling away the stone with a touch of his finger. And then he "sat upon it." Surely he laughed as he sat there, and surely there was mockery upon his heavenly, terrible, laughing face, the mockery both of the psalmist and of Puck. "The fool hath said in his heart, there is no God. . . . Lord, what fools these mortals be." Men think they can get rid of God by burying him and saying he does not exist, and sometimes there comes a long black night when it almost seems that they are right. But then, to the terror of men and the joy of angels, God breaks out.

Two men came running into the garden, running like the wind as Mary had done. The youngest got there first, but when he reached the entrance to the tomb, after one glance that showed him nothing but the gleam of the white graveclothes, he checked suddenly and leaned breathless and panting against the rock, his face hidden in the crook of his arm. He could not go in. What if the women, crazed with their grief, had imagined it all? When he went inside would he see the stiff swathed body of the beloved lying there as he had seen it when he said good-by on Friday night? Or, far worse, a desecrated tomb from which thieves had stolen the body. That would kill him. That would kill his dead heart all over again.

But the older man, catching up with John, ran past him and

stumbled down the stone steps into the tomb. Then his shaking knees gave way beneath him and he sank down to the rock floor, and gazed stupidly out of his red-rimmed sleepless eyes at what he saw—just a pile of graveclothes lying on the stone. It conveyed nothing to him. He was more desperate than John, more bruised in mind than Mary, more grief-stricken even than the Mother of Our Lord. For he had denied his Lord. Three times over he had denied him. Peter had not gone to the cross with the others. Where he had been all that time we do not know. He had been in some private hell of his own somewhere and what he suffered in it only he and Jesus knew.

John recovered his courage and followed Peter down into the tomb. If the two glorious ones were still there John did not see them. He was intent only on the graveclothes, and to his clearer, calmer mind they brought slowly and steadily a realization that was like the rising of the sun. For they were not lying in a confused heap, as they would have been if thieves had unwound them and stolen the body. They had not been unwound at all. The linen that had been so carefully and lovingly wrapped about the body of Our Lord was still as the Marys had arranged it, with little bunches of herbs undisturbed among the folds, but it lay flat on the stone as though it had sunk gently down by its own weight. And the napkin that had been wrapped about Our Lord's head lay a little apart from the other linen, in the place where Our Lord's head had lain, still in its folds. When God had wanted his human body again he had withdrawn it through the folds of the linen without disturbing them, gently and quietly, in just that same gentle way in which he opens a flower or moves a cloud. St. John says of himself that looking at those graveclothes he "saw, and believed."

3.

That same evening Mary and Cleophas, her husband, were walking home to Emmaus, a village close to Jerusalem, where their home was, and they were talking together of all that had happened. Mary had seen the angels and the empty tomb, but perhaps she found it hard to convince her husband of the truth of what she had seen. Perhaps, now, she doubted herself. They had believed that Jesus was the Christ, yet how could it be that he should suffer death? They were puzzled and worried and could not understand it at all.

Busily arguing, they did not notice the third wayfarer until they found him quietly walking along beside them, suiting his stride to theirs. It seemed so natural to have him there that when he gently asked them what they were talking about, and why they looked so sad, they told him. He seemed to them a stranger and yet they told him everything. They poured it all out in a flood. He listened to it all, and when they had finished he smiled at them and said, "O fools, and slow of heart to believe all that the prophets have spoken! Ought not Christ to have suffered these things, and to enter into his glory?"

And then patiently he explained it all to them, taking the prophecies of the Christ that were in the Scriptures one by one and showing them how exactly the suffering and death of Jesus of Nazareth had fulfilled them all. Their "hearts burned within them" while he taught them, burned with love and joy and faith. It was all so clear now. They wondered how they could have been such fools as not to understand.

It was getting late when they reached their home but the wayfarer "made as though he would have gone further." Here again is that humility of God which breaks our hearts. Were they going to ask him into their home to rest a bit? He would not ask to come in if they did not want him in their home. Would they offer him anything to eat, and a seat by the fire now that it was getting dark and cold? If they had not, he would have gone away into the night, and they would never have known who he was. But it was all right. They were disciples of Jesus of Nazareth, and they knew better than to turn a wayfarer from their door. They said, "Abide with us: for it is towards evening, and the day is far spent."

And he went in with them and sat by the fire and talked to them while Mary got the supper. When it was ready the three of them sat down together, and Cleophas asked the stranger if he would say the blessing, and he said that he would, and took the bread in his hands and blessed it and broke it and gave it to them, with that light upon his face which was always there when he could give something to his children. "And their eyes were opened, and they knew him; and he vanished out of their sight."

4.

That wonderful resurrection body was the perfect instrument of his will. He could be recognized, or not, just as he willed. He could come and go just as he willed. No physical weakness, no pain or weariness, could hinder him now in the doing of his Father's will; no stone walls or locked doors could separate him from his children. He had now a body as swift and untiring as his love and the perfect expression of it.

Mary his Mother would have known him instantly when he came to her, and her joy when he came back again would have been comparable only to her joy at Bethlehem when after his birth Joseph laid him in her arms or to the joy she had felt in the Temple at Jerusalem when for three days he had been lost and then restored to her again. There is no record in the Gospels of their resurrection meeting. There are some things so holy that only the language of a world other than this can describe them.

Of Our Lord's resurrection meeting with Peter there is only this brief description, given by the disciples to Cleophas and his wife when they hurried back to Jerusalem that very night. "The Lord is risen indeed, and hath appeared to Simon." For that meeting, too, with its anguished penitence and divine forgiveness, its pity and its peace, words that could describe it were not found.

But Peter was with the other disciples in the upper room, healed and happy, and forgiven, when Cleophas and Mary burst in upon them with their glorious news. He listened, his worn, bearded face lit up with his smile, but he who had always been the talker had very little to say tonight. He was not the same man now. The Peter whom we see later in the Acts of the Apostles, the strong and resolute hero who was the foundation stone of the church, the martyr who asked to be crucified upside-down because he had denied his Lord and was not worthy to die quite as he had died, is not the old headstrong unreliable Peter of the days before the resurrection. His suffering during the passion, and the resurrection meeting of which he could not speak, and then the gift of the Holy Spirit transformed the shifting sand to rock. And so, as they all talked excitedly, he listened; and not so much to their voices as for another voice for which now he would always be listening. And his eyes, going from face to face, would yet have been looking beyond them for another face for which now he would always be watching. If he heard what they said he heard other words more clearly, words that were the only ones he wanted to hear.

"Peace be unto you."

He had come to them. He was there. Peter, and Cleophas, and Mary knew already the heavenly quietness of his entering in, but the others were terrified. The door of the upper room had been locked for fear of enemies, and only ghosts, they thought, could so pass through locked doors and enter so silently. "Why are ye troubled?" he asked them, "and why do thoughts arise in your hearts? Behold my hands and my feet, that it is I myself: handle me, and see; for a spirit hath not flesh and bones, as ye see me have."

They knelt around him and clasped his warm strong human hands, and with unspeakable gladness knew him for their Lord given back to them from the dead. And then he shared their supper with them, their poor man's feast of fish and bread and honey, and explained to them the meaning of all the terrible things that had happened since last they had eaten their supper together in this very room. He "opened their understanding" so that the suffering and death that he had conquered seemed to them no longer terrible, and taking their stand upon his victory they could face it for themselves with courage and faith and joy. And then, as quietly as he had come, he left them, and they waited for the next time as men wait through the long hours of the night to see the sun again.

One of the disciples, Thomas, had not been present when Our Lord came to the upper room that first time, and when the others told him about it he would not believe a word of it. Thomas was what is called a realist, one of those people to whom reality is what has happened before and what they are accustomed to. It had not happened before that God had walked the roads of his world and talked to his children clothed with the glory of a resurrection body, and Thomas was not accustomed to it, as he was accustomed to sunsets and rainbows and other wonders of Almighty God, and so he would not believe it. He said, "Except I shall see in his hands the print of the nails, and put my finger into the print of the nails, and thrust my hand into his side, I will not believe."

Eight days after Our Lord's first appearance in the upper room the apostles were gathered there again, and Thomas was with them. And once more the doors were shut and locked. They were talking together, and just eating their supper, when they felt again the joy of heaven, that glow of warmth that told them God was near.

"Peace be unto you."

And there he was in the midst of them, Jesus Christ the same yesterday, today, and forever, their light and their joy, come all the way from heaven to earth again to bring faith to one poor doubting sinner. "Thomas," he said, "reach hither thy finger, and behold my hands; and reach hither thy hand, and thrust it into my side: and be not faithless, but believing."

From birth to death Our Lord's body had always been humbly and lovingly given for and to his children, and now after death and resurrection it was just the same. With the same humble love God gave his most glorious body into the hands of Thomas to touch and to hold. Perhaps it was this unchangeableness of the divine humility, even more than the feel of the wounds against his trembling fingers, that shattered Thomas's composure. It was from Thomas, the doubter, the unbeliever, that there broke now the great cry of faith, "My Lord and my God!"

5.

Of Our Lord's many visits to his children during those forty days when he went to and fro between heaven and earth, weaving them together in a union that has never been broken, the loveliest is the last.

The disciples had gone back to Galilee again, as Our Lord had told them to do, and one night seven of them went out fishing; Peter and Thomas, Nathanael, James, and John, and two others. They worked all night and caught nothing, and just as the day was breaking, weary and discouraged, they rowed back toward the shore. They were too tired to talk. There was no sound but the creak of the oars in the rowlocks and the slap of the little waves against the ship's side. The man at the tiller was perhaps John, and he watched the lovely colors of the dawn steal into the sky, and the curve of the shore coming nearer, and saw how the growing light touched with silver the edges of the waves breaking there. They broke very gently, for the dawn was windless and a great and growing peace brooded over all the world. How peaceful that man looked there, moving about on the shore. He wore a white robe and that too was touched with silver light. What was he doing? He was building a little fire on the shore, the sort of fire that men make when they are preparing a picnic meal in the open. Presently the glow of flames lit his silvery white robe with warm gold. There was something very familiar and homelike about that fire, and about the man who was making it. John remembered a day years ago when he had seen a fire just like that upon this very shore. It had been evening then and the man who had made it had been preparing supper for his guests. Now, it seemed, he was preparing breakfast. John said nothing—not yet. That familiar warm glow crept over his body and his heart beat hard with joy.

The tall stranger on the shore straightened himself and coming down to the edge of the waves called out to know if they had caught anything, and gloomily they said "No."

"Cast the net on the right side of the ship," he called back to them.

They shipped their oars and did what they were told, and the net enclosed a great shoal of fishes, as it had done once before. For a little while they had all they could do getting the fish into the boat, but when this excitement was over and they had calmed down again John said quietly, "It is the Lord."

Peter could not wait for the slow business of getting ashore with the fish. He flung his fisherman's coat about him and slipped overboard and swam ashore, and sitting down near the little fire he watched Our Lord cooking fish, as the men of Galilee knew so well how to do, carefully roasting them over the glowing coals and then laying them on flat cakes of bread. He watched the deft movements of the hands that had made so many beautiful things in the carpenter's shop, and brought life and loveliness again to so many broken bodies, and looked at the face he loved so much lit by the warm glow of the flames, and as he watched he worshiped and adored.

The others came ashore in the dinghy, towing the net, and Our Lord asked them to bring some more fish; it seemed he did not think he had quite enough to feed his children. When Peter had brought some more he went back to help the others get the net to land and count the fish; for they must do their work and finish it properly, even though their Lord and their God was there, only a few feet from them, cooking their breakfast. There were 153 fishes, all big ones, and though there were so many the net was not broken. And when they had finished their work, and Our Lord had finished his, he called them to breakfast.

As they ate their breakfast round the fire, warm and comforted and happy, their living Lord there in the midst of them and the spring dawn brightening all about them, did they think to themselves that to die and come home to Paradise would be rather like this? Not frightening at all, just a passing out of night and darkness, weariness and failure, into the light. Nothing strange, but a land that was familiar, and Our Lord standing on the shore to welcome them.

When breakfast was over Our Lord said to Peter, "Simon, son of Jonas, lovest thou me more than these?" And Peter said, "Yea, Lord; thou knowest that I love thee."

And Our Lord said, "Feed my lambs." And then he paused and said again, "Simon, son of Jonas, lovest thou me?" And Peter said the second time, "Yea, Lord; thou knowest that I love thee."

Our Lord said, "Feed my sheep." And then for the third time he said, "Simon, son of Jonas, lovest thou me?"

Peter was heartbroken that his Lord should ask that question three times over, as though he doubted his love, and he cried out in deep distress, "Lord, thou knowest all things; thou knowest that I love thee."

And Our Lord said for the last time, "Feed my sheep." And he did not repeat the question. Peter had atoned for his threefold denial by a threefold affirmation of his love, and could now no longer doubt that the sin was wiped away. And then all his distress was wiped away too, for he was hearing once more the great "Verily" that he had thought would never ring out again, and it was ringing out for him with love and comfort.

"Verily, verily, I say unto thee, When thou wast young, thou girdest thyself, and walkedst whither thou wouldest: but when thou shalt be old, thou shalt stretch forth thy hands, and another shall gird thee, and carry thee whither thou wouldest not."

Peter understood. He was to glorify God by a martyr's death.

And not only that, but he was to be given the honor of dying for his Lord as his Lord had died for him, upon the cross.

"Follow me," said Our Lord.

The apostles had not understood, when they first left their nets and followed him, just how hard that following would be. But they knew now and their hearts did not fail them. Once they had wanted wealth and power and ease in an earthly kingdom, and they had argued about who should be greatest. They were changed men now. What they wanted now was humility and poverty and pain and death, because the death and resurrection of their Lord had taught them that only when the grains of wheat fall into the ground and die can the harvest fields be bright with golden grain. And only by this grain, bought at this cost, can the souls of men be fed.

Peter looked at John the beloved disciple and wondered how he would glorify God in his death. "Lord," he said, "and what shall this man do?"

Our Lord did not, and never does, answer this question, for the way by which God calls each soul to himself is a secret between him and that soul, and another may not trespass on that holy ground. "If I will that he tarry till I come, what is that to thee?" he said to Peter. "Follow thou me."

There is a divine orderliness in all the works of God. On a spring morning three years ago, with the sunshine glinting on the lake, when they had first come to shore with a net full of fishes, Our Lord had first said to his disciples, "Follow me." Now the heavenly pattern comes round full circle and we are back where we started, by the same lake, in the spring sunshine again, hearing the same words, "Follow me." They are, for us as for them, the beginning and the end.

6.

The heavenly visitations of the forty days had to end. That particular mode of communion between Our Lord and his children had to pass and give way to another. Had they always been listening every evening for the sound of his voice and watching in every dawn for the shining of his robe, they could not have got on with the work they had to do for him. The lambs and the sheep would have been neglected. There had to be another way, the way of the Comforter who would not come and go but would be always with them. Our Lord as a man with a physical body could be present only in one place at one time, but in the power of his Spirit he could be everywhere, in every soul that was his own in all the worlds, in time and out of it, "closer than breathing, nearer than hands and feet."

But though they had the promise of the Comforter their good-by to the physical presence of their Lord must have been a rending pain. For the rest of their earthly lives they would not hear his voice or touch his hands or see his face. Though his Spirit would be with them his body, which they loved so much, would no longer be going in and out among them. But that had to be borne, and they were ready now to bear all things.

Upon a certain day they went, as he had told them, to the Mount of Olives, and there he came to them and led them up to the top of the hill. From here they could see the country where they had lived, the roads and winding paths they had walked together in the sunshine, and by night under the moon and stars. They could see Jerusalem the holy city built upon the Mount Sion, and little Bethany among the olive trees, and the Jordan Valley, and far away in the distance the blue waters of the Dead Sea and the mountains of Moab streaked with their lovely colors of rose and violet. This was the world they knew, and none of them, not even Our Lord as a man, had ever known another. Yet beyond the mountains lay so many countries and so many peoples, civilizations half as old as time in India and China, Italy and Greece with their glorious cities, and further west, in Gaul and Britain, a barbarian people not yet conquered by Rome, living in clearings in the forests in their huts of wood and clay. Our Lord saw it all, the whole glory of the world, all the nations rising and living and dying, all the centuries coming to the birth and passing away, and knew that he held it all in the hollow of his hand. "All power is given unto me in heaven and on earth," he said to his disciples as they gathered about him, worshiping him. But still he must win his great kingdom slowly, patiently, by the power of love, through these children of his, and all those other children whom they would win for him through all the ages and for whom he had prayed to the Father in the upper room. He looked at the little band of simple men gathered about him, men who had never left their own country, and he said to them, and to all his other children who through the centuries would believe in him and be his church, "Go ye into all the world, and preach the gospel to every creature."

And then in the hush that followed came the last words that he ever spoke to us as a man upon this earth, "Lo, I am with you alway, even unto the end of the world."

He lifted up his hands and blessed them and for the last time they saw the love in his glorious face shining upon them, and then they found that he had left them. It seemed to them that a cloud, that cloud that through all the history of their people had symbolized for them the terrible presence of the living God, had come about him and received him out of their sight, and they were bowed down in fear like Peter and James and John upon the Mount of Hermon.

When the fear and the cloud had passed then they knew that

they were really alone. Above them, as they looked up, was only the emptiness of the blue sky and it may be that they suffered then an almost unbearable agony. But God never leaves his children to suffer more than they can bear. A great angel strengthened Our Lord in the garden of Gethsemane, two angels were in the tomb to save the women who came there from shock and grief, and now two more stood by the disciples in the glory of their strength to help them to bear this grief.

"Ye men of Galilee," they said, "why stand ye gazing up into heaven? This same Jesus, which is taken up from you into heaven, shall so come in like manner as ye have seen him go into heaven."

Then they too were gone. The visible traffic of the angels back and forth from earth to heaven, which had accompanied both Our Lord's coming to this earth and his leaving it, was over now. But the door is not shut in heaven. Just as we are aware, as we go about our daily work, of Our Lord's presence with us until the end of the world, so we are sometimes aware of theirs too. And when we feel them near us we remember their promise, and we say, "Even so come, Lord Jesus."

7.

The disciples were happy in the days that followed. After the ascension they "returned to Jerusalem with great joy; And were continually in the Temple, praising and blessing God." And patiently they waited for the coming of the Comforter. Their meeting place was the house of the upper room, now so holy to them. Tradition says that this house had now become the home of the Mother of Our Lord, and that Mary lived here with John until she died.

They were all there together when the Spirit of the living

God came upon them, in power and flame and light. No words of this world could describe what happened to them then, but they have tried to tell us what it was like. It seemed to them that a great wind filled the whole house where they were sitting, clean and strong and fresh, bringing with it as all great winds do that sense of tremendous and terrifying power, of awe and mystery. They seemed to see a tongue of flame lighting upon each one of them, for the gift of the Spirit of Our Lord Jesus Christ was to the whole church forever, and to each one of us individually too, our own precious possession, to be guarded as a secret fire within us, to be loved and adored forever. Our Lord promised us, "The Spirit of Truth ... dwelleth with you and shall be in you. I will not leave you comfortless. I will come to you." Flame is so many things; it is warmth and light, without which there is no life, and it is cleansing, which is both joy and pain. All these the Spirit is to us, and he is wisdom too, symbolized upon that day by the gift of tongues, when the disciples found themselves speaking in all the languages in which they must spread the news of the Kingdom of God. If we ever doubt the power of the Spirit of Our Lord with us we have only to read the Acts of the Apostles, and see those simple Galilean men transformed into men of power and unshaken courage and unwearied love, like their Lord before them. We have only to think of the infant church, that group of poor and humble men and women gathered in the upper room, and think how it grew and spread into all the world, like the grain of mustard seed of which Our Lord had spoken, growing into a great tree whose leaves are for the healing of the nations. We have only to think of all the heroes and saints and martyrs from that day to this, men and women whose greatness would have been impossible of achievement unless Our Lord had lived in them in the power of his Spirit. And still the church, Our Lord's body in the world, lives on. She suffers persecution, but the blood of the martyrs is the seed of the church and she becomes only the stronger for it. Through the centuries the world ridicules her, ignores her, tries to use her for its own purposes, and sometimes corrupts her with wealth and power, but she still goes on. Within her body the sin of her children rends her and weakens her, but even that she survives. Sometimes it seems that the life is crushed out of her but always she rises again from the dead. She cannot be destroyed, for her walls are built up of the souls that love Christ, who are held in the hollow of his hand and indwelt by his Spirit, us his children whom he loves and for whom he died that we might live eternally.

"Who shall separate us from the love of Christ? shall tribulation, or distress, or persecution, or famine, or nakedness, or peril, or sword? ... Nay, in all these things we are more than conquerors, through him that loved us. For I am persuaded that neither death, nor life, nor angels, nor principalities, nor powers, nor things present, nor things to come, nor height, nor depth, nor any other creature, shall be able to separate us from the love of God, which is in Christ Jesus Our Lord."

—Romans VIII:35-39